Also by Anthony M. DeStefano:

King of the Godfathers:
Joseph Massino and the Fall of the Bonanno Crime Family

Mob Killer:
The Bloody Rampage of Charles Carneglia, Mafia Hit Man

VINNY GORGEOUS

The Ugly Rise and Fall of a New York Mobster

ANTHONY M. DESTEFANO

LYONS PRESS
Guilford, Connecticut
An imprint of Globe Pequot Press

Lyons Press is an imprint of Globe Pequot Press.

All photos courtesy of the US Attorney's Office, Eastern District of New York, unless otherwise noted.

Project editor: Meredith Dias
Layout: Sue Murray

Library of Congress Cataloging-in-Publication Data

DeStefano, Anthony M.
  Vinny gorgeous : the ugly rise and fall of a New York mobster /
Anthony M. DeStefano.
    pages cm
 ISBN 978-0-7627-8541-4
1. Basciano, Vincent. 2. Criminals—United States—Biography. 3.
Organized crime—New York (State)—New York 4. Mafia—New York
(State)—New York. I. Title.
 HV6248.B346D47 2013
  364.1092—dc23
 [B]
                                                                    2012051760

Printed in the United States of America

10 9 8 7 6 5 4 3 2 1

In memory of Frank Bari, a repository of so much of the knowledge of the hidden history of the mob in New York. A former member of the Coast Guard, Vietnam veteran, attorney, husband, father, and good friend.

"Only Your Friend Could Hurt You."

—*TESTIMONY OF SALVATORE VITALE ON THE
INHERENT TREACHERY OF MOB LIFE*

1

In New York City if you have secret business to take care of late at night on a lonely street, then certain spots in Greenpoint are among the best places.

Not the southern part of the Brooklyn neighborhood close to the Williamsburg Bridge where the chic artistic crowd hangs out in Asian fusion restaurants. No, instead there are streets in the northern section of the neighborhood surrounded by industrial parking lots and old brick buildings dating from the nineteenth century. Greenpoint once was home to the old New York industries of printing, pottery, petroleum, glass making, and iron working. Collectively they were known as the "black arts" because of the grit and noxious by-products.

Most of that manufacturing base left the area after World War II, but this zone bordering the polluted Newtown Creek still remains largely industrial. The city planned to revive the area in the latter years of Mayor Michael Bloomberg's administration, but in 2004 street lamps too widely spaced apart to give much illumination lit the mostly deserted streets after dark. Metallic towers of a sewage treatment plant towered over the neighborhood. Oblong and tall, the structures resembled giant eggshells or the domes of some misplaced Russian Orthodox church.

On the evening of November 30, 2004, Randolph Pizzolo arrived in the neighborhood driving a black BMW and made the turn onto Monitor Street, a byway named for the fabled Civil War ironclad ship, built in one of the area's old shipyards. A dark-haired man with a husky build bulked by years of construction work and overeating, Pizzolo had arranged to meet a friend to discuss something important.

"Friend" wasn't exactly the right term for the man called Ace. Pizzolo never got much from the relationship. With intimidating, penetrating black eyes and a head that merged, sans neck, into his shoulders, Ace Aiello was a new member of the Mafia, and he acted like it—certainly around Pizzolo. He never missed a moment to dress down Randy in public, like when Pizzolo first shook the hand of a lowly soldier before greeting a Mafia captain and Ace castigated him. Arguments between the two men commonly took place at bars and restaurants.

But things weren't like that with Dominick. The handsome, strapping guy from the Bronx seemed to be the only one who treated Pizzolo decently. Maybe it was because he was secure in his position as a Mafioso or he just happened to like Pizzolo. But if someone took the time to dine with Pizzolo and listen to his problems and his dreams, it usually was Dominick. If there was a fight to break up, Dominick was there. Since Aiello fell under the command of Dominick, Pizzolo knew to come when he was called. After all, Dominick was really controlling things.

Ace and Pizzolo had talked earlier in the evening, and he told Pizzolo to drive to Greenpoint, to a street behind the lumberyard. Pizzolo likely didn't know what was so urgent, so sensitive, that it required an evening rendezvous on a Brooklyn street. But he had for years been flirting with life as a mobster, although he was not really a member. He had worked as a factotum and driver for some of the made men. If those more closely connected to the mob life wanted something from him, he obeyed. If he did enough favors—including the odd bit of violence if necessary—he figured it would get his ticket punched for a trip to joining La Cosa Nostra. He wanted to build a bar in Astoria, Queens, and if he established true ties to the mob fraternity, that could mean a lot of business.

God knows, Pizzolo had waited long enough for just such an initiation. For years he had been pestering some members of the Bonanno crime family like Dominick—who chewed Pizzolo out for asking—about whether he would get to attend a secret conclave where the old ritual of membership took place. The old gangsters used a gun as a prop and pricked the initiate's finger to draw blood. In recent years, they stopped using the gun to avoid getting busted for weapons possession if cops happened to arrive. They also did away with the medieval ritual of drawing blood for health reasons. But participants still burned the card with a picture of a saint in the hands of the initiate, who had to swear loyalty to the life of crime and his new boss.

Pizzolo was ready. He had paid his dues. Randolph Pizzolo wanted to become a made man in the worst way. Yet, if truth be told, Pizzolo had problems, which had been weighing increasingly on his mind. The previous months had seen a convergence of festering issues that had plagued Pizzolo and were seriously inhibiting his wiseguy aspirations. Career criminals needed to exhibit a certain decorum, and Pizzolo showed a lack of discretion and a propensity to call unnecessary attention to himself. Once, at a Manhattan restaurant, he told a soldier in the crime family that he should keep quiet and not ever think about becoming a government witness as others had done. Realizing his mistake, Pizzolo apologized.

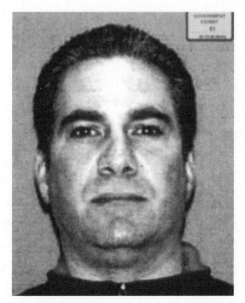

Randolph Pizzolo

At another fashionable Manhattan restaurant mob hangout, Pizzolo thought he would be cute and hassle an FBI agent dining at a table nearby with some friends.

"I will buy you all a drink—except the fed," Pizzolo boasted in an effort to embarrass the official.

The agent, whose investigative specialty covered Colombian drug cases and not La Cosa Nostra, wasn't the least bit intimidated and put Pizzolo in his place. "I should get your ass violated because you know you shouldn't be in here." The agent knew Pizzolo was already on probation and should not have been in close proximity to other criminals that evening. It was a moment of vulnerability that Pizzolo stupidly had opened himself up to. To make matters worse, he had done so by violating one of the rules of Mafia civility: Be respectful of the cops who are doing their job.

Pizzolo also bragged about knee-capping a Lucchese crime family soldier at a restaurant alternately described as "Terrace on the Park" or Caffe on the Green, a trendy eatery in an old Queens house once owned by silent screen star Rudolph Valentino. Then there was the episode at another little restaurant in the same area where Pizzolo showed up with a gun and, after some drinks, once again opened his mouth. His claim that he had been a Navy SEAL probably wasn't as bad as the way that he insisted that he was the only person among all in the Bonanno family who knew how to kill. That didn't sit well with the other members of the *borgata,* as crime families are known.

Pizzolo had tried to explain his actions by relating how he had showed up at the restaurant Napa & Sonoma with a gun after his friend called him and sounded as though he was having a problem. There wasn't a problem; the friend took the gun from Pizzolo, carefully wrapped it up, and placed it behind the bar. Filled with drink, Pizzolo later admitted that he might have bragged about his ability to kill. Although he admitted his transgression and had an explanation for it, the incident formed another black mark against him.

Nor was Pizzolo's day job going all that well. Experienced in doing excavation work and installing foundations and footings for buildings, he normally had a good reputation as a contractor and had hooked up with some big projects in the Bronx. Depending on who was giving the critique, either his work got sloppy or he did a good job. Robert Van Zandt Jr., a businessman in the Bronx who used Pizzolo to put up some steel work at a new office building, thought Pizzolo was somehow stealing from him by padding bills. But then again, Van Zandt always seemed to think someone was trying to pull one over on him. In Pizzolo's case, the suspicion wasn't misplaced. Randy was fiddling with the money needed to pay workers.

Vincent Basciano was Pizzolo's overall boss in the Bronx construction work—and not just that kind of boss. Unlike some of the worn-out elders of the Bonanno family, Vinny cut an imposing figure in his world. With neatly styled hair, vivid eyes that telegraphed ambition and cunning, Vinny had a rough handsomeness. He ran a beauty salon on East Tremont Avenue named Hello Gorgeous, but mostly because of his looks Vinny earned the moniker "Vinny Gorgeous." Animated hand and arm gestures always punctuated his conversations at the social clubs or in private. He liked taking charge and being the most charismatic person in the room. In bars and nightclubs—always with a vodka and club soda with a piece of lemon—Vinny held court and attracted women.

To be sure, Vinny actually liked some of the work that Pizzolo had been doing. Randy saved projects money and moved enormous amounts of dirt from excavation sites, Basciano told acquaintances. There may have been problems with Van Zandt, but the developer complained about everybody. Yet, somewhere along the way, things were going wrong. A wall supposedly had to come down because of sloppy construction. With all his gaffes and misadventures, Dominick told Pizzolo that it might be a good idea to move to Florida, where he might be able to resurrect his flagging business. Moving away from trouble is called being "chased," but Pizzolo wanted none of that. He wasn't going to leave town and let everybody know it.

The next car onto Monitor Street was Ace's, who had, by prearrangement, followed Pizzolo to the rendezvous. It had rained some, but Pizzolo was hatless as he left the BMW, its engine running. This was his third meeting of the night. Earlier, Pizzolo met with another businessman to see about getting some financing and then went to a coffee shop to talk about a $1 million life insurance policy—just in case. This last meeting on Monitor Street he didn't expect to last long; he had plans to have drinks later with Dominick, who had been good enough in recent weeks to act as a buffer between him and his recent problems. Ace exited the second car, dressed in a hooded sweatshirt, keeping his hands out of the rain in the front pockets. Another man remained in the driver's seat of Ace's vehicle listening to music.

It seems possible that forty-three-year-old Randolph Pizzolo knew, as he opened his car door, that he was living on ever-diminishing borrowed time. There was too much negativity in his life: his arrogant public displays of impulsiveness, problems in the construction work, his refusal to leave town when asked. One story making the rounds had it that when he invited some of the local associates to his granddaughter's christening,

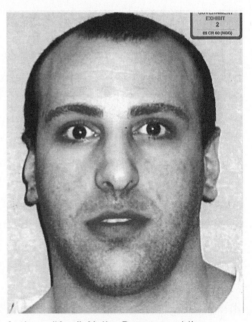

Anthony "Ace" Aiello, Bonanno soldier

none showed up, forcing an embarrassed Pizzolo to plead with other friends to attend so the table wouldn't sit empty.

When he left his home in Bayside a few hours earlier to take his drive in the rain, he made a simple request of his girlfriend, Roxanne, something that later seemed out of character for such a macho man. "Kiss me," he told her. She did.

Pizzolo walked around to the left of his car and went about twenty-five feet past the bumper. He extended his hand to greet Ace. Handshakes in the mob form a large part of protocol. Since he was a lowly associate, Pizzolo was doing the right thing by making the first move.

Ace didn't reciprocate the gesture this time, though. Under the glare of a solitary street lamp, he pushed Pizzolo back and then fired a 9-mm Luger concealed in the hoodie pocket. The shot hit Pizzolo in his chest, and he crumpled to the wet payment. He wasn't dead yet, but he soon would be. Anthony "Ace" Aiello pulled the gun from his front pocket and walked closer.

<hr />

Some twenty miles away from Monitor Street, two men drove from the Meadowlands Arena, where the New Jersey Nets were playing the fourth quarter of a basketball game with the Charlotte Bobcats. The Nets were approaching a 99 to 86 victory, but the two men opted not to stay for the win, beginning the drive back to the city. It was enough that, if anyone should inquire about where they had been, they had indeed on this particular night been far away from Brooklyn. They could prove it with ticket stubs. A friend even called them to say she saw them both seated courtside on television. In the car, a pager lit up with the number "711." Seeing the code, Dominick Cicale knew that Pizzolo wouldn't be having drinks with him later.

Cicale had tried to save Pizzolo from himself. He had suggested that Pizzolo move to Florida, where both men had been looking for investors for a real estate deal. If he stayed there, Pizzolo could have supervised the project. But Pizzolo didn't want that. He knew that when the mob chased you from New York, your chances of initiation became virtually nonexistent. No, Pizzolo wouldn't leave. He had roots here; his married daughter Constance still lived on Staten Island. There was also his relationship with Roxanne. So Cicale could only keep Pizzolo away from places like the Bronx, where he moved too prominently on the radar—in a bad way—with some powerful people. But with that kind of notoriety, it was hard to protect him. When orders came, even a Mafia captain like Cicale knew that there was no choice in the matter.

Driving through the rain back through the Bronx, Cicale had to take care of the one tangible piece of physical evidence tying him to Pizzolo's demise. He had already spent years in prison for a homicide, and he didn't want to repeat the experience. His friend Al was chatting

The Randolph Pizzolo murder scene in northern Greenpoint

on his cell phone in the passenger seat. On the Cross Bronx Expressway, as if trying to discard evil from his life, Cicale opened the car window on the driver's side and let the pager slip from his hand onto the busy roadway.

The next morning, December 1, shortly after 6:00 a.m., a worker at the Feldman Lumber yard noticed the BMW with its engine running and, lying face down in a puddle, the body of a slightly obese man clad in a black bomber-style jacket, blue jogging pants, and white tennis shoes. The puddle under the head, tinged with blood, had the color of a deeply steeped tea. Police arrived quickly, and crime scene investigators took a quick inventory, noting the two Luger shell casings on the street. Turning over Pizzolo's body, the cops discovered three deformed copper jacketed bullets, two from the body and another on the ground beneath the corpse.

There was plenty of cash on Pizzolo, amounting to $1,040.70, which the cops took from one of the front pants pockets. He was wearing an expensive ring, and a hand stiffened by rigor mortis—fingers bent as if palsied—held a cigarette lighter. Detectives quickly ruled out a robbery. Pizzolo's elderly mother had made some cryptic remarks about her son wanting to live the fast life and make fast money. Other family members were less helpful. Faced with a dearth of information and no eyewitnesses, the NYPD had little to use as evidence other than what lay in the street.

The medical examiner had an easier job of it. The autopsy quickly determined that Randolph Pizzolo had died of gunshot wounds to the back of his head, lungs, heart, aorta, and other organs. Seven bullet holes riddled the body. From the examination on the morgue table, the doctor noted that most of the entrance wounds to the body were in the back, which meant that the shooter likely finished off Pizzolo while he was face down in the puddle. To ID the body of the man labeled "unknown" at the coroner's office, Pizzolo's father drove in from Queens a day after the corpse had been found. To spare the elderly man the emotional

GOVERNMENT
EXHIBIT
308(c)
05 CR 60 (NGG)

Pizzolo's body

trauma of having to look directly at his son's bullet-ridden corpse, the medical examiner showed him a photo. It was he.

Meanwhile, detectives at the crime lab examined the bullets found at the scene and came to the conclusion that they all came from the same gun. The bullets and the casings found on the street went into an envelope and storage for future use if a break in the case came.

The Mafia had learned over the years that funerals and weddings, once the best places for members to meet and transact business, had inherent problems for a secret society. As portrayed in *The Godfather,* law enforcement officials began using them to gather photographs of made members. Cops also made inferences about the mob's power structure by seeing who showed or who stayed away from a funeral home or reception hall. Like Kremlinologists from the Cold War, detectives watched to see who in the crime family received the most respect, a status revealed by the number of people who kissed a particular man of honor on the cheek.

In the weeks before he died, Randolph Pizzolo was treated as a pariah. But, in a counterintuitive move designed to deflect suspicion from himself and those involved, Dominick Cicale showed his betrayed friend one last sign of respect. He attended the wake.

What happened? Why had he died? Pizzolo's kin asked Cicale as he stood among the mourners. He didn't know, Cicale lamented. Walking up to the casket, Cicale stared at the body. Filled with regret and sadness, he stayed only a short time—but he wouldn't forget the moment.

2

OF ALL THE INDIGNITIES THAT JOSEPH MASSINO HAD TO SUFFER IN THE federal detention center on the Brooklyn waterfront, the worst, doing his own laundry, reminded him just how much his situation had changed.

He might still be the boss of the Bonanno family, but he had no wife or maid now to do his chores. To wash his skivvies Massino took them into the jail shower and cleaned them with soap under the running water. He couldn't get his ample girth into briefs comfortably, so he wore boxer shorts, which air-dried faster in his cell. It was hardly the way a man who considered himself the last godfather should be living.

Then there was the food. For a man who built his size around eating and his life around a catering business, jailhouse cuisine, or what passed for it, was an abomination. Whatever the Metropolitan Detention Center served gave Massino digestive problems. One way around that indignity was to take snacks from the vending machines and commissary. He thrived on bread and peanut butter. When his lawyers came, Massino had them bring two of everything that he wanted: candy bars, potato chips, and ham sandwiches with cheese that he melted in the microwave.

The effect over a two-year period was predictable. Rather than lose weight behind bars, Massino, who as a free man never met a meal he didn't like, added to his nearly three hundred pounds. This state of affairs did nothing good for his blood pressure and diabetes. It also played havoc with his gastrointestinal tract, forcing him to rely on Maalox for relief of periodic stomachaches and other predictable ailments.

The one good thing about Massino's racketeering trial six months earlier was that he could always rely on good eats. Most days when court was in session, his wife, Josephine, and his two daughters, Adeline and Joanne, brought him lunch. These weren't just any lunches, though, but special dishes from Brothers Italian Food World, one of the best in Massino's neighborhood of Howard Beach, Queens. They also brought meals from the Park Diner across from the courthouse.

It turns out they were fattening him for the kill. The two-month trial resulted in the jury finding him complicit in seven murders, not counting the ones for which the government didn't have enough evidence to include in the indictment. With his old friends turning on him and becoming star witnesses for the prosecution, Massino could see the inevitable coming. The future wasn't good for the man known as "Big Joey" on the streets of Queens. A life sentence seemed almost assured, and then Massino faced the ominous prospect of a second trial, which called for the federal death penalty.

It was against that backdrop that, on the morning of January 3, 2005, Joseph Massino looked forward to a visit in the exercise pens of the MDC facility with an old friend, who as fate would have it had been arrested a few weeks earlier. He and Vincent Basciano had a lot to talk about. They could commiserate together and discuss what was happening on the street.

Massino hadn't felt particularly close to Vinny for a long time. Massino came from the old-school days of bosses like Philip Rastelli and Nicholas "Nicky Eye Glasses" Marangello. Basciano, a new kid from the Bronx, made his mark as a gambler but didn't have the institutional memory of what the mob was like. He also had too quick a trigger finger—or so the stories went, since Massino had never given him an order to kill anybody. Basciano was joining him now because of the murder of a Bronx drug abuser named Frank Santoro outside his home in the Throgs Neck neighborhood.

Massino had heard about the Santoro slaying and frankly wasn't too happy about it. No one had asked his permission. Made men have to get clearance to hit someone, and Massino learned about the murder only after the fact. It had made him wary of Basciano—if in fact he was involved. There were also stories that Massino had heard of Basciano a decade earlier taking part in a spur-of-the-moment killing of some man in a social club off Francis Lewis Boulevard. No name was ever attached to the alleged victim, and the body supposedly disappeared. But still.

Those stories made Massino think Basciano a volatile man, a "mad hatter" with an unpredictable nature. A few years earlier, Massino had been chatting in his Casablanca Restaurant with one of his captains, Richard "Shellack Head" Cantarella, about Basciano. Massino saw good things and bad in the Bronx gangster. The crime boss liked Basciano's strong-mindedness, his strong will.

"If anything happened to him, meaning Joe Massino, he would hold this family together," Cantarella later remembered Massino telling him about Vinny.

"The only thing, he's got to slow down; he's too quick," Massino said, putting his forefinger and thumb up to mimic a gun. Massino never uttered the words "murder" or "kill," and, as Basciano reminded people later, the crime boss never ordered him to kill anyone. Basciano showed up at Massino's restaurant in the Fresh Ponds Road section of Queens on alternate Saturdays, and the crime boss was so wary of him that he wouldn't come to the eatery on those days.

But in the face of any misgivings, Massino knew that Basciano was a loyal man, someone wedded to mob life and in love with the notion of what it meant to be a made man. From about 2000 until he was arrested in 2003, Massino saw a usefulness in Basciano and spent more time in his company. There was also the tribute money, about $3,500 a month that Basciano gave to Massino, and the Christmas cash turned over to the boss during dinner at a restaurant near Wall Street. Massino respected the Bronx man's fearlessness in taking command of the street during such a trying time. Under a calamitous assault by the federal government, the Bonanno family was verging on chaos, and few able men in the borgata could take the initiative to keep business running as usual with Massino in jail.

But with information not getting to the incarcerated crime boss fast enough, his men insecure and dreading an FBI knock on the door, the situation was worsening for the Bonanno crowd. Basciano had done what he could while on the street, but now he too lay behind bars. Massino needed to talk with him, to discuss some unsettling things he had heard, to rein in his eager acolyte. Massino had to make sure he knew everything.

Massino arrived first at the exercise area on the roof of the MDC. He wore a jacket to ward off the cold, although he told one of the other inmates that the weather seemed unseasonably warm. The area consisted of a group of metal cages that separated inmates physically but easily allowed them to talk through the partitions. For an older prisoner like Massino, the guards could be accommodating. When Basciano entered, they put him next to Massino.

"What's up, brother?" said Basciano, his neat pompadour, alert eyes, and polished look in stark contrast to the portly, gray-haired, fleshy boss.

"What's up, pal."

"How are you feeling?"

"Good. Good."

Well, not so good, really. Massino unleashed the litany of his usual physical complaints. He had diarrhea, chills, a fever. His back hurt. The Motrin they gave him was causing him stomach problems. Medication for his stomach was causing more distress.

"I went to the bathroom fifteen times," Massino complained.

"Holy Christ," said Basciano, who offered to take care of Massino if they ever were put together in the same jailhouse wing.

To a fly on the wall, the conversation between the two Mafiosi was like listening to the laments of residents in a poorly run nursing home. Basciano needed a nail clipper. The showers bothered Massino, who complained about having to sit down while he washed because of a bad back. If he ever dropped the soap, Massino said he would be in big trouble because he couldn't bend over. The next day, said Massino, his attorney was going to bring up the conditions in the jail before a federal judge.

There was also a problem with Massino being able to attend meetings in the jail with the other codefendants like Basciano. Such meetings commonly took place in a large conspiracy case, and for a while Massino had been able to attend them, even picking up gossip and news from the street, like word about the killing of Pizzolo. But now Massino was being kept away.

"What they were doing was investigating me for the sneakers," he explained. "They wanted to take the sneakers."

"Why?" asked Basciano, genuinely perplexed.

"They said I escape, I could run quicker."

"What are they, fuckin' nuts? They don't know when to stop! How much more do they want, how much more," Vinny said.

The image of the rotund Massino somehow managing to escape the heavily guarded MDC, getting past the security force at the front gate, then running in sneakers through the streets of the Red Hook section of Brooklyn stretched credulity. Yet they had moved Massino around in the jail, and he didn't know why. He suspected it might be in retaliation for making a complaint about his medical condition. The two men chatted more about the deplorable state of the jail showers and the food, something that Massino always worked into his conversations. But this wasn't just a social visit. Massino wanted to know what was happening.

"What is going on out there? A few guys, they want to know what is going on, but they want to take orders only from me."

Massino had known that Basciano, before his arrest, had been issuing orders, initiating new members into the crime family, and generally keeping the Bonanno family together. That wasn't a bad thing, given the disarray within the family, but Massino wanted to ensure that Basciano wasn't trying to pull a coup and usurp the role of boss.

"They want to know who is calling the shots," Massino said.

"You are!" replied Basciano defensively.

Then the conversation turned into a lecture, Massino acting both as tutor and inquisitor, alternately praising and gently chiding the ambitious Basciano. Massino said that he didn't agree with Basciano putting certain gangsters in control as street bosses. Some of the candidates Massino didn't know much about. Others, like aging mobster Nicholas Santora, while nice guys, never made any money and had reputations as "brokesters," a term coined by the mob.

"You can't put brokesters. That don't work. You can't make a captain a brokester, that don't work," said Massino. "Learn from my mistakes."

Massino had known of Basciano's initiating new members into the crime family with good reason: He had told him to do it earlier by passing a message through a lawyer who visited the jail on occasion. "For that, you always had the okay for," Massino reassured Basciano.

As far as promoting people to captain, the candidates Basciano picked might not have been Massino's choice, but he said he wasn't going to undo what his loyal friend had done.

Feeling chastised, Basciano emphasized that what he had been doing was for the good of the crime family in such a trying time. "I did it, Joe, just to get structure. Without the fucking structure, beau, you are dead."

"There are reasons," Massino agreed.

The exercise pen meeting wasn't the first time both men had the chance to talk in jail. A few weeks earlier, they had met in an area of the courthouse known as the "bullpen." Massino remembered something he claimed both of them had discussed. The nemesis of the Bonanno family, an ambitious young federal prosecutor in Brooklyn named Greg Andres, had convicted Massino. A workaholic who thrived on coffee, Andres had led the offensive, turning six of Massino's cohorts against him and ripping apart a structure the crime boss had carefully built over a decade of activity, unfettered by the FBI. If anyone had become the scourge of La Cosa

Nostra it was Andres, a man cursed within the precincts of the mob and whose name, Massino reminded Basciano, had been on their lips a few days earlier. Andres mentioned in court and in front of Massino's wife that the boss had a girlfriend. The rest of the conversation in the bullpen had not been, Massino intimated, particularly pleasant.

"You want to take the prosecutor out," Massino said pointedly, as if to remind Basciano of what had been discussed earlier. "What are we going to gain if we take the prosecutor out?"

"Nothing."

"What are you going to gain?" Massino repeated.

In the world of organized crime, killing a cop or a prosecutor represented a cardinal sin. Mobsters don't like getting arrested, and they know that cops are only doing their jobs, that the act of killing one in retaliation only brings more trouble. The public also wouldn't stand for it. It was off limits, Massino emphasized.

"Forget about it, forget about that," said Basciano, feeling a bit uncomfortable and eager not to hear more criticism from his *padrone*.

Massino shifted his lecture onto another subject that he had to discuss with his young acolyte. Massino may not have been anywhere near Monitor Street on the night that Randolph Pizzolo died, but the boss knew—from reading the newspapers, the jailhouse grapevine, and a meeting a month earlier among his various codefendants—that the aspiring gangster from Queens had been gunned down. Another Bronx gangster had first whispered to Massino that Pizzolo had been killed, at which point Massino shot a glance at Basciano, who then had a private meeting with the Bonanno boss.

"Randy, you okayed it," Massino said.

The statement seemed to come from nowhere, sounding as much like a statement of fact as it was a question. Vinny said nothing as Massino continued his lecture.

To insulate himself from trouble, Massino throughout his career as boss appointed at various times committees of three trusted captains to run the family business on a day-to-day basis. The crime boss had done that before he was arrested, setting up a panel of Anthony Urso, Richard Cammarano, and Peter Calabrese, all Bonanno captains. The troika—not a term Massino used but which he would have appreciated—was a group of wise men who checked with each other if some really big action like a murder had to be taken. But according to Massino, the killing of Pizzolo had taken place without the approval of the ruling panel. He didn't want that to happen, because the family could degenerate into a three-way war once their collegiality dissolved.

"What do we got, we got three fuckin' families here," Massino warned about the dangers of anyone in the borgata taking drastic action without consulting the panel. "Now, I hear things," Massino continued. "You used Dominick to clip Randy." Massino then threw another name into the conversation, Joey Gambina, the "cocaine cowboy," whom he didn't trust. Was he involved in the Pizzolo murder?

"No, all bullshit," Basciano said with irritation. He stumbled over his words. "It was fuckin'—no . . . it's all, they. I don't know what happened there. I am not sure exactly what happened there. . . . But I gave the order."

Basciano finally volunteered the key piece of information, not reluctant now to put himself in the picture.

Massino sounded worried. The death of Pizzolo might fall at his feet. He already had convictions on seven mob hits and was facing the death penalty for another. An additional murder charge he didn't need. But Basciano insisted that there was nothing about the Pizzolo affair that would come back to haunt him.

It was here that Massino tried to sound like the wise man, the seasoned mob warrior weary of bloodshed. He had killed a lot of people in his time. Murder wasn't always the answer. "It took twenty years to put this together," Massino said wistfully.

In the spring of 1981, Joseph Massino engineered a spectacular purge that led to the deaths of three rival Bonanno captains—Dominick

"Big Trin" Trinchera, Alphonse "Sonny Red" Indelicato, and Philip Giaccone—who had been plotting to take over the family. Basciano didn't need reminding; he had been Trinchera's driver and errand boy at the time the ill-fated gangster disappeared. His power solidified by the executions, Massino became the crime family's rising star. Despite a short stay in prison, he had an undisturbed run that enabled him to rebuild the Bonanno group after the scandal of the 1970s, when undercover FBI agent Joseph Pistone had penetrated the organization.

But now, facing life in prison, Massino was sounding like a peacemaker. "It is easy to take a life. I can take a life every day."

"I know that," said Basciano.

"What am I going to gain, taking a life every day?"

If the point of Massino's philosophical rambling was about Pizzolo's worth as a human being and the sanctity of life, Basciano knew his boss was being disingenuous. Massino had killed a lot of people in his rise to the top. Basciano knew well how in one instance the old mobster supposedly had borrowed $10,000 from a business partner, James "Doo Doo" Pastore, just days before having him killed. Life was precious only when it pleased Massino. As far as Pizzolo was concerned, Basciano didn't see any value to him at all.

"Randy was a fuckin' jerkoff, beau," said Vinny.

"But did it warrant, wait a minute, did it warrant the clip?"

Basciano started to tell his boss about the incident at the Napa & Sonoma, but, when Massino interrupted in his avuncular way and asked why Pizzolo wasn't simply chased out of New York, the young captain couldn't contain himself. "You want to know why? Because he is a fuckin' dangerous kid that don't fuckin' listen. He talks stupid. He talks like a fuckin' jerkoff. He's a fuckin'—he is just an annoying fuckin' kid."

Massino repeated that, from what he had heard, the Pizzolo hit hadn't gone before the ruling Bonanno panel first. Why else have a panel if it wasn't to be consulted? The family could degenerate into warring factions, Massino reiterated.

Basciano agreed, but as street boss he felt that he had a certain amount of leeway, the right to do what he wanted without having to consult the panel.

"Why?" asked Massino.

"What I tried to do, Joe, I tried to give a fuckin' structure because everybody was all over the fuckin' board. And what I did, by me taking the reins, I anointed myself, through you, as acting boss."

Basciano had appointed Michael "Mickey Nose" Mancuso as his underboss and "Fat" Anthony Rabito as consiglieri, or adviser. They took those jobs to help him run the family, but at the same time Basciano insisted that he didn't want them taking any action without consulting him.

"There was a lot of fucking dissension. There was a lot of bitterness. I put these guys in a position," Basciano continued. But if Basciano had the confidence to put these men in those jobs and made them part of the Bonanno ruling panel, then it made sense to consult with them. That was how Massino had always done it. To do it any other way invited a kind of Mafia anarchy.

"Then what is the reason of having a panel?" Massino stressed.

"Right, you right, all right. Okay," Basciano said, anxious to drop the issue.

The two men continued their conversation for well over an hour. Massino again raised the issue of Pizzolo and the preferred wisdom of disciplining the miscreant rather than having him killed. They talked about the deadbeats in the family. One soldier Massino called a "piece of shit," another Basciano called a "punk." They both liked Jimmy the General, a soldier from Queens, but Massino opined: "He is just a degenerate gambler."

Running a crime family wasn't easy now with all the federal investigations. As a result, Basciano had to meet people in cemeteries. He even had captains strip down before meetings to ensure no one was wearing a wire, which bruised the pride of the older Bonanno members and compelled members of the other New York families to say that the job of street boss was going to Basciano's head. He was also dressing too much like the late John Gotti, who also let power get to his head. Massino didn't tell Basciano, but one of the big bosses of the Genovese family had offered to have the Bronx hairdresser killed.

They talked about money, Massino saying that he wasn't getting his share of old gambling profits. But the conversation steered back once again to the Pizzolo hit. Massino wanted to know who had ordered it.

"Who gave the okay to clip 'im? You did?"

"Michael," answered Basciano.

Michael the Nose had been underboss and, when Basciano got arrested, took care of all the old family business that needed handling, Basciano explained.

"It wasn't me, you know what I am saying," the young captain said.

Both men went on about the minutiae of mob life, old girlfriends, and the drudgery of jail. Massino complained about the leaks in his cell from the showers and how he needed to use five towels to soak up the water. Basciano brushed off similar indignities as challenges that he had met. "I am getting stronger every day," he bragged.

When it was time to go, Massino said he would see Basciano again, likely on the following Monday.

"I love you, beau," said Basciano, using a term of endearment that applied to everyone in the family.

"I love you, too," Massino replied.

The crime boss looked around the exercise area. Although he had done nothing but talk about mob business and all his problems, Massino felt invigorated, unburdened.

"It felt good, this air, beau," he said.

"It felt good," Massino repeated. The boss, for the first time, sounded relieved by the simple blessing of fresh air.

"Take care," Basciano said as he left the pens.

"Be good," answered Massino.

The conversation had gone well. Massino talked about the issues on which he needed to get a handle. It still seemed a bit unclear what had happened to the intensely disliked Pizzolo; Basciano seemed to know but then indicated that he didn't. Who ultimately was in charge of the Bonanno family? Basciano felt he had to take charge in Massino's name. The federal prosecutor, Andres, Basciano didn't like, but he didn't even want to talk about harming him. They were all subjects that Joseph Massino needed to hear about.

So did some of his new friends.

Separated from the recreation area, a jail guard escorted Massino into a corridor. The crime boss zipped off the jacket and gave it to a corrections lieutenant. The garment helped ward off the January chill, but his hands felt like ice. He went back to his cell, where a new mattress lay on his bunk. Massino poured himself some water and drank it, giving a solitary sigh, the only sound in the cell amid the background noise of the jail. His sigh was pregnant with meaning and resignation. After he urinated, an affable female correction officer asked him if he needed a shave and passed him a razor. Then he waited.

About twenty minutes later, a guard unlocked the cell door and escorted Massino again to a medical area. Sounding sick, a female inmate coughed. Massino told her that he had been ill as well. The medic came in to talk about some flu medicine, blood gases, and the challenges of treating bronchial infections. Massino then went into an elevator, taken into a secure area where most prisoners never tread.

Entering a room he had only seen once before, Joseph Massino saw three people, two of whom he had met for the first time nearly two years earlier when they came to his front door to arrest him. FBI agents Jeffrey Sallett and Kim McCaffrey had rung the bell at Massino's Georgian-style house on 84th Street in Howard Beach the morning of January 9, 2003,

to take him away for possibly the rest of his life. Young agents and certified public accountants, Sallett and McCaffrey had used their forensic
accounting skills to put together the case against Massino over a four-
year investigation.

Throughout the trial some months previous, Massino had developed a grudging respect for the two agents. They had always treated him
courteously, and Massino returned the favor. It helped that McCaffrey, a
petite, black-haired woman of Irish lineage, didn't have an officious atti-
tude. The crime boss always believed that there was little benefit to being
a brute with law enforcement agents. Everybody had a role to play in the
game of cops and robbers, and, a lord of crime, Massino had standards to
maintain. He once offered a beer to an FBI agent who had come to one of
his social clubs to retrieve a defective wiretap device. The agent declined.

But on July 31, 2004, Massino made the FBI another offer it couldn't
dismiss out of hand. A Brooklyn federal court jury had just convicted
the crime boss when he told a federal marshal in the courtroom that
he wanted to speak to Sallett. Massino saw the sandy-haired agent, who
seemed to wear a perpetual smile and never once smirked at him, as his
best hope. What happened next no one expected. Massino told Sallett
that he wanted to talk to the judge. From that moment, the man considered the last Mafia boss in New York began a long process of trying to
convince the FBI and federal prosecutors that he could offer something as
a cooperating witness. It was the only card that Massino had left to play.

The other face in the room at the MDC was that of an FBI agent
Massino had likely heard about but never had any dealings with. James
DeStefano had been working in another organized crime investigative
unit in the bureau tasked with probing the flagging and nearly moribund
Colombo crime family. Named for the late Joseph Colombo, that borgata
had suffered a bloody civil war in the 1990s that involved the faction
led by the imprisoned boss Carmine "The Snake" Persico and Gregory
Scarpa, a Brooklyn mobster of some renown and notoriety. (Ironically,

Scarpa, who died in 1994, turned out to be an FBI informant as well, although his cooperation appeared selective.)

The Colombo War and the various dead bodies that had popped up all over New York and Long Island had kept DeStefano and his fellow agents busy. But for a variety of reasons—some of no importance to Massino, but which the wise men and women of the Department of Justice knew could be of great legal significance—DeStefano had to be brought in to help handle Massino. A taciturn agent with short-cropped blond hair, a no-nonsense demeanor, and a body sculpted by years of working out, DeStefano earned the affectionate nickname "Robo-Cop" from some of the courthouse reporters who followed his cases.

The familiar faces of Sallett and McCaffrey in the room helped put Massino at ease. Once one of New York City's most wealthy, feared, and crafty crime bosses, now Massino was like any other criminal trying to save his skin by helping the FBI. DeStefano knew how to work quickly with Sallett to place the recording device on the rotund Massino and to remove it just as speedily. Speed was of the essence in an operation like this, because if Massino went unnoticed back in his cell area for too long, inmates would talk and think something was up. It takes very little to start a rumor that a prisoner has turned informant—which Massino most certainly had. DeStefano disengaged the recording device and removed it from Massino's crotch. Then the quick discussion started.

When he was being wired for his meeting with Basciano, Massino was jittery, like a drug informant about to make a cocaine deal. After the meeting in the pens, he seemed calmer. The three agents wanted to know from Massino how the meeting in the pens went. He gave them a brief recap about what had transpired. He noted the conversation about the Pizzolo murder, the talk about Andres, the moves Basciano had made to take over and run the crime family with Massino off the street. Among the more realistic mobsters, an old saying holds that in the gangster life the best liar wins the fight for survival. Massino, with his impressive acting skills, had walked the unsuspecting Basciano down the proverbial garden path for a free-wheeling conversation that could lead only to more trouble for the young captain.

The significance of what had just occurred was lost on no one in that secret room on that January morning. Joseph Massino had not only become an informant for the FBI but had secretly taped one of his most important captains. The conversation had been unfiltered and wide-ranging. The tape had to be closely analyzed, but if Massino's recollection was correct, then the evidence might contain the motherlode of intelligence that the FBI had been seeking for many months.

"There had never been an official New York city boss to cooperate," Sallett said later.

Nor was the importance lost on DeStefano, the man brought in at the last minute to help Sallett and McCaffrey. He also sensed that Massino, whose life as he knew it was over, knew the historic significance of his actions.

Vincent Basciano went back to his cell at the MDC suspecting nothing. He wasn't a new face in the mob. He had become a full-fledged Mafia member in 1991 during an initiation ceremony conducted at Cantarella's home. Massino's brother-in-law Sal Vitale had presided over the ritual. But no one considered him a major power in the crime family . . . until Massino's arrest. It was then that the brash captain from the Bronx started to make things happen for himself in Massino's name, as he would have everyone believe.

Even as an acting boss, Basciano's forte had been gambling, a favorite family activity. However, the landscape had changed drastically in the past few months, giving the obscure Bronx businessman a more ominous presence. It was time for Sallett and his colleagues to dig deeper and find out more about Vinny Gorgeous—who turned out to be more than just a pretty face.

About two weeks after the first secret taping by Massino, Sallett and DeStefano took a drive in a government vehicle to Monitor Street in

Brooklyn. Pizzolo's blood had long ago dried up and disappeared. There wasn't anything special to see in the street behind the lumberyard. But any good investigator knows that it's always good to visit the scene of a homicide. You need to get a feel for the locale, bring a fresh set of eyes to the situation. NYPD detectives catch a lot of cases, including murders, but they tend to get overworked and might miss something. They also weren't as up to date on what was going on with the Mafia as the two feds.

Both men had their qualms about Massino. They hadn't recorded his first conversation in jail with Basciano, so they had to take his word about what they had discussed. As Massino remembered it, Basciano said without hesitation, in private and sotto voce, that he had ordered Pizzolo's murder. True, Massino had alluded to that first conversation a few times during the exercise area meeting, but was he being truthful in his debriefing about the first meeting, the one in which the prosecutor had been discussed? Sallett and DeStefano knew that Massino had failed a lie detector test not once but twice.

The nighttime desolation of the Greenpoint location struck both men. Daytime offered plenty of bustle as contractors picked up lumber, but at night there were only these streets. Anyone coming into the area must have known whom they were going to meet and—to a degree—trusted them. Pizzolo didn't have a gun—a telling fact. He was smart enough that he wouldn't let a stranger get the drop on him.

"It doesn't take Sherlock Holmes to know it was a mob hit," DeStefano said later about his visit to Monitor Street. "This was obviously a set up meeting. . . . He was obviously going to meet someone he knew."

Sallett and DeStefano noticed surveillance cameras on poles at the lumberyard. But as luck would have it, none was working in the moments when Pizzolo was killed. They were lacking direct evidence about who had killed Pizzolo, but they had the Massino tape containing a tantalizing series of conversations about the dead man and those who carried out the dirty deed. It was a good start. Pizzolo had made his share of enemies, and, while the list of those who could have wanted him killed was long, the agents had heard enough from Basciano's own mouth to make him a prime suspect, even though he had been in jail when the shooting took place.

Under federal law, prosecutors like charging mobsters with conspiracy to commit murder as part of a larger racketeering case. Basciano had already been charged with racketeering, including an earlier murder. But showing that he was involved with planning the Pizzolo murder would take more than his statements to Massino, which a good defense attorney could argue were contradictory. After all, Basciano said at one point that he ordered the hit and later that it was Michael Mancuso who actually did so.

With Massino neutralized, Basciano had become the most important Bonanno leader and the new man to target. But Sallett and DeStefano knew that nothing from their visit to Monitor Street or their check of Pizzolo's financial or telephone records—hell, even Massino's tape—could make a compelling case against him. Massino in particular was too problematic, too crafty to rely on alone. They left Brooklyn knowing they needed more. They had to look deeper into Basciano's past and the coterie of men who surrounded him to find what they needed.

The FBI now had Vinny Gorgeous in their sights.

3

WHOSE KID WAS THAT?

Puzzled, FBI agent Charles Rooney looked at the color photograph taken at the wedding reception held a year earlier at the Hotel Pierre in Manhattan. He had been inspecting a stack of over one hundred photos in his Rego Park office, but one in particular, depicting an eager, smiling young man, simply stumped him. Giuseppe Bono and his new bride, Antonino Albino, had been married at St. Patrick's Cathedral hours before the sumptuous hotel festivities on November 16, 1980.

It was the male cast of characters who had been in attendance, including the groom, that drew the FBI's interest. Rooney, along with colleague Carmine Russo, was leading what had turned into a long-term investigation of a major cocaine and heroin trafficking operation that used pizza parlors as a cover. It later became known as the Pizza Connection case and led to one of the longest criminal trials in federal court history.

But before the FBI could arrest any of the drug traffickers, Rooney, Russo, and the rest of the squad had to identify the various Sicilians and other Italians showing up in surveillances and wiretaps. On top of that, various members of the Bonanno crime family were involved, particularly out of the East New York section of Brooklyn.

The Italian police knew Bono himself as a major figure in Milanese organized crime. When Rooney inquired about him through Italy's law enforcement intelligence channels, the US authorities knew they had a major target on which to focus. Bono reportedly spent over $63,000 on the wedding, including over $4,000 for a professional photographer to cover the event.

The images included the requisite shots of bride and groom, who posed with various guests at a number of tables. The FBI ultimately subpoenaed the photos, which proved to be a treasure trove. At one level nothing more than happy snapshots, the pictures also provided a society register of major international organized crime figures, including major players in the Bonanno crime family. Vito Rizzuto, a Montreal mobster with thin, angular features, cut a suave figure in his tuxedo. Another Canadian, Gerlando Sciascia, also attended, as did Joseph Lopresti, considered a liaison between the Sicilians in Montreal and the Sicilians working with the Bonanno family in Brooklyn.

Scanning a photo of one table, Rooney noticed several American men known to be members and associates of the Bonanno borgata. Seated was Frank Lino, a soldier from Brooklyn; leaning closer to him was an associate with a bad cocaine habit, Anthony "Bruno" Indelicato, the son of prominent captain Alphonse Indelicato. To Lino's right was J. B. Indelicato, another Bonanno soldier and Alphonse's brother. Sitting nearest the camera was a tight-lipped Joseph Benanti. To his immediate left was a very stout Dominick "Big Trin" Trinchera, who, like Alphonse Indelicato, served as one of the Bonanno family's more important captains. Standing behind those who were seated was Philip Giaccone, along with Trinchera and Alphonse Indelicato, a key family captain.

This was likely the last time that all three men had their picture taken together. In eight months they all lay dead, brutally killed on May 4, 1981, in a struggle for control of the Bonanno family. Their bodies were buried in a deserted lot as a favor to the winning faction—led by Joseph Massino, as it turned out—from the crew of an Ozone Park gangster known as John Gotti. Cops found Alphonse Indelicato's rotting body just a few weeks after the slayings. It took the FBI nearly a quarter of a century to dig up the remains of Trinchera and Giaccone after Massino started to cooperate.

Plenty of well-coiffed, nicely dressed ladies appeared in the photos, some sultry, others more matronly. But one young man in the back row stood out because he looked out of place to Rooney. The other male guests wore tuxedos or business suits, but this kid—no more than twenty years old—stood behind Trinchera in an open-necked shirt. He sported no tie and yet seemed happy among the made men. Because he was so under-dressed, Rooney thought this had to be a son of one of the guests, meaning his lack of sartorial respect wouldn't cause offense.

A career FBI agent from Brooklyn, Rooney turned around at his desk and showed the photo to Russo, himself an Italian by birth. Neither man knew the kid's identity. With more pressing work ahead of them, the two men shifted their focus to the drug dealers. It took the agents a while to identify Vincent Basciano as the grinning kid—and his proximity to Trinchera in the photo was no accidental placement.

Vincent Basciano was born on November 14, 1959. Although he earned the moniker "Vinnie from the Bronx," Basciano wasn't raised there. His parents lived in Yonkers, the city on the Hudson River just north of the Bronx, at that time predominately a mix of working and middle-class Polish, Italian, and Irish families as well as blacks who had immigrated from the South.

Basciano's father, Gennaro, worked as a stone cutter in New York City. His mother, Shirley, a homemaker, raised him and his two brothers. By the time Vincent turned thirteen, the Basciano family had moved farther north to New City in Rockland County, more of a bedroom community to the city after the Tappan Zee Bridge opened in 1955. Gennaro Basciano had a reputation for being a good craftsman, but he also had some personal devils. As later stated in federal court records, Gennaro drank and became abusive, although a family member later said it was only a bad temper that caused problems. Vincent sometimes had to intercede.

During his teen years, Basciano developed a brashness and quickness with his hands that allowed him to take care of himself on the street.

According to Barry Levin, an attorney who later defended Basciano, the gangster as a young man intervened when weaker, more defenseless teens were being bullied. He did that for one of his cousins and also helped out the nephew of the up-and-coming mobster Dominick Trinchera, remembered Levin. As a result, Trinchera took a liking to Basciano and allowed him to hang around his social club and to accompany him to nightclubs on Allerton Avenue in the Bronx. Soon Basciano became Trinchera's driver, which put the young man constantly in the company of the older man, which explains their proximity in the wedding photo that had so mystified the FBI.

The Pierre Hotel photo presents clear evidence that by 1980 Basciano was associating with the Bonanno family. Once he forged this link to the world of organized crime, it hooked him into a lifestyle that he wouldn't relinquish—even after Trinchera, his mentor, was brutally murdered with his two cohorts in the infamous Three Captains homicide.

Like most mob associates, Basciano didn't start out with a particularly noteworthy employment history, particularly after Trinchera's murder. But over time he built his own life, unafraid to take chances as a businessman. It was also in 1980 that Basciano, while having drinks one evening in a small pub at the Cross County Shopping Center in Yonkers, met a trim and pretty Italian woman. From the Bronx, of Neapolitan lineage, department store saleswoman Angela Tocco had gone there to keep a girlfriend company. Although Angela was already in a relationship, Basciano was smitten by the doe-eyed brunette. Initially wary of Basciano, five years younger and a bit brash for her tastes, Angela began a relationship with Vinny that led to marriage in December 1980. A short time later the couple had their first son, Vincent Jr., and took up residence in the Bronx.

Coming from a family with no significant business background, Basciano struggled to find a legitimate livelihood by relying on his own ambition and drive. He had some connections to illegitimate cash, though, and soon after Trinchera's demise he fell in with another associate who knew his way around gambling operations. Anthony "Tony Cole" Colangelo was tied firmly to bookmaking in the Bronx, an activity with a long history that crossed ethnic lines and formed a staple of street life in a lot of ethnic communities: Puerto Rican, Italian, Jewish, black, Chinese.

Each gambling operation had its own cast of characters. In New York City, many prominent bookmakers came from either Jewish or Italian families, particularly in the Bronx. The overall system involved nothing more than the taking of wagers from customers for agreed-upon odds. When necessary, runners collected bets from the patrons. The gambling house made its money on the spread, and—as anyone from Nevada knows—the house wins no less than 51 percent of the time, thereby collecting more than it pays out to winners.

Typically, each mob gambling location—or "store" as they're called—had clerks who took bets from patrons at windows in the establishment and used their initials, placed on slips. The stores might masquerade as record or music vendors and keep some token samples or merchandise to mask the real business at hand. A trusted associate picked up the slips and took them back to a central location to await the results. Business could be substantial, with hundreds of patrons showing up on a busy day to place bets. Compensated well for their work, the store clerks could pay out on hits from the money collected at the store. But a large hit required the clerk to contact the "office," which sent over more money to make the larger payments. Sometimes one gambling operation laid off a bet to spread the risk with other bookmakers. There were also guns on the premises of the stores, since they often contained thousands of dollars in cash, making them prime targets for robberies.

Many mob-connected social clubs and coffee shops began to stock gambling video games like "Joker Poker." While a machine could in theory make big payouts, again the odds were stacked against the bettor. The devices became cash cows, generating hundreds and thousands of dollars per week in profits. Cafes, bodegas, and social clubs all had the machines on the premises. Massino had them in his social clubs, and he expected his captains and associates to "do the right thing" by throwing him a couple of hundred dollars a week as tribute from the machine profits.

To avoid competition for customers in a particular geographical area, crime families divided up a given territory. They generally respected the boundaries of the territories, but disputes did arise, which called for meetings among emissaries of the various borgatas in what was euphemistically known as a sit-down.

One of the bigger bookmakers in the Bronx, the late Frank Caruso inherited operations from some older Jewish gamblers. Caruso was indicted on federal gambling charges in 1975 and pleaded guilty, which got him only six months in prison, recalled attorney Murray Richman, who represented one of the codefendants in the case. An inveterate gambler with numerous arrests and seven convictions to his credit, Caruso operated out of a luncheonette on White Plains Road. Colangelo earned his stripes as a controller or money manager for bookmakers like Caruso, as did Alfred Bottone Sr. But it was Colangelo, remembered one Bronx source familiar with the mob scene, who took over Trinchera's gambling operation when he was killed in 1981.

A snappy dresser, Colangelo had more than just bookmaking on his plate. As far back as the early 1970s, he played a role in cocaine trafficking and in 1972 was arrested on charges of participating in a large-scale

Anthony "Tony Cole" Colangelo

drug ring that operated from suburban New Jersey and New York to supply distributors in Harlem. In a prosecution that involved a number of reputed mobsters—some murdered during the course of the investigation—Colangelo was convicted of one count of conspiracy to supply cocaine to the ring. He received a ten-year sentence in 1973.

Unfortunately for Colangelo, he didn't learn his lesson the first time around. At approximately the same time he was inheriting Trinchera's operations in the early 1980s, he was also scheduled to go away to federal prison for a second time for drug trafficking. But prison can't stop a good bookmaking business. As luck would have it, Colangelo, through his old friend Trinchera, had become friendly with Basciano and thought highly of his abilities as a manager. When Colangelo started having trouble with his numbers stores around Bedford and Montgomery Streets in Brooklyn, he put Basciano in charge of the locations, one federal informant later told the FBI.

Basciano worked magic with Colangelo's stores. According to the informant, who was close to Colangelo, the old man's troublesome locations became lucrative, and he decided to turn the businesses over to Basciano and his friend Anthony Donato. The locations included gambling stores on the Grand Concourse and in Baychester, both in the Bronx. Colangelo, who was losing interest in bookmaking, then split the proceeds with Basciano and Donato. Once Colangelo went away to prison for a second time, his share of the gambling proceeds went to his longtime girlfriend, Anna Caruncho. The weekly envelopes she received contained tidy sums, ranging anywhere from $2,000 to $7,000 a week, she later told investigators.

The arrangement with Colangelo worked smoothly, but Basciano's success drew the attention of the New York City Police Department. In a Brooklyn storefront just before midnight on February 20, 1983, cops from the Public Morals Division arrested Basciano and two other men. The charges represented a garden variety of gambling offenses. The original complaint alleged that Basciano and his codefendants had in their posses-sion 198 policy slips, representing bets totaling $883, averaging just over $3 a bet. Cops also found $2,543 among the three men. Court records show that Basciano told police that he was living with his wife on Swin-ton Road in the Bronx, apparently the home of his in-laws.

Basciano also reported to police at the time of his arrest that he had been unemployed for at least three months. But it appears he had already begun taking steps to open a video rental business. In January 1983, about a month before the gambling bust, Basciano incorporated B&V Video, Inc., in the Bronx, according to state records. Stiff competition from stores like Blockbuster Video pushed Basciano out of media rentals and into a tanning studio and beauty salon that ultimately inspired his nickname.

An upstate petty larceny arrest in 1978 had been dismissed, so the gambling case was the first significant arrest cops had on record for Basci-ano. Officially, the charges constituted one count of promoting gambling and one of possession of gambling records, both low-level felonies. There was no disposition for the case listed, and state records show that Basci-ano didn't receive jail time. But more serious trouble was coming his way.

David Nunez made a living being a numbers clerk in the Bronx. It wasn't bad as far as wages went. A good clerk in 1984, when Nunez started working, could pull in about $750 a week for just over six days of taking bets. (Sunday was a half day for obvious reasons.) If bettors hit big, he could expect to receive tips. Saturday was the big day for the store on White Plains Road with over six hundred customers, with food provided.

One day in November 1985, Nunez had the job of bringing around $15,000 to another gambling location nearby on White Plains Road at around 8:00 a.m. to pay off a customer's large winning bet. That kind of money run wasn't uncommon, and Nunez took a livery service and a shotgun for protection as usual. The drive lasted only a few blocks. Nunez stepped from the cab in front of the Happy Garden Chinese restaurant.

"Dave," someone said.

The cab driver heard somebody mention something about money. A high school student waiting nearby for a bus also recalled somebody asking for money.

Turning to his right on the sidewalk, Nunez saw a man beside a blue Chevrolet Impala with tinted windows and a New Jersey license plate. He also saw for just an instant the .38-caliber Charter Arms revolver the man was holding that fired five times. The bullets hit Nunez in his right shoulder, chin, chest, and grazed his head. Another round struck the window of the open cab door. Showing surprising self-awareness, Nunez first dropped to his knees, then drew his own .38, stood up, and tried to move toward the shooter, who had jumped through an open window into the Impala, which sped off, his two legs dangling. Witnesses nearby noted that the driver of the Chevrolet, the shooter, and another man in the car all wore ski masks.

Although wounded in four places, Nunez slid back into the livery cab and waved a $100 bill to convince the driver to take him to Our Lady of Mercy Hospital, the closest emergency room in that part of town. The driver radioed to his dispatcher to say a passenger had been shot.

"I don't believe they shot me," Nunez said in disbelief.

At the hospital, one of the controllers of the bookmaking operation arrived before the police and took the money that Nunez was carrying as well as the shotgun. Police officers arrived to provide some security for Nunez while doctors treated his non–life-threatening wounds.

The curbside shooting wasn't the first time Nunez had run into trouble. Later he told an investigator how two men in the months before the shooting twice had showed up at his regular gambling store and either threw out the workers or fired at Nunez, protected by bulletproof glass.

"Get out of here, you don't belong here," one of the armed assailants had said.

Nunez drove off his attackers with a rifle he kept behind the counter of the store.

Back at the scene of the storefront shooting, though, an eyewitness gave police the license plate number of the suspects' car. About ten minutes later a patrol car from the 47th Precinct noticed a vehicle that matched the description and pursued it to Provost Avenue and East 233rd Street in the Bronx. The driver, whom police later identified as Patrick DeFilippo, made a hard right into a private driveway . . . that a bulldozer just so happened to be blocking. The police car pulled up behind it, preventing any escape. Seconds later, according to a police account, the cops noticed a revolver thrown from the driver's side. At the same time, police saw a man they identified as Basciano flee the car from the front passenger seat with another gun in his hand and run toward a construction site. Basciano threw the gun to the ground, but police recovered the fully loaded .38-caliber revolver. Back at the vehicle driven by DeFilippo, police found him and Donato, the latter in the back seat. Outside the car, cops also found another .38. It contained one live round and five spent shells. A search found two ski masks. All three men were arrested.

Given his background and arrest record, investigators doubted Nunez's initial claim that he was the victim of a mugging. To investigators with the Bronx District Attorney's Office, eyewitness accounts of masked men seen switching cars had the earmarks of an organized crime operation. Threatened with prosecution for obstruction of justice or worse, Nunez agreed to look at a photo lineup of possible shooting suspects.

Nunez looked at a spread of fifteen to twenty images, which, from the looks of it, were taken during street surveillances. The names of the people in the images were written on the front. Despite the statement of witnesses that his assailants wore ski masks, Nunez identified the three men who attacked him: Vincent Basciano, Anthony Donato, and Patrick DeFilippo. A day later, an unshaven, bleary-eyed, and rumpled Basciano appeared in a lineup with three Hispanic men who, a defense attorney later remarked, did not look much like the suspect. Nunez, just

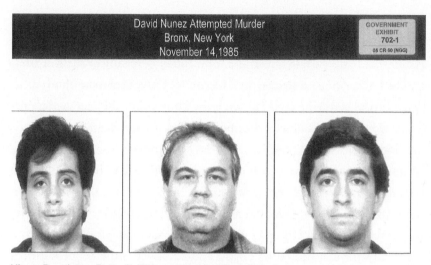

David Nunez Attempted Murder
Bronx, New York
November 14,1985

GOVERNMENT
EXHIBIT
702-1
05 CR 60 (NGG)

Vinny Basciano, Patty DeFilippo, and Anthony Donato

a day or so out of the hospital, nervously identified to police that Basciano had shot him.

Armed with the results of the lineup and other evidence, Bronx prosecutors hit Basciano with his first serious felony case: the attempted murder of David Nunez on November 14, 1985. Also charged were Patrick DeFilippo, the older Bonanno gangster who was the suspected driver of the getaway car, and Anthony Donato. Although it was unclear at the time, another Bronx gambler, Alfred Bottone Sr., with whom Basciano worked, may have ordered the hit.

Freed on $35,000 bail, Basciano hired Murray Richman, one of the better-known defense attorneys in the Bronx. A likable schmoozer who had long practiced in the borough courts, as well as in the federal system, Richman battled hard and often worked out favorable plea bargains for a wide range of clientele, from drug dealers to politicians. A short, stocky man who had the appearance of everybody's likable Jewish uncle, Richman prided himself on being what he called "a friend to the friendless."

Though few knew it, Richman had a penchant for growing tomatoes, a horticultural skill that put him in good stead with some of his Italian clients. He had a certain affection for mobsters, generally of the Bonanno family. Earlier, he had represented Dominick Trinchera, who showed his appreciation before he died by giving the attorney a gold ring with a precious stone, which Richman fondly showed to friends years later.

The defense strategy of Richman and the attorney for DeFilippo was to attack the eyewitness identifications. They did so in February 1987 at a hearing before a Bronx state court judge. The session set the prosecution back. Lineups are supposed to be conducted scrupulously, with no possibility that a victim or witness might in anyway be influenced to identify a suspect. In the case of DeFilippo, the alleged driver of the car, prosecutors conceded that one of their witnesses actually saw him for about twenty minutes while he was in a holding cell just before the lineup. The situation flabbergasted the judge.

"In a situation where any civilian witness comes to the police station, that witness can, by his own, wander through an area and look into a holding pen. How can that be right?" Bronx State Supreme Court judge Bernard Fried asked of assistant district attorney Michael Kalmus.

Despite Kalmus's argument that the witness already knew DeFilippo by having sold him a car, the court wouldn't allow the lineup to be used.

A different kind of problem developed with the lineup identification of Basciano. While Nunez had initially identified Basciano as the shooter, the victim started to have doubts. He later gave the defense a statement in which he recanted his earlier identification. Nunez said that he believed the assailant was a short man with a mustache—which the clean-shaven Basciano never had. He just wasn't sure anymore, said Nunez in the statement given to the defense.

Richman told the court about Nunez's change of heart. Then additional problems came to light. The prosecutor told the court that he had been having trouble actually finding Nunez to prepare him for trial.

Detectives had tried to serve a material witness arrest warrant on Nunez a day earlier, and when they went to his house they learned from his father that Nunez was gone.

"Mr. Nunez's father indicated to the detectives that the witness was frightened and he was scared to testify. He was scared for his own safety and his family's safety," prosecutor Kalmus told the judge. "He was scared because he indicated to the detectives that these people were connected with organized crime, the people who had shot him."

Since prosecutors didn't know when they might be able to locate Nunez—and arrest him if necessary to bring him to court—Judge Fried adjourned the case for six months, until September 1987. Fried indicated that if prosecutors still weren't ready with Nunez by then, he might consider dismissing the case entirely.

Circumstantial evidence pointed to the involvement of the three men in the shooting, but forensic evidence wasn't helping the prosecution's case. A ballistic examination found that the guns recovered couldn't be linked to the shooting. State records later revealed that Basciano, admitting that he had a fully loaded handgun when chased by the cops, said that he carried it because he often carried large amounts of cash for his businesses, which at that point included legitimate stores. Basciano also said that he was in the vicinity of the cab stand when the shooting occurred because he was considering purchasing it.

The problems in the case worked in the favor of Basciano and his two codefendants. Richman worked out a plea bargain, in which prosecutors dropped the attempted murder charge and reduced the case to one of criminal possession of a weapon in the third degree. While still a felony, the weapons charge carried a more lenient sentence than attempted murder, punishable by a minimum of ten years. On June 19, 1987, Basciano pleaded guilty to the weapons count and received a jail term of one year—a cakewalk considering what would have happened if the trio had gone to trial and lost for attempted murder. The cases against DeFilippo and Donato were dropped.

Why so much trouble with Nunez as a cooperating witness, though? A number of stories later emerged. Years later, federal witnesses testified that Nunez was shot because of a conflict in the gambling business with Basciano and Donato. Since Nunez worked at a gambling store run by DeFilippo and had a set practice of taking the livery cab each day at around the same time, any assailant could easily track his movements. According to investigators, Nunez had left the city for the safety of his family while police were trying to locate him for trial. Court records show that in the following years he was arrested on charges of sexually abusing a young girl and sentenced to a term in state prison.

On the gun case, Basciano received a prison sentence ranging from one year to three years, not bad for a first felony. On January 15, 1988, he reported to McGregor Correctional Facility, a medium-security prison about forty miles north of Albany. Correction records show that Basciano—characterized as pleasant, cooperative, and friendly—adjusted well to life at McGregor, working on outside cleanup crews.

But Basciano rubbed one prisoner at McGregor the wrong way, provoking threats. Because of the threats, Basciano went into protective custody and later moved to Great Meadows Correctional Facility, a maximum-security prison near Lake George and close to the Vermont border. While at Great Meadows, Basciano again proved to be a good worker and friendly, factors that worked in his favor when it came time for parole and getting into a work-release program.

In April 1987, some months before Basciano reported to McGregor, his old mentor Anthony Colangelo emerged from Danbury federal correctional facility. The seventy-three-year-old mob associate had finished his second prison term for heroin trafficking and had reached a crossroads in his life. He had been losing interest in the gambling business, formerly his mainstay that had provided him and his common-law wife, Anna, with a nice income, even while he was locked up.

But Colangelo had heard from a friend that people had been steal-ing from him. Colangelo's son, government records show, had also come across a newspaper account that related how two of his father's trusted business associates—Basciano and Donato—had been accused of Nunez's attempted murder. Another interesting wrinkle formed in that account: The codefendant was Patrick DeFilippo, someone with whom Basciano and Donato might be aligning themselves in the gambling world, the son told federal investigators.

One day in May 1987, Colangelo told Anna that he had some busi-ness to take care of. It involved some kind of trouble, but she shouldn't worry because he had "the kids" with him. Colangelo wore a fancy Jules Jurgensen wristwatch inlayed with diamonds on the face, which he only donned for special occasions. He was sporting fancy socks also, and he took two pairs of glasses with him. Colangelo's son later told federal investigators that he thought it unusual that his father doubled up on the glasses, and he believed "the kids" referred to Basciano and Donato.

Colangelo and Anna drove to her video rental store on Central Avenue in Yonkers at around lunchtime on May 23. Each drove in a separate car, Colangelo taking his white Mercedes. After helping Anna rent some videos to customers, he told her that he had to leave but would be back and take her out to dinner. Anna knew enough not to ask his business.

"He would not have told me, and I was used to him just leaving on his own without telling me where he was going," Anna later said. She also later changed her statement, maintaining that she and Colangelo didn't go to the video store but instead said their good-byes that day at home. Either way, she never saw him again.

The Sprain Brook Parkway, a major roadway north of New York City, cuts through a picturesque area of Yonkers. The road passes the Sprain Brook Reservoir, the prime water supply for Yonkers, and continues northbound through wooded areas. No service stations punctuate the route, and when a driver has to answer the call of nature, it isn't much of a problem to pull a car off to the side of the road to take a break in the trees.

The morning of July 2, 1987, a driver did just that, easing off the road about a half mile north of the Jackson Avenue exit. While relieving himself, the driver looked around and noticed a large black plastic garbage bag tied in several places with clothesline, giving the mass a trussed-up appearance. The shape of the bag and its contents were unmistakable, and the shaken motorist called the police.

The Town of Greenburgh Police Department responded to the area on the northbound side of the parkway. Peeling away just a portion of the plastic—actually more than one bag—the cops saw decomposing human remains. The body lay in a fetal position amid extensive maggot infestation. Skin had slipped away from the body in some areas. At least one of the forearms had gone skeletal, and a watch encircled a wrist. Despite the poor condition of the remains, the coroner focused on the skull, which still had on a pair of glasses. A determination of the cause of death came quickly. Four bullet tracks marked the skull and neck, and bullets for each were found in the skull and the shrunken brain tissue within.

"Multiple gun shot wounds of Back of Head and Neck Involving the Brain," was the state cause of death on the autopsy report. A police report also indicated that marks on the bullets suggested that either a silencer was used on the gun or that it had a defective muzzle. It was unmistakably an execution-style slaying.

Ascertaining the identity of the body also proved relatively easy. The clothing contained personal papers and items of interest, among them an address book that contained enough information for the coroner to make a tentative identification of Anthony Colangelo. Dental records confirmed the identity, and later one of Colangelo's sons identified the Jules Jurgensen watch and glasses as belonging to his father.

Early in the investigation, police couldn't figure out who would have wanted Colangelo dead. Anna was of no help. Her accounts of Colangelo's last hours with her contradicted themselves, a product it seems of her initial confusion and shock after learning of his demise. In later recounting for investigators, Anna remembered that a day after Colangelo didn't return home, she began to panic and contacted Basciano. According to her, Basciano didn't seem too concerned but offered to ask around to find out why Colangelo hadn't come home.

Investigators knew that both Basciano and Donato had been involved with Colangelo in gambling stores, so they approached them both. State police interviewed Donato at his home in the Bronx about a week before Basciano. A summary of the interview later filed in Brooklyn federal court indicated that Donato lied to the cops, denying working for Colangelo, although he did admit knowing the dead man. When the cops asked Donato if he, Basciano, and Colangelo had gone somewhere together, he became angry and said that he was being courteous talking to the cops and had nothing further to say to them, according to the police summary.

State police interviewed Basciano while he was on a work-release program for his gun possession conviction. According to a police report of the interview, Basciano "seemed relaxed and to display his intent to cooperate." Basciano told the officer that he had last seen Colangelo about a week before he disappeared. "Subject [Basciano] claimed that he knew absolutely nothing about Anthony Colangelo's business and didn't know why anyone would want to execute him," the officer reported. In terms of what Anna Caruncho later told investigators, Basciano's claim of ignorance about Colangelo's business dealings was also a lie.

No one has ever been charged with the killing of Anthony Colangelo. Caruncho, his longtime girlfriend, died in 2009. So what happened to the gambling enterprise that Colangelo had overseen for so many years? According to government informants, Vincent Basciano ran the operation for a time as his very own.

4

THOUGH VINCENT BASCIANO'S SMALL-TIME GAMBLING ARRESTS HAD
started to put him on the radar of law enforcement, the attempted murder
of David Nunez and the killing of Anthony Colangelo certainly enhanced
his profile further, both among his associates and the law. The murders,
as well as the charges and innuendo that linked them to Basciano, gave
him credibility useful in his burgeoning career as a street gangster. He had
risen to another league and not just as a petty gambler.

At the end of 1988 or early 1989, not long after state police interviewed him about the Colangelo case, Basciano, released from his work-
release program on the gun charge, went back home to his wife, Angela,
and their three sons in the Bronx—their youngest son, Michael, not yet
born. Parole officials, state records show, were impressed with the "excel-
lent support base" Basciano had at home, meaning his wife and children.
He also had two video rental outlets to which he returned for work, and
he was preparing a Blimpie sandwich franchise store nearby as another
venture in his business empire on East Tremont Avenue.

The Blimpie operation was little more than another food joint in an
ethnic Italian and Hispanic neighborhood. Basciano worked behind the
counter himself, slicing the provolone and salami and serving customers.
The neighborhood liked that kind of service from an owner, and Basciano's chattiness endeared him to customers. When business was slow in
the sandwich store, he could always go next door to the video store.

Unable to compete against bigger video chain stores, Basciano began
transitioning his businesses soon after he left state custody. Records

Vinny and Angela Basciano celebrate the First Communion of their son Joseph.
HANDOUT PHOTO

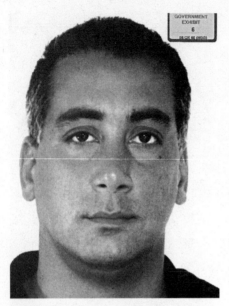

GOVERNMENT
EXHIBIT
6
05 CR 06 (NGG)

Vincent Basciano around 1991

show that in November 1991 he incorporated Tremont Nail & Tanning Salon, Inc., which he ultimately named Hello Gorgeous, on East Tremont. With both Vinny and Angela on the premises, Hello Gorgeous did well for a while. Nicknames don't always stick, and his businesses sometimes provided him with new ones. Vinny from the Bronx had become "Vinny Blimpie," and now the salon inspired his latest moniker, the one that stuck: "Vinny Gorgeous."

After his release, Basciano became a more frequent presence on the street in the company of Bonanno family members. Through the gambling connection, Patty DeFilippo, one of the crime family's mainstays in the Bronx, squired Basciano around town, although DeFilippo had an apartment in Manhattan. DeFilippo's connection to the Bonanno family went back to the time of patriarch Joseph Bonanno. DeFilippo's father had been a close associate of Bonanno, and in the 1960s he and a few other select men accompanied the boss's son, Salvatore, to Canada. Police never determined the exact reason for the trip, but Canadian officials expelled the group after finding two guns in their cars.

Salvatore Bonanno's trip coincided with a serious power struggle in the crime family that ultimately led to a major shift in leadership. In the face of hostility from the ruling Commission of the New York crime families over how they had tried to position Salvatore as boss, both Salvatore and his father decamped to Arizona. The elder Bonanno lived there in forced retirement while his son flirted with returning to power—while never actually doing so. By mid-1968, the so-called "Bananas War," which got its name from one of Bonanno's monikers, had ended, and police realized that Paul Sciacca, a low-key Long Island mobster who ran a garment company, had taken over as new boss.

But Sciacca wasn't in good health and appointed Frank Mari as his successor, a move the Commission approved, in May 1969. But Mari's tenure

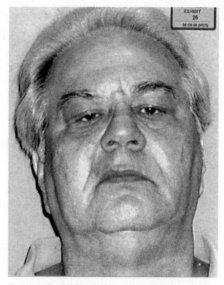

Patrick DeFilippo, Bonanno captain

proved short lived, however, when four months later he disappeared, possibly over his alleged involvement in the murder of gangster Sam Perrone or the way he had rocketed to the top as deputy boss. To fill the leadership gap, the Commission appointed a three-man panel of garment trucker Natale Evola (an old friend of Joseph Bonanno), Philip Rastelli, and Joseph DiFilippi. Rastelli eventually won control of the Bonanno family, although long stretches in prison fractured his reign from the early 1980s until his death in 1991.

With a pedigree like that, DeFilippo had a secure place in the crime family, welcomed at all of its social clubs. In the mob, if you have any pretense of advancement, you need a mentor, and DeFilippo seems to have played that role for Basciano. Law enforcement intelligence reports showed that by the early 1990s, DeFilippo was taking Basciano around town, including a discreetly located social club down an alley in Maspeth, Queens.

The club off Grand Avenue was a favorite of Salvatore Vitale, an aspiring captain and the brother-in-law of Joseph Massino. Vitale's club had drawn the attention of the FBI from 1990 through 1992 during an intelligence operation known as Grand Finale, part of a budding agency offensive against the family. Vitale and his crew knew that the FBI might be watching, so instead of making telephone calls inside the club they turned to a pay phone outside the public library on Grand Avenue. This public move didn't escape the attention of the FBI agents, who promptly put a wiretap on the pay phone to glean what information they could. The tap didn't yield any major evidence against Vitale, who was acting as Massino's surrogate on the street. The surveillance did ensnare a few crime family members, notably Michael "Mickey Bats" Cardello, who pleaded guilty in 1994 to a charge of racketeering, receiving forty-one months in prison.

The FBI in New York—stretched thin because of a bloody war within the Colombo crime family—had to use their agents elsewhere, but, while focused on Vitale's club, FBI cameras had a field day snapping photos of all the Bonanno family members who showed up. The agents had spent months in the neighborhood and finally had the chance to rent an apartment across from the alley that led to the club. Since some of their subjects knew them by sight, the FBI surveillance teams carefully parked their cars a few blocks away from the neighborhood and entered the apartment building through a side door.

Among others, the cameras captured DeFilippo and his Bronx friend Basciano. Often wearing sunglasses and flowery shirts, Basciano was clearly well liked. Agents photographed him with big-name captains like James Tartaglione, draping his arm around the younger man's shoulder. A made man wouldn't comport himself in such a way with just anybody. That level of familiarity, seen in 1991, signaled that Basciano had been inducted into the borgata.

DeFilippo's gambling operations formed his major source of income and his major moneymaker for the crime family. Basciano of course had

ANTHONY M. DESTEFANO

his legitimate sources of income. But they operated in tandem, DeFilippo placing some of his Joker Poker machines in places that Basciano controlled. Basciano also served as a source of the machines if any other family members needed them. DeFilippo protected Basciano when needed. When the Lucchese crime family complained about a Joker Poker spot controlled by Basciano, DeFilippo attended the sit-down that hashed out the dispute in favor of the Bonanno family. A portion of the money from the machines was put aside each month for Vitale and Massino.

Sometimes disputes weren't settled easily, though. In conversations some years later with the FBI, former Bonanno soldier Joseph D'Amico recalled a night in the mid-1990s when he and Basciano went to a bar on Spring Street in SoHo controlled by a member of the rival Gambino crime family. Basciano got into a fight with a bartender, and the NYPD soon arrived, remembered D'Amico. Perhaps fearful that an arrest might mar his parole status from the Nunez case, Basciano jumped behind the bar and ran out the back. Bonanno crime family soldier Frank Lino had a talk with the Gambino family that settled the tiff.

While supervising a significant gambling operation, DeFilippo had his own crew of soldiers, apart from Basciano, considered his men. According to government records, that group included Michael "Mikey Nose" Mancuso, a product of East Harlem, his notoriety resting on his 1986 manslaughter conviction in the death of his wife, Evelina, after he shot her in the head and then dumped her outside a Bronx hospital. The killing earned Mancuso a ten-year prison sentence that kept him behind bars until 1996.

Basciano became an official member of DeFilippo's crew when the crime family formally inducted him into their numbers. Exactly when that event happened remains unclear. One informant told the FBI that Basciano went through the Cosa Nostra initiation with Sally "The Horse" Tozzi, but he didn't give a time period. Former Bonanno underboss Sal Vitale, whose recollection about family events seemed more precise, told

51

Michael "Mikey Nose" Mancuso

the FBI that Basciano became a made man in the early 1990s—likely in 1991—after his old mentor DeFilippo formally sponsored him. Since Massino was in prison at this point for a federal conviction and wouldn't be released until 1992, it was up to Vitale to handle the initiation.

As a legitimate businessman, Basciano was earning a comfortable income of about $3,500 a week. Angela Basciano had her own earnings, and the family, which by 1991 saw the addition of fourth son, Michael, seemed cohesive. Despite aligning with DeFilippo's crew and making required appearances at social clubs, Basciano usually made it home for family dinners and often showed up at his sons' Little League games and school events. He never went further than a high school diploma himself, but Basciano helped his sons when they ran into trouble with homework.

It was the kind of environment, one psychologist later remarked, in which Basciano provided a source of authority and structure.

Real estate records show that Basciano, Angela, and their sons moved from their home on Swinton Avenue in the Bronx in 1991 into a larger and more expensive home on Gatehouse Road in Scarsdale, some twenty miles north. Many area middle-class families aspired to live in Scarsdale. Aside from its relatively bucolic setting in Westchester County, a Scarsdale address meant affluence and achievement, as well as the status that went along with both.

His work habits made Basciano an achiever. In the mob world, he certainly had status—although his Scarsdale neighbors might not agree. But federal investigators were starting to have serious questions about the source of his fortune. The government's attempt to find out how Basciano made his money was about to put his wealth, status, and liberty all at risk.

5

MENTION HEROIN AND THE MOB TO A NEW YORK CITY COP, AND you'll likely get images conjured from *The French Connection,* the quintessential crime film about the obsessive hunt by Detective John "Popeye" Doyle for the traffickers of narcotics from France. The film was based on a true story involving attempts to bring in 220 pounds of heroin originating in Turkey through the French port of Marseilles. The case led to a number of convictions, but in a still unsolved mystery, the heroin was stolen from the NYPD evidence storage facility.

As iconic as *The French Connection* remains, the reality upon which it was based changed dramatically over the years. The source of much of New York's heroin in the 1980s and early 1990s wasn't Europe but rather Southeast Asia, specifically the area known as the Golden Triangle in the border zone of Laos, Burma, and Thailand. Major traffickers included Asian gangs and syndicates working out of Hong Kong who had a ready market in New York City. The shipments also dwarfed anything Detective Doyle might have seen. Intercepted cargoes weighed up to a ton, and in three locations in Queens authorities found over 820 pounds of the stuff.

The standard legend in the American Mafia was that drugs were off limits. The old mob bosses, fearful of the draconian sentences they or their members could face if caught, put out word that anyone trafficking did so at his peril and could be killed. The main proponent of the hands-off policy was allegedly Joseph Bonanno, the crime family patriarch. Sometime in 1947, according to an account by his son, Bonanno prevailed upon the Commission to pass a resolution of sorts to ban narcotics involvement.

That became the source of the prevailing wisdom that the American Mafia wasn't involved in drugs.

But the wisdom prevailed on no one in the crime families. The ban on drugs turned out to be a charade. Major mob families had members, some very high ranking, involved in trafficking heroin, morphine base, or other drugs. In 2007 a published US Treasury Department Bureau of Narcotics compendium gave an A-to-Z listing of hundreds of reputed mob members and associates, of whom some were allegedly involved in narcotics as far back as the 1950s. The names included the late Lucchese crime family boss Anthony "Tony Ducks" Corallo, Bonanno crime family captain Carmine Galante, and even the late Carlo Gambino.

In 1959 in a federal case in Manhattan, the mob's ties to narcotics trafficking reared their hydra heads with the conviction of Galante, John Ormento of the Lucchese family, and the powerful Genovese crime family namesake Vito Genovese. All received substantial prison sentences, and both Genovese and Ormento eventually died behind bars. But those prosecutions did nothing to dissuade American and Italian Mafiosi from trafficking. FBI agents Charles Rooney and Carmine Russo found clear evidence of continued mob drug dealing as they put together the Pizza Connection case. They discovered that a group of Sicilian gangsters in Brooklyn had cemented ties to a number of Bonanno crime family members in an international ring that smuggled heroin into the New York City area through a chain of pizza parlors. At the heart of the investigation stood Salvatore "Toto" Catalano, a Sicilian Mafioso who had become a major player in the Bonanno family.

When in 1984 Rooney finally drafted the criminal complaint in the case, it ran to over three hundred pages long and spelled out in detail how key players in the Bonanno family, notably Catalano and other Sicilians like Cesare Bonventre and Baldo Amato, had played central roles in the heroin conspiracy. In June 1987, after an eighteen-month trial in Manhattan federal court, Catalano, Amato, and others were convicted.

Bonventre never made it to trial, but he didn't make out well either. He was killed and dismembered before the trial started.

The evidence in the Pizza Connection case showed how deeply involved the American mob was with drugs. For some of the old-timers, the Bonanno family's drug dealing was just too much. Anthony "Fat Tony" Salerno, an old Genovese crime family boss, hung out in a social club in East Harlem, which the FBI knew for years. They saw it as a prime location to plant a bug. Salerno didn't hold back at times, and the recordings reveal how much disdain the Bonanno family incurred over its drug involvement and other transgressions, notably the undercover penetration by FBI agent Joseph Pistone posing as wiseguy Donnie Brasco.

"There are too many junk guys," said a gruff-talking Salerno in a May 1984 bugged conversation as he talked about the Bonanno family. "They got a crew of eighty guys like that."

Drug dealing and the Pistone penetration provided the chief reasons that Salerno and other mob bosses wouldn't let the Bonanno family back into the ruling Commission. While a major slight, it actually worked to the Bonanno family's benefit. By keeping the borgata away from participation in some major rackets, the other crime bosses unknowingly insulated the family from the spectacular Commission indictment of February 1985, the brainchild of then–Manhattan US attorney Rudolph Giuliani. In that case, prosecutors indicted Salerno and heads of three other families: Gambino boss Paul Castellano, Lucchese boss Corallo, and Carmine "The Snake" Persico, who led the Colombo family. Bonanno boss Philip Rastelli was also charged, although he was later dropped from the case.

One of the main charges against the Commission members held that they ran a conspiracy in the concrete industry that required that the mob receive kickbacks on all major construction jobs in New York City. Because the Bonanno family didn't have a seat on the Commission, it didn't suffer from the conspiracy charge. The same situation also occurred about two years later when the Bonanno group evaded charges

in the Windows Case, so-called because it involved the window replacement industry. This insulation allowed the borgata to prosper when the
FBI was laying siege to other groups. Once Massino emerged from
prison in 1992, he had a relatively unscathed crew, and his members,
which included an eager thirty-three-year-old Basciano, had been busy
making illicit money any way they could during, for them, this peaceful
interregnum. However, trouble never lay very far away, which Basciano
would find out soon enough.

The police in Pittsburgh in the fall of 1987 saw trouble on the streets.
Drug overdose deaths from heroin were starting to show up from a new
product in the area. The heroin came in glassine envelopes bearing a Blue
Thunder logo, and a cursory investigation put its origins in New York
City. Unlike some heroin cut to low purity levels, Blue Thunder was tipping the scales with a purity of over 90 percent. For someone who didn't
know how to handle drugs, such high purity could spell trouble. Unsuspecting Pittsburgh addicts were winding up in the morgue. Blue Thunder had become popular enough in Pennsylvania that police arrested one
sixteen-year-old pusher with vials of the product and hundreds of dollars
in cash in his pocket.

Back in New York City, the Blue Thunder brand had also come to
the attention of law enforcement officials battling the flow of heroin from
Southeast Asia. Agents with the DEA, detectives with the NYPD, and
New York State police banded together into the New York Drug Enforcement Task Force (NYDETF) to pool their resources and intelligence to
target major trafficking operations. New York City, home to hundreds of
thousands of heroin addicts, proved to be a bonanza.

Alfred Bottone Sr., the portly gambling friend of Vincent Basciano,
felt uncomfortable about the increased NYDETF activity. In late July
1991, while lunching with an attorney friend in the Bronx, Bottone

confided that he was seeing a lot of "cars" around, by which he meant law enforcement vehicles on stakeouts and surveillance. Bottone thought the agents were tailing him, to which his lunch companion perceptively said that he shouldn't be messing with drugs.

"I swear I have nothing to do with drugs!" Bottone exclaimed.

But to the attorney, Bottone did protest too much. On the morning of August 2, 1991, at around 5:30 a.m., his barking dogs awakened Bottone at his Westchester home in Shrub Oak. A few moments later NYDETF agents swarmed the house. Arrested and handcuffed, Bottone sat in the house for over five hours as agents went room by room and gathered up reams of documents and other evidence, placing it all in his luggage for transport to DEA offices in Manhattan. They scooped up every bit of cash and almost every item of jewelry, even his son Christopher's stamp collection. Based on an informant's tip, agents returned to Bottone's home a few weeks later to look for cash and records in a secret compartment within his kitchen table, but apparently they found nothing of interest.

That day the task force led several hundred agents and cops in raids around the city, arresting over forty men and women and executing more than fifty search warrants in the five boroughs as well as nearby areas of Westchester County. They also carried out searches in towns just over the George Washington Bridge in New Jersey. The raids and searches targeted suspects in the Blue Thunder distribution system and confiscated an enormous amount of cash, drugs, records, guns, and narcotics packaging materials. The heroin ring was processing so much cash—estimated by officials at $20 million a month or $500,000 a day in some locations—that one raid on Grand Street in lower Manhattan found two money-counting machines and thousands of pages of records describing the Blue Thunder operation's work schedules, payrolls, and sales. Agents also seized a Thompson .45-caliber semiautomatic rifle and assorted ammunition.

Around 6:00 a.m. a team of agents also awakened Basciano with a warrant for his arrest and another to search his Scarsdale home, dubbed "the mansion" by cops. Although he knew not to talk before speaking to an attorney, government records show that he did engage in some chatter with the arrest team. The house on Gateway Road had a mortgage on it, Basciano said, and he worked in construction. You got the little fish, he offered as he watched agents search his spacious manse. It must be a case of mistaken identity, he further volunteered. Then he shut up. Apart from some valium, the search of Basciano's Scarsdale home didn't turn up much in the way of drug evidence. Agents didn't even find any guns, although they seized dozens of pieces of jewelry owned by Basciano and his wife and about $230,000 in cash, money from drug proceeds, they suspected, but which Basciano protested later was only gambling winnings from Las Vegas.

Revealing how drug proceeds were laundered through seemingly legitimate businesses, the government seized an estimated $40 million in real estate and businesses, which included a Bronx sound studio, a Manhattan production and merchandising company, and an antique car dealership. A number of condominiums also fell under seizure orders. "We will take your drugs," NYPD commissioner Lee Brown boasted at a news conference announcing the massive sweep. "We'll take your money. We'll take your cars. We'll take your liberty, and, I guess I should add on this occasion, we'll take your condominiums."

The suspects arrested in the case weren't household names in the city but turned out to be major players in what authorities said was the largest heroin operation uncovered in New York to date, dwarfing anything attributed to the players in *The French Connection* some two decades earlier. According to the original criminal complaint filed in Manhattan federal court, the operation kingpin was Eric Millan-Colon, an enterprising twenty-nine-year-old from Yonkers who, investigators believed, built the Blue Thunder operation on the ruins of a similarly named Bronx ring broken up five years earlier. As his second in command,

Millan-Colon had Ralph Rivera, who coordinated the processing of the heroin into stamped envelopes and their distribution to street-level retail spots. Rivera also collected the cash and paid the suppliers.

Officials believed the Millan-Colon operation distributed over $100 million worth of heroin around New York City and its suburbs from about 1985 until his arrest in 1991. Some of the heroin, based on the findings of police in Pennsylvania, made its way west. It's also possible that the product made it to other US cities, especially if customers created a secondary market. An estimated $65 million of the sales came back to the Blue Thunder ring, with 35 percent of that, over $22 million, coming back to Millan-Colon himself, prosecutors said.

The complaint charged that Millan-Colon was putting his profits into Ejay Enterprises Ltd. of 330 West 58th Street in Manhattan. Ostensibly involved in concert promotion, international joint ventures, and marketing deals, Ejay chiefly laundered drug cash, the complaint stated. In one deal, Millan-Colon purchased the rights to market the Teenage Mutant Ninja Turtles merchandise in Argentina for $1 million, an amount of cash that Ejay Enteprises didn't seem capable of producing legitimately, according to the complaint. As agents were driving Millan-Colon to the task force office for processing, they couldn't resist asking him how the turtles were selling. "All right," came Millan-Colon's response, adding that he expected a bigger market to open up soon. Whether he could profit from that had now become problematic.

As federal agents and police had come to expect, some of the Blue Thunder heroin originated in the Golden Triangle of Southeast Asia. But how did the heroin get to New York? According to federal officials, the major trafficker turned out to be the fifty-one-year-old "Fat Al" Bottone, a mainstay in the world of Bronx bookmaking in which Vincent Basciano had operated for years.

Bottone always hovered on the edge of illegitimacy in his dealings. One lawyer remembered how he once tried to pay a legal fee with a diamond that Bottone swore was worth the $30,000 he owed. The attorney had the stone appraised, and the appraisal found the stone was flawed, worth at most $5,000. Bottone protested, saying that he had received $30,000 for it from an insurance company when he had reported it stolen. Aside from his illegitimate dealings, the senior Bottone owned and ran two Bronx businesses: the Bronx Sound Studio at 601-603 Morris Park Avenue and Auction Cars at 2015 East Tremont Avenue. Both companies, the criminal complaint charged, covered heroin deals. Bottone's two sons, Alfred Jr. and Anthony, were also charged in the complaint with assisting their father's heroin operation.

The complaint also accused Basciano of assisting Bottone and said the young gangster had a useful specialty. "In particular, Basciano uses sophisticated radio equipment capable of monitoring law enforcement transmissions to advise Bottone and the others of the presence of surveillance agents." An affidavit from a DEA agent later spelled out in more detail what Basciano's role was alleged to have been in helping Bottone. At the crux of the matter lay a series of intercepted telephone conversations that led police to believe Basciano had been intercepting law enforcement radio traffic. In one call between Bottone and Basciano, agents heard Basciano say, "We got some problems, pal."

"They [the police] were just all over the fuckin' place . . . heard them and they caught me by Cropsy [Avenue]," said Basciano, according to the affidavit. It's no wonder then that just a few weeks later Bottone bemoaned being followed by cops.

Basciano was also monitored mentioning that he heard the agents say "we're going to check down by the marina location, and we're going up to the mansion," as well as "you think you can be up at Scarsdale." A group of DEA agents was attempting to conduct surveillance of Basciano himself, the affidavit noted.

There were other calls, some involving Basciano and others between Bottone and his son Alfred Jr., which led agents to believe that the suspects had special radio equipment that allowed them to break into encrypted DEA communication devices. Basciano and Bottone likely were using either stolen devices or those given to them by an unauthorized source, the document added.

Faced with such a high-profile case, Basciano and some of the other defendants found it hard to get out of jail after their arrests. Magistrate-judge Kathleen Roberts ordered Basciano held without bail, not uncommon in major drug cases. But being in custody was giving Basciano a taste of what his life could be like if convicted in a case where his maximum sentence could last at least twenty years in prison. He needed a good advocate on his side, both to help him make bail and then to help him beat the Blue Thunder case for good.

Murray Richman, the attorney whom Basciano had used to beat the attempted murder case, couldn't represent him because of other commitments. But Richman recommended that Basciano see Benjamin Brafman, a hardworking Manhattan lawyer who, while not a superstar at the time, was certainly gaining that kind of stature. Not a physically intimidating lawyer like the late John Gotti's attorney, Bruce Cutler, Brafman came from Brooklyn, where he grew up in a household with parents who escaped the Holocaust about two years before World War II erupted.

Raised by Orthodox Jewish parents, Brafman remained true to his faith. Working his way through Brooklyn College at night, during summer months Brafman waited tables in the Catskills, where he discovered in himself a knack for stand-up comedy, not a bad talent to have if you want to be an effective advocate; jurors do like humor at times. "I went out onstage with another guy, and we did all this waiter humor, and we weren't killed," Brafman later recalled in a *New York* magazine article about the night he filled in for a comic who didn't show.

After deciding to study law, Brafman attended Ohio Northern University Law School. Married and in need of a job after graduation, Brafman aggressively courted a Manhattan criminal defense firm for a job.

Then he took a job with Manhattan district attorney Robert Morgenthau, the formidable prosecutor with whom a job was a one-way ticket to traction in the criminal justice field. In 1980 Brafman struck out on his own in private practice.

Well before Basciano approached him for representation in Blue Thunder, Brafman was gaining a name for himself in that part of the criminal defense bar that takes on wiseguys as clients. One of his first major mob clients was Anthony Senter, an associate of the Gambino crime family, who in 1986 stood trial with Gambino crime boss Paul Castellano on charges that they and others took part in a large-scale stolen car ring that incorporated some murder and dismemberment as a way of doing business. On December 18, 1985, Gotti assassinated Castellano while the trial was under way, an unlucky turn for Castellano, since the scuttlebutt on the street held that he likely would have been acquitted. With Brafman as his advocate, Senter, a handsome but menacing-looking man, got out from under most of the case, acquitted of twenty-one of twenty-two counts.

The Senter verdict as well as other wins by Brafman drew Basciano to him as a client. This was the era before cellular phones, and with Brafman's career on the upswing, he was so busy attending to the needs of his many clients that he came to court with rolls of quarters to feed the pay phones during trial breaks, one colleague remembered. But the success that came with high-profile, multidefendant mob cases had a price. They were physically and emotionally taxing, and the lengthy trials often forced lawyers to scrimp on the time they could spend on the business of other clients. Very often the ugly allegations brimmed with violence. Given the opportunity of another big case like Blue Thunder, Brafman had some hesitation.

"When Vinny Basciano came to me into my life professionally in the early 1990s, I had made a decision that I didn't want to be involved in any more several-month, multidefendant organized crime cases," Brafman said some years later. "I had been there, done that. I had been very successful. I had managed to keep my distance from these people on a personal level."

But looking more closely at Basciano and the Blue Thunder case, Brafman saw details that made the client and the case different from the so-called "mega cases" that had come into fashion in the legal world. "When Vinny presented himself to me as a prospective client, he was presented to me as an extremely successful, young entrepreneur; there were not organized crime allegations in that case; there were no crimes of violence in that case," said Brafman.

Earmarks of that success included Basciano owning substantial real estate holdings and his involvement in several successful stores. Brafman also remembered that his legal fee came from a law firm that had handled one of Basciano's real estate deals, likely involving one or more of his construction projects. "There was nothing nefarious about him," Brafman recalled. "To the contrary, the only thing I saw and did know about him was that he did have some involvement in either sports gambling or numbers gambling. But there were no allegations that he was a high-ranking organized crime person."

Having dealt with some Gambino crime family members and associates in the Castellano case, Brafman wouldn't necessarily have known which mobsters played a part in the other crime families. But by the time of the Blue Thunder case, Basciano had already joined the Bonanno family. He just wasn't a prominent player . . . yet.

Sizing up Basciano, his lawyer saw a charming, handsome, smart, and interesting man with a lovely wife and young children, who lived in a magnificent home up in Scarsdale. Basciano wasn't well educated, but Brafman noted that he could talk to anyone about almost anything, from the hot dog vendor outside the courthouse to attorneys walking the hallways. He had a natural charisma. "To be perfectly candid with you, he maintained from the very beginning he had nothing to do with the narcotics conspiracy that he was charged in."

Moderately wealthy at this point, Basciano could afford the kinds of legal fees Brafman commanded. Brafman's first task was to get Basciano free on bail. Being locked up was keeping Basciano away from his businesses, which he needed to attend to since at least one, a construction company, was having financial problems. It's also difficult to defend against an indictment from behind bars; access to lawyers is cumbersome and restricted, and psychologically a cell is a terrible place. Then there was the issue of home life. With her husband behind bars, Angela Basciano suddenly became a single mother with four growing sons. She had relied on her spouse to help give structure to the boys' lives. Basciano's absence was straining the entire family structure.

Brafman worked his magic with federal prosecutors and the court. A month after Basciano had first been detained, a different federal magistrate-judge held a hearing and released Basciano on $2 million bond, secured by pledges of property from six friends and neighbors, including one of Angela's relatives. Confined to his home under strict supervision by federal court officials, he had to surrender his passport. He also had to wear an electronic ankle bracelet and report to pretrial service officials once a week.

But even with the bail restrictions, Basciano got around. He could request "black out" periods in the electronic monitoring so he could visit Brafman and other lawyers, his accountant, doctors, and attend to pressing family matters like the funeral arrangements in June 1993 for his mother, Shirley. Basciano held the wake in his old Bronx neighborhood, just a few blocks away from the Hello Gorgeous salon.

With forty defendants involved in the Blue Thunder case, it took until March 1993 for the matter to reach trial before Manhattan federal judge Shirley Wohl Kram. Jury selection involved an anonymous panel of jurors, the government insisting on anonymity after alleging that Basciano's strenuous objection to the way the prosecution team got certain prospective jurors removed by peremptory challenges must have meant that he thought he could corrupt them. Nothing like that ever surfaced in the case.

The government was prepared to end the case before trial with what was called a global plea bargain, one in which either all the defendants agreed to plead guilty or they all went to trial. In Basciano's case, prosecutors wouldn't offer him any plea involving less than twenty years in prison, according to Brafman. Basciano rejected that position, forcing the case to trial. "His [Basciano's] position was that twenty years is as good as life and I would go to trial, and he wanted to go to trial and see if he could win," explained Brafman.

But it quickly became apparent that the trial wasn't going to go smoothly. On March 2, 1993, just days before prosecutors were scheduled to give their opening statements to the jury, a bombshell disclosure shook the case: Two NYPD cops and one state police investigator were charged with corruption in a criminal complaint. Specifically, the government accused the investigators—all members of the task force that put together the Blue Thunder case—of conspiring to distribute about four ounces of heroin.

Three days after the government had delivered its opening statement, the three task force agents were arrested formally. Neither the trial judge nor the defendants had had a heads-up about the arrests. That development threw the case—one of the biggest narcotics investigations in decades—into confusion. Basciano and the other defendants moved to have their indictment thrown out on the grounds of prosecutorial misconduct. That move forced the government to disclose more detailed allegations about the police misconduct, and the results were disturbing. Two of the officers, Detective Jeffrey Beck and Sergeant Joseph Tremini, stood accused of giving an informant the heroin in exchange for $25,000. Other allegations about the task force members included charges that they conspired to rob a money-laundering suspect and a drug trafficker and planned to burglarize places linked to drug trafficking.

Further complicating matters for the government, the state police investigator involved, Robert Robles, had made some undercover drug buys that formed the basis for the original wiretap application in the Blue Thunder case. The taps amassed over three hundred recordings for use at trial, including some that picked up Basciano. But since Robles allegedly was corrupt and involved in crucial parts of the case, Judge Kram ordered a special hearing in which defense attorneys called two witnesses who made even more troubling allegations about criminal conduct by task force agents.

Brafman directly challenged the wiretaps and moved to suppress the tapes because of the allegations surrounding the cops, arguing that the agents' misconduct may have infected all of the wiretaps. But Judge Kram agreed with prosecutors. She found that "virtually every investigative action taken by Robles," including his undercover drug buys, had been "extensively corroborated" by the other members of the task force. Those actions included the purchase of the drugs, the processing of the narcotics at DEA headquarters, and secret recordings made during the drug buys. Kram found no evidence to suppress the wiretap evidence.

But Kram did find troubling that the government was conducting a secret investigation of the agents without telling the court or defense counsel until prosecutors had made their opening statements, which expressly involved the credibility of Robles. The US Attorney's Office had committed a major mistake. According to one prosecutor on the Blue Thunder case, supervisors had been told to ask all the trial teams in the office before any case was ready for trial if they had used the indicted cops as witnesses or case agents. If that kind of query had been made, then the Blue Thunder prosecutors would have been forewarned and could have informed the court and defense in a timely manner and made other adjustments. But for reasons never clear, someone dropped the ball and never informed the Blue Thunder trial team of the looming problem. Kram found the omission inexcusable and a cause for disrupting the trial—but she stopped short of dismissing the indictment.

Then the situation got worse—or better, depending on your point of view—for the government's case. No sooner had Kram, despite misgivings about prosecutors not being forthright, refused to dismiss the indictment because of the secret investigation of the agents than more allegations surfaced. During a conference of the defense lawyers in Kram's robing room at the courthouse, attorney David Breitbart, representing Bottone's son Anthony, revealed that he had come up with even more disclosures of wrongdoing attributed to the agents, claiming that $29,000 in cash was missing from a safe at his client's business.

"There was $29,000 in cash that they say they seized from my client; they can't find it," said Breitbart. "There was $60,000 in another car that [agent] Beck drove; they can't find it."

In the second instance, Breitbart was referring to money missing from a car driven by defendant Carlos Rivera at the time of his arrest. Faced with Breitbart's stunning claims, prosecutors quickly investigated and found that what he said was largely true. Then, on April 14, 1993, the government told the court that between $50,000 and $80,000 seized from a car during the arrest of Rivera, later a cooperating witness for the prosecution, was missing. Another $12,000 was also not vouchered, court records showed. On top of that came the amazing announcement that DEA records indicated that *no* money ever was recovered from Rivera's car. (Kram later noted that the original allegation of the missing money from Bottone's safe wasn't substantiated.)

In the face of what looked like the kind of law enforcement corruption not seen since the days of crusading New York cop Frank Serpico, the Blue Thunder case was dissolving into disarray. Basciano and almost all the other defendants moved for a mistrial. When the news first broke that Robles, Termini, and Beck had been arrested, Kram fashioned an evidentiary ruling that allowed the trial to continue. But now there seemed to be no end to the allegations of corruption and the trouble they were causing.

"Each week the government reveals new allegations of misconduct involving an ever widening circle of police officers over an ever longer period of time," said Kram. "The ongoing, unpredictable nature of the Robles investigation places defendants in the untenable position of having to restrategize and recall and reexamine witnesses on a daily basis.

"In fact, it is the defendants and their counsel, rather than the government, who have brought to the court's attention specific instances of misconduct, which allegedly occurred during the [Blue Thunder] investigation," said Kram.

Confronted with the prospect of having jurors face months of delay and no other way to rectify problems facing the case, Judge Kram declared a mistrial and dismissed the jury. It was a stunning reversal for the government in a case that less than a year earlier had the makings of the largest heroin conviction of all time. The mishandling of the case represented one of the biggest screw-ups that the court had seen, amounting to an enormous waste of money and court resources. Basciano and the rest of his codefendants now had to go through another round of jury selection.

The seemingly never-ending life of the Blue Thunder case was causing all kinds of problems for Basciano. Under house arrest with electronic monitoring, he found it difficult to handle his business interests. In a letter to the court, Brafman's associate Charles Ross bemoaned that Basciano couldn't attend to those matters properly from home. One of those businesses requiring Basciano's immediate attention was MSV Development, a contracting company that Ross said was threatened with bankruptcy. A coffee supply company and a trucking company in Bayonne, New Jersey, just north of the Kill Van Kull from Staten Island, also needed Basciano's attention.

But the court wasn't going to allow Basciano to roam at will around the metropolitan area. He already was under a $2 million bail restriction and home detention rules that almost no other defendant faced. Even

Millan-Colon and Al Bottone Sr., who faced more elaborate charges of heroin trafficking, walked on $700,000 bail. Further, Judge Kram had admonished Basciano for not making timely calls and checking in with his pretrial service officers when he visited his lawyers and accountants. As a compromise, Ross suggested that Basciano be allowed to work out of his Hello Gorgeous salon so that he could deal with his businesses and seek permission from government officials if he had to go to business meetings outside of the office. The court agreed, giving Basciano an extra measure of liberty.

Some seven months after the debacle of the first trial, the Blue Thunder case came before a second jury on November 15, 1993. For Brafman, the case represented an interesting challenge and also seemed winnable. "The case had hundreds of tape recordings. I was viewed as someone who was very good in dealing with government tape recordings and trying to develop a defense from within the recordings themselves, and that is exactly what I did in this case," said Brafman.

Since Basciano and most of the other defendants were free on bail, he could leave the courthouse for lunch breaks. To make sure he didn't get into trouble, attorney Maurice Sercarz, representing Al Bottone Sr., chaperoned Basciano to a local restaurant. Since the Manhattan federal court lies within three or four blocks of Little Italy, they often selected Ottomanelli's, a well-known Italian restaurant. There Basciano, back in his element, exhibited his outsized personality.

"Basciano was such a big tipper that whenever the waiter saw us coming, if there was no table available, they could get one out of the back and set it up," remembered Sercarz.

Despite good lunches, the trial was serious business. Bottone Sr. was in deep trouble. The prosecution had a treasure trove of tape recordings compiled over a six-month period that captured him talking with operators of the various heroin-packaging mills in the Blue Thunder ring's area of operation. Bottone talked cryptically about heroin shipments and disparaged some of the ring members, sarcastically referring to one as "Einstein" or "the professor." At one point Bottone was so angry with a member of the heroin operation that they almost came to blows.

But while he was wallowing in deep trouble, ironically it was Bottone who provided some help for Basciano's defense as devised by Brafman. The car dealer from Westchester had attempted to proffer—that is, provide evidence to the government without the statement being used against him—that all the conversations he had with Basciano on the tape referred not to the drug business but their gambling stores. After all, it wasn't a secret to law enforcement that Basciano and Bottone had been tight in Bronx gambling operations.

While prosecutors wouldn't reveal the complete statement that Bottone made to them during the proffer sessions, it came to light during the trial that he had claimed that "Basciano had nothing to do with the heroin business and that all of the intercepted conversations involving Basciano pertain to Basciano's gambling business." According to Bottone in his proffer session, Basciano's gambling operation was a "bad package," apparently not very profitable. He was advising Basciano on how to improve.

One intercepted conversation of June 11, 1991, recorded Basciano talking with Bottone about all the customers lined up outside a "store" with their "odds." They also discussed scheduling workers.

Basciano: "If they're not with, down with their odds tomorrow, ten o'clock Thursday morning, you know, let that crew go over there. I might need them for Friday too, 'cause I want the same guys to go back to the store again on Friday to see if they came down with their odds."

Bottone: "Tentative Thursday at ten."

The conversation didn't include any of the regular coded conversations about "pieces" or other phrases that prosecutors claimed referred to drugs. The Basciano-Bottone conversations, by contrast, appeared rather mundane and showed nothing more than a mutual interest in gambling.

In another twist that buttressed the gambling admission—although probably not the intent—the prosecution called former defendant turned witness Carlos Rivera to the stand. A young man in his twenties when arrested in the Blue Thunder case, Rivera had served as one of the main supervisors of the day-to-day dealings of the heroin ring. His role was substantial, and he had three felonies on his record, so he was looking at life in prison if convicted. About a month after his arrest in August 1991, prosecutors brought in Rivera and played one of the Bottone-Basciano recordings in an apparent effort to get him to confirm that both men were talking about a drug deal.

Questioned in his interviews about Basciano's wealth, Rivera related to prosecutors a conversation that he had had with Basciano when both were sitting in a courthouse holding pen, a small cell known as the bullpen where defendants are held before arraignment or court appearances. Both men talked, and the conversation came up in testimony after Rivera had decided to become a government witness.

Asked at trial if Basciano had said anything to him about how he made his money, Rivera said he admitted to gambling.

"Well, tell me what he said," asked Brafman on cross-examination.

"Well, I remember him telling me the day of the bullpen that he said that he is guilty for selling or giving numbers and machines and things like that but that he said he is not guilty from selling drugs," Rivera answered.

Brafman then asked if Rivera had said so to the government, and he answered that he had.

"I remember that he was telling me that I shouldn't cooperate and that I should just handle time and then if anything, if I had a problem with anybody, I should just handle it when I get out," said Rivera.

While Basciano apparently didn't say what he meant by "handle it," Rivera told the jurors that he raised his hand and made a well-known gesture. To make sure the jury understood the patently obvious, Prosecutor

Snell interjected, on the record, that "the witness has just raised his right hand and extended his forefinger and moved his thumb up and down in this fashion."

The gun gesture attributed to Basciano was meant to paint him as a bad actor. Brafman moved for an immediate mistrial. Kram denied the motion. Rivera also testified that he gave drug money to Bottone Sr. and indicated that another suspect believed some of the money went to Basciano.

The Rivera testimony showed the problems that the government was having in the Blue Thunder case tying Basciano directly into any drug dealing. Circumstantial evidence such as the tapes had Basciano and Bottone talking about police surveillance, but that was a slim reed on which to play the case. The government had painted the conspiracy as the Basciano-Bottone drug ring. But in the three hundred recordings introduced into evidence, virtually none contained Basciano's voice. Only two witnesses out of nearly forty mentioned Basciano by name.

"I was able to demonstrate that the conversations in large measure related to Joker Poker machines that were gambling paraphernalia and the numbers racket that Vinny was admittedly . . . involved in," said Brafman.

An operative of the heroin ring who had potentially damaging evidence, Anthony Damiani was the other witness who talked about Basciano during trial testimony. Damiani testified that Basciano became his prime source for heroin after the arrest of another man. It was also Basciano, testified Damiani, who stopped by his house around February 24, 1987, to pick up $200,000 in cash that ringleader Eric Millan-Colon had dropped off earlier. Damiani knew the specific date because it was his child's birthday, and Millan-Colon passed the money to him outside because the birthday party was under way inside the house. Either that night or the next day, Basciano picked up the cash, said Damiani.

The testimony about the drug money transfer was damaging and incriminating, placing Basciano squarely in the middle of the heroin conspiracy—if Damiani could be believed. On cross-examination, Brafman revealed to the jury that Damiani, during the first trial, testified differently. To show the glaring discrepancy, Brafman read from a transcript of Damiani's earlier testimony.

"Let me ask you if you remember being asked these questions and giving these answers," Brafman prefaced his questioning. If used effectively, the tactic can raise substantial doubts in jurors' minds about the candor and accuracy of a witness.

Flipping through the earlier testimony, Brafman recounted how Damiani had stated that at the February 24, 1987, birthday party Millan-Colon had dropped off the $200,000. So far, so good. Damiani had just stated as much at the second trial. But six months earlier, in the first trial, Damiani said "Alfred took the money," referring to Bottone Sr.

Caught in a major contradiction on the witness stand, Damiani had no choice but to hold his ground and insist that his testimony the second time around—that Basciano took the cash—was accurate.

"Well it couldn't be that you were telling the truth on both occasions you were under oath, could it?" Brafman asked facetiously.

Damiani gamely tried to say that he didn't remember his earlier testimony and insisted that Basciano had taken the money. But the contradiction gaped so large that, when it came time to sum up the arguments for the jury, Brafman exploited it to the hilt.

"Anthony Damiani was one of the only people to claim direct drug dealing with Basciano, was maybe in the last thirty-five years one of the worst witnesses I have ever come across," said Brafman, who called him a "skilled cross-examiner's dream target." "Damiani's testimony on direct [examination] was very powerful, until you took it apart. . . . He just fell apart as witness. . . . He was a terrible witness," Brafman summed up one of the most crucial pieces of evidence against his client. When it came time to sum up for the jury, Brafman had a field day pointing out the lack of proof against his client, and he didn't mince words. The government stubbornly refused to admit that it had made a mistake by indicting Basciano and went ahead anyway.

For a criminal defendant, the summation that his or her lawyer gives can make or break a case. A poor summation, in which a lawyer drones on from notes to bored jurors, can sink a client. Empty dazzle, popularized by the lawyer character Billy Flynn in the musical *Chicago*, also won't carry the day. On the other hand, a summation that zeroes in on crucial pieces of evidence and shows how they prove a person's innocence—or at least creates reasonable doubt about guilt—can mean the difference between a life of liberty and one behind bars.

In the Blue Thunder trial, Ben Brafman began writing his summation the day Vincent Basciano walked into his law office in Manhattan. At least that's how Brafman once said he began the process of preparing his closing arguments. Sizing up Basciano for the first time, Brafman could see he was a personable man with a loyal family. That definitely could help in selling him to a jury. Brafman knew of the mob connection, but that wasn't going to play a role in what the jury heard in the case. What also helped was the way the evidence in the case started to unfold in the six-month trial. The best that the government had to offer against Basciano were witnesses like Carlos Rivera and Anthony Damiani, all clay in the prosecutors' hands, malleable and interested only in pleasing the government.

It was April 25, 1993, when Brafman began his summation in the Blue Thunder case. It followed three days of government summations, encompassing all the defendants. His presentation started late in the afternoon, broke for the night, and then went until lunch the next day. What transpired in those hours could fill a casebook on how to execute a great summation. Invoking the wisdom of his Jewish grandmother, the words of Thomas Paine, and the jurors' own common sense, Brafman dissected the government case so well that at times some of the jurors actually nodded in agreement with him.

Brafman didn't ascribe bad motives to the government in indicting Basciano. But he did say that prosecutors simply didn't want to admit they made a mistake.

"I am not asking you to conclude that they took Vinny Basciano out of the Yellow Pages to put him in this case," he said. "I am telling you that they assumed that he was guilty, and, when it was clear to them they were wrong, they concluded, well, maybe he is a bad guy anyway, so we will convict him and what is the harm."

Brafman closed in on Damiani's testimony, so markedly inconsistent about who had picked up the $200,000 in drug money. The startling contradiction made Damiani sound like a liar. "As my grandmother used to say, 'If you are lying, you better have a good memory,'" he said to the jury. "I swear it was Al; I swear it was Vinny. It can't be both. It has got to be a lie," Brafman argued.

Brafman had to deal with Carlos Rivera as well, who said that Basciano had made deliveries of heroin. That kind of testimony, alleging hands-on activity, had to be refuted or else the newly minted Bonanno mobster was sunk. It all turned on handwritten records in which Rivera made the notation "Vin," which he said referred to Basciano.

But Brafman pointed out that no evidence established that "Vin" ever pointed to Basciano. There was another man, Vincent Roman, who, Brafman argued, was "Vin." Brafman also repeated to the jury that comments on taped conversations between Basciano and Bottone clearly were referring to their gambling interests and not drugs, as government agents believed.

Finishing up, Brafman said the case was really about what Thomas Paine called the "avidity to punish," which leads men to misinterpret and stretch the laws. "That is what Basciano's case was about," the lawyer emphasized. "They assumed he was bad. They went with the case, and as the case began to fall apart they put their head in the sand, and these guys so eager to punish began to stretch and misapply even the best of laws."

Brafman's summation dealt with the evidence, but he had to show a connection between himself, the plight of Basciano, and the lives of jurors in a way with which they could empathize. Any successful trial lawyer strives toward that advocacy point.

"I hope that none of you and nobody you love is ever in the position that Mr. Basciano is in in this case, where he is, I submit, falsely accused of a crime in a terrible atmosphere and in a terrible setting," concluded Brafman. "But if, God forbid, that should ever happen, I wish you two things. I wish that whoever represents them cares as much about their work as I do, and I hope whoever they are that they get a jury just like this."

Basciano certainly got his money's worth. On the day the jury began their deliberations, Basciano signed a courtroom artist's sketch that depicted him and Brafman seated together. His message, scrawled in black letters, conveyed his gratitude. "I am writing this while the jury is still out. If I am convicted I'll have no regrets as far as my counsel is concerned. You did a brilliant job. Thank you, your friend Vinny B."

During the trial, Basciano had been his usual wisecracking and magnanimous self. Brafman remembered visiting the courthouse cafeteria with him and watching his client pay for a couple of cups of coffee with a $100 bill, telling the cashier to keep the change. He chatted with the federal marshals. Women even came up to him and slipped him their numbers. But with the case in the hands of the jury, Basciano knew that a guilty verdict meant the end of his life as he knew it. Each morning, before going into Manhattan from Scarsdale, Basciano went into the bedrooms of his four young boys and kissed each of them good-bye, not knowing if that day was going to be the last he would see them as young children.

"He knew if he was convicted, he knew he would be immediately remanded," explained Brafman. "I said 'Wow, there is a soft, serious side to this man.'"

After about the second day of deliberations, the notes coming from the jury didn't make any mention of evidence related to Basciano. To

Brafman, that was either a good sign or a bad sign. You can never be sure in the game of predicting the jury. He felt confident, though, that he had given the case his best shot.

"They didn't try to take my defense seriously. They kind of laughed it off," observed Brafman. He was referring to the $236,000 in cash seized from Basciano's house that prosecutors indicated came from drugs. But during the trial Brafman presented records that showed that several days before the agents seized the money, Basciano had won it at a Las Vegas casino.

On the morning of May 9, 1994, Basciano kissed his kids good-bye. When he arrived at court, he learned that jury deliberation had come to an end. Six of the defendants were found guilty of the most serious charges, among them Eric Millan-Colon, Alfred Bottone Sr., his son Alfred Jr., and Ralph Rivera. But in a shocker to some observers, Basciano was acquitted, as was Bottone's other son, Anthony. The final line-score was six convictions and four acquittals. The results thrilled and surprised both Brafman and Basciano.

"To be honest with you, going into that trial, could I have predicted an acquittal across the board for Basciano? I could fantasize about it, I couldn't predict it," recalled Brafman. "Then as the trial broke, as the evidence came in, it became more apparent to me that if I walked this very fine line of him being involved in gambling and not drugs that there was reasonable doubt that could develop."

After the verdict, his bail exonerated and no restraints at all on his liberty, a smiling Basciano walked out of the federal courthouse at Foley Square with Brafman by his side. As they talked, Brafman had some words of advice for his client. "'I am not certain you understand what has happened,'" Brafman recalled. "'You have been acquitted in a trial in federal court where you were facing life in prison—this stuff does not happen every day in this building.'"

The grim statistic for anyone going to trial in the federal system was that the conviction rate was around 90 percent: A person had a one-in-ten chance of winning an acquittal.

"God smiled on you," Brafman continued as they walked in the fresh air of victory. "Get out of this life, go away from New York, sell your stores and your buildings, and go have life that is away from the Bronx. You don't have to be Vinny Gorgeous."

Then, as Brafman remembered it, Basciano looked at him in a way that said that, while the attorney had saved his life, it was up to him to live it his way. Vinny Gorgeous was who he was.

Cleared at last, Basciano went back home to Scarsdale. His wife got back her jewelry, and the money seized by the government on suspicion that the cash represented drug proceeds was also returned.

The Bonanno crime family ties never came up in the trial. But back on the street and at Massino's restaurant, the news of the acquittal became a double-edged sword. Had Basciano been convicted, his stint as a made man could have fallen into serious trouble. The Bonanno borgata already had some major heat from law enforcement with drug dealing and didn't need more. Massino let it be known that if Basciano had not beaten the Blue Thunder case, well, there could have been trouble for the young Bronx gangster.

Basciano was never arrested again for drug dealing. But the allegations about heroin continued to dog him. In one DEA intelligence document prepared in May 1995, an informant alleged that during the Blue Thunder case some of the defendants—including Basciano—were sitting on approximately sixty to eighty units of heroin. Preliminary conversations about a possible sale of the heroin had taken place—an initial sale garnering $52,000 for half a unit—but because Basciano was being monitored while on bail, the seller didn't want to get involved with him, according to the document.

Basciano walked free, but the same didn't hold true for the NYPD cops and state police officer accused of stealing drug money and other crimes. Jeffrey Beck, Joseph Tremini, and Robert Robles all pleaded guilty to crimes related to their corrupt conduct and received varied prison terms. In a 1993 newspaper interview, Beck said that some of the motivation for the corruption—which involved stuffing cash into his pockets that he was supposed to be confiscating as evidence—was a sense of entitlement.

"We busted our ass on this case, and we won't get a pat on the back from anyone," Beck said in a *Los Angeles Times* story. "We thought they were the spoils of war."

After Beck was sentenced to fifty-seven months in federal prison, his wife divorced him. His own guilty conscience also preyed upon him, which, even before getting caught, prompted him to give $100 bills to homeless people as a way of assuaging his disloyalty.

Meanwhile, Vincent Basciano went back to being Vinny Gorgeous, legitimate businessman and mobster. He had dodged yet another bullet, a free man when the Bonanno crime family was beginning to thrive again. It was the life he couldn't leave.

6

By the time Basciano exited the troubles of the Blue Thunder case in mid-1994, the Bonanno crime family was developing under new boss Joseph Massino into a force with which to be reckoned. Federal investigations had roiled the Gambino, Lucchese, and Colombo crime families, which saw their bosses either imprisoned or sent into hiding. Numerous ranking members of those families had also been convicted.

By the FBI's calculation, the Bonanno family had about 150 members, comprising approximately fifteen crews. One crew belonged to Patrick DeFilippo, who had about nine men under him, including Basciano, Anthony Donato, and Bruno Indelicato, son of the murdered captain. Undamaged to any significant extent by the investigations of other crime families, the Bonanno borgata continued to consolidate its rackets in gambling and extortion as well as making headway in Wall Street stock scams.

The family also had made the *New York Post* newspaper delivery operation its cash cow. Just about the time that Massino was anointed boss—even though he was still in prison—an investigation by Manhattan district attorney Robert Morgenthau was finding evidence that members of the family had no-show jobs at the paper for themselves or family members. Others had clout or control over the union that handled delivery workers.

Fears that Robert Perrino, a supervisor at the *Post*, might cooperate with the Morgenthau probe led high-ranking Bonanno leaders like Sal Vitale and Anthony Spero, a pigeon fancier from the Bay Ridge section

Joseph Massino, Bonanno boss

of Brooklyn, to plot his murder. Perrino was killed in May 1992 and his body buried in a drum filled with concrete. Massino was still in jail and knew nothing about the Perrino plot at the time it was executed. Later, Massino told confidantes that the slaying angered him, and had he known about it he would never have let it happen.

With problems like the *Post* investigation and unsanctioned homicide to worry about, Massino didn't have time to pay much attention to the family's Bronx operations. DeFilippo seemed nominally in charge, and, so long as the tribute money flowed his way, Massino didn't need to know the details about what the Bronx boys were doing. But no sooner had Massino walked than he got the first indication that he had some loose cannons around DeFilippo.

Thomas and Rosemary Uva had a livelihood destined to put them in an early grave. In 1992 the young husband-and-wife pair had been burglarizing mob social clubs all over the city. They even hit Spero's club in Brooklyn, a Bonanno hangout. The Mafia families put out an open contract on the pair, meaning that anyone could kill them. On December 24, 1992, as many families were having Christmas Eve dinner, the Uvas were shot dead on a Queens street.

Investigators were stumped and so were the mob bosses about who killed the couple. It wasn't that the Mafia families cared about the bloodshed: They wanted to know who had boasting rights for ridding the underworld of the troublesome pair. Not long after the Uvas were gunned down, both Vitale and Massino met with John Gotti Jr., son of the then-imprisoned mob boss, in Howard Beach. According to an FBI summary of what Vitale later told agents, Gotti said "we took care of it" when the Uvas came up. That admission indicated that the Gambino family had been responsible for the Uvas' demise. But on hearing that, Massino became angry. Some time earlier DeFilippo told Massino that Anthony Donato, one of his men in the Bronx crew, and his good friend Vincent Basciano—at the time out on bail from the Blue Thunder case—had

Vinny Basciano and Anthony Donato captured on surveillance

taken care of the Uva situation. Somebody was lying, and both Vitale and Massino believed that Donato had fibbed to DeFilippo.

A lie of that magnitude could have cost Donato his life. But when Massino called DeFilippo on the carpet, the Bronx captain admitted that his associate had spread a falsehood. For reasons that remain unclear, Massino didn't ask for Donato's head, possibly because in the end the lie didn't cause the Bonanno family any trouble. (In 2007 Gambino soldier Dominick "Skinny Dom" Pizzonia was convicted of racketeering charges that included the murder of the Uvas.)

Massino's style of leadership operated on a central paradox: While he wanted to insulate himself from knowledge of what the family was doing, he raged when he wasn't aware of certain things. What he was hearing about Basciano and the others in the Bronx was a case in point. One story making the rounds was that Basciano and another Bonanno soldier had killed a man in a social club off Francis Lewis Boulevard in Queens. The information was sketchy at best: There was no name for the victim, the date covered the period between 1992 and 1995, and it remained unclear as to what motive might have precipitated the homicide. DeFilippo felt duty bound to report what had happened to Vitale, who told him not to give him any more information. If Vitale knew more, he would have had to have told Massino, technically on supervised release from his latest federal prison sentence and not supposed to be dealing with organized crime matters.

But Massino heard about the story anyway and told Vitale to bring DeFilippo to Howard Beach for a meeting. Always conscious of the possibility of surveillance, Massino liked to conduct business outside of his home or social club, preferring walk-and-talk meetings. One of his favorite locales was a weedy area known as the Baja at the southwest end of Howard Beach. Another was Charles Memorial Park, a sliver of green at the south end of Old Howard Beach, a residential area to the east across Shellbank Basin. The place had tennis courts, and, because of its location, law enforcement had a hard time getting close for surveillance.

When a nervous DeFilippo arrived with Vitale at the park, Massino was there with James "Big Louis" Tartaglione, a lanky, bespectacled gangster who steadily had worked his way into crime family membership by helping clean up murder scenes. Vitale and Tartaglione, knowing that Massino wanted privacy, walked a short distance away as both the boss and DeFilippo began to talk. It wasn't a pleasant conversation. Vitale later told the FBI that he overheard DeFilippo explain to Massino that what had happened was a "spur of the moment" thing and that Basciano and an associate had killed the still unidentified man. The body was taken from the club. In later conversations with the FBI, Vitale believed the dispute that led to the killing centered on money, perhaps because of bookmaking operations.

Although never charged for the murder, Basciano and his quick trigger finger came to Massino's attention once again. The crime boss liked the brash young hood from the Bronx but was having continuing concern about his hair-trigger tendency to resort to violence. It wasn't that Massino didn't like violence. The boss had killed or ordered the deaths of at least six men at this point in his career and eventually notched up almost as many more. But as he consolidated his power and increased his fortune, Massino realized that if police and prosecutors linked him to the deaths, he would be vulnerable to a racketeering prosecution that could mean spending the rest of his life in prison. Murder didn't cut it as a modus operandi for the new Bonanno family, a borgata he had decreed should now be known as the "Massino crime family"—although the title never really stuck. Only as a last resort would Massino approve a murder and only when it suited his grand designs or private motives, as seen some years later.

One of the demographic shifts occurring in the Bronx in the 1990s was the ascendancy of organized crime elements with roots in the Balkans, most notably the ethnic Albanians who—since the 1970s and then in increasing numbers since the fall of Communism in Albania in 1990—had settled in the city. The Bronx became one of the first destinations for new Albanian immigrants, and they tended to settle in the Pelham Park area that surrounded Basciano's social clubs. The Albanians quickly gained a reputation for toughness, loyalty to their group, and fearlessness about standing up to the Italians. They occasionally beat Mafia members senseless, showing up with twenty or thirty allies in a dispute and intimidating even the biggest Mafiosi.

In one incident, they stripped an old Gambino mobster and threw him into the street as a sign of disrespect, his wallet purloined as a trophy. In another, the underboss of the Gambino family had a standoff with Albanians at a gas station, where one of the Balkan gangsters threatened to shoot the gas pump and cause a catastrophic explosion. In parts of

Queens, the Albanians began to overtake the fading Lucchese crime family's gambling racket.

One of the main Albanian crime groups, the Rudaj organization took its name from Alex Rudaj, an ethnic Albanian from Montenegro. Beginning in the early 1990s and continuing until 2004, the Rudaj crime group worked in Westchester, Queens, and of course the Bronx. It became known to law enforcement officials as an aspiring "Sixth Family" aimed at becoming a power like the traditional five Mafia families. Throwing their weight around the city, the Rudaj group, which included some Greeks and Italians, made a brazen grab to bolster their status as a crime family when Rudaj and some of his lieutenants threatened the owners of Rao's Restaurant—an East Harlem place to be seen for mobsters and trendsetters as Elaine's once was—when the restaurant refused to give up a table once reserved for the late Gambino boss John Gotti. Faced with about fifteen Albanians in an intimidating display of force, the management relented and allowed the group to have the table, according to court records.

It wasn't long before the Albanians began to rub up against the Bonanno family. Rudaj as well as Nardino Colotti got into a conflict over territory with Basciano. Colotti, an Italian immigrant from Foggia, made a living owning and running a series of Italian cafes in the Bronx. The establishments served their fair share of espressos, cappuccinos, and pastries, but they also doubled as gambling speakeasies. A patron entered and, if allowed by the manager, bypassed the regular bar and tables, buzzed into a back room through a door disguised as part of the wall. The inner room contained Joker Poker machines. If a patron won, the house manager remotely checked the machine's records and paid out at the front counter.

The machines were for suckers, essentially rigged to pay out only 33 percent of what went into them. Sometimes a bettor won, but more often he lost continuously. Gaetano Peduto watched one old man sink his entire paycheck into a machine and then borrow more money, at usurious rates, to try to win some back.

"Let's put it like this: If you just played $500 in the machine. I would watch you play and then after you would lose, I would stick $100 in there and I would probably win some of your money back and I would cash out and that was it. It is a sucker's bet," Peduto recalled later in federal court testimony. "It was funny."

But problems developed when it turned out that one of Colotti's cafes was in territory run by Basciano for the Bonanno family. A classic bit of mob arbitration ensued. Basciano and a representative of the Genovese family met with an emissary of the Gambino borgata and came to an agreement on splitting the winnings, recalled Peduto. This arrangement understandably complicated the system of collecting the winnings. Instead of one man doing the machine collections, representatives of all three crime families had to verify the collections.

Building a working relationship with the Albanians under the circumstances would make for a useful alliance. Basciano seemed to be the right man for the job. He had what the Albanians understood: a lack of fear and a reputation for violence. Massino soon realized that his Bronx soldier had a way of finessing the Albanians and earning their respect, saying as much to Richard Cantarella at the Casablanca Restaurant.

Peduto began stealing cars in his native Throgs Neck area of the Bronx when he was thirteen years old. He was nineteen years old when he met Basciano and his old mentor Bottone Sr. Bottone owned a used car lot, so Peduto made himself useful and served as Bottone's driver for daily tours of gambling locations. Bottone picked up winnings from various stores and collected the clean-out of coins from the slot and Joker Poker machines. On the daily gambling collection drives, Peduto learned that the Bronx was divided up for gambling operations. The Gambino group had the Morris Park area, while the Genovese and Bonanno families had parts of the South Bronx, including Throgs Neck.

From Bottone, Peduto also quickly learned the law of the land about what it meant to be a mob associate.

"If anybody tried to shake us down or tried to get something from us or anything, that we were basically already claimed," Peduto later recounted about his relationship with Bottone and Basciano. "So they would have to go through either Vinny or Alfred, and we'd have to work that through them."

It was a classic mob associate relationship: You're on record with your mob contact—in this case Bottone and Basciano—and if anyone gave you trouble the Bonanno family got involved. Peduto also admitted to federal investigators that he committed a number of crimes for Bottone and Basciano, notably the theft of cars.

In later testimony at the 2004 trial of Alex Rudaj and other members of the Albanian mob, Peduto recounted how his first meeting with Basciano at the Del Chino restaurant on Arthur Avenue was auspicious and laden with promise about the money that could be made in auto larceny. "We discussed the fact that, you know, about—you know, the thing about the stolen cars, about there was a lot of money to be made and so forth," recounted Peduto.

In a follow-up meeting at the same restaurant, Basciano spelled out what he wanted, mentioning high-end BMWs and also fast eight-cylinder GM cars, remembered Peduto. For each car Peduto sold to Basciano or his friends, the Bonanno soldier got a kickback ranging from between $1,000 to $2,000 per vehicle, he told the court. Basciano wanted speedy cars because he wanted to use them as hit cars, said Peduto, adding that the mobster asked that he use gloves when he stole them so that no fingerprints could trace back to him when the vehicle was abandoned. "If they had to do something with it, maybe kill somebody or a car that, you know, don't touch with your hands, make sure you use gloves."

Peduto wasn't a run-of-the-mill car thief, either. Federal court documents show that in the mid-1990s he was arrested on charges of participating in a sophisticated auto theft ring that stole over 2,100 vehicles in the metropolitan area, retagged them with fake vehicle identification numbers, and sold them to willing buyers. Peduto specialized in stealing luxury cars like Mercedes-Benz and Lexus, and through a contact he secured fake title certificates and VINs. Investigators estimated that the stolen vehicles had a combined retail value of $20 million.

Peduto had stolen vehicles for the elder Bottone and told investigators that over a period of a year he also supplied Basciano with about twenty so-called hit autos and many more luxury cars, according to court records. There was more to the relationship with Basciano, though, said Peduto. He said he knew of insurance fraud, arson, gambling, and murder for hire, all of which Basciano had told him about or ordered him to do, court records stated.

Working in the Bronx stealing cars, Peduto and his street partners, Sal Onofrietti and Frank Rotondo, soon ran up against the Albanian organization. Boss Alex Rudaj and Nardino Colotti allegedly tried to squeeze Peduto and his cohorts for cash from the car theft operations by claiming the Italians were lifting vehicles in an area controlled by Colotti, according to what Peduto told the FBI. Since Peduto was on record with Basciano, he told him about the pressure from the Albanians. Basciano sent two men with machine guns to confront Colotti and tell him that the Bonanno family protected Peduto's crew.

Despite being beholden to Basciano, Peduto said that he worked out a private deal with Colotti. He and Onofrietti stole not only cars for Basciano but also for Colotti in the early 1990s. That arrangement gave prosecutors enough evidence to accuse Rudaj and Colotti of having more than just a casual relationship with Basciano. Although the federal government never proved in court to the jury's satisfaction that the Rudaj gang profited from or was involved in Basciano's alleged car thievery, both men and various associates ultimately were convicted of other racketeering offenses and received lengthy prison terms.

To Massino it became quite clear that Basciano had developed associations with the Albanians that could work to the family's advantage. You keep your friends close and your enemies closer. By not dissuading Basciano from his ties with the Albanians, Massino was using him to keep tabs on the upstart crime group that was causing so many problems for the other crime families. Apart from some jostling in the Bronx over gambling, the Bonanno crime family kept the upper hand with the Balkan gangsters.

One person Massino didn't know whether to consider friend or foe. Gerlando "George" Sciascia, one of the Bonanno members from Canada, had long played a role in the family. When Massino orchestrated the murder of the Three Captains in 1981, he turned to Vito Rizzuto, Sciascia, and others from Montreal to take part in the killings. A surveillance photo taken a day after the assassination showed Massino leaving a Queens motel with Sciascia and Rizzuto, both of whom grew up in the Sicilian town of Cattolica Eraclea. The trio had spent the night there in an attempt—futile, as it turned out—to avoid FBI spying. With the bodies of the victims nowhere in sight at the time, police could only speculate about why the group wanted to spend time at the motel.

A handsome man, Sciascia traveled between Canada and the United States, living in Manhattan and Westchester with his wife and family. He showed up in the famous Hotel Pierre wedding photo

Gerlando "George" Sciascia, a Bonanno captain from Canada

of 1980, dubbed by Special Agent Charles Rooney as the "dead men walking" shot because so many of them met early, violent deaths. That was the photo of a number of suspected drug dealers in which Basciano first came to the attention of investigators. Among that group of international heroin dealers was Sciascia, who luckily beat the one serious arrest he had on that count when in 1987 a Brooklyn federal court acquitted him of conspiring with Gene Gotti and John Carneglia, themselves both convicted and imprisoned. Once cleared of the Gotti heroin conspiracy, Sciascia was deported to Canada, but in 1997 he was allowed back into the United States, where he oversaw some of the Canadian faction's activities. He also had strong ties with the Zips, the Sicilian mobsters who immigrated in droves to New York and Canada beginning in the 1970s.

Sciascia had been close to Massino over the years, and Basciano and others in the Bronx liked him. Basciano's eldest son even socialized with Sciascia's daughter. But Sciascia's relationship with Massino started to sour in 1999. Sciascia grew increasingly alarmed at the seemingly erratic actions of Anthony "T. G." Graziano, the father of *Mob Wives* reality star Renée Graziano. Sciascia complained that Graziano was often stoned and likely dipping into his cocaine supply, which should have been sold to produce money for the family. "Every time I see this guy he is stoned," Sciascia said. The problem was that Graziano was an old favorite of Massino: Both men socialized together with their wives, and they even took trips together.

Vitale took Sciascia's complaint to Massino, who looked into it and reported back that Graziano was being medicated for a stomach ailment and not taking illegal drugs. While that should have defused the situation, Sciascia remained wary of Graziano. Never shy about speaking his mind, Sciascia also criticized Marty Rastelli, brother of the late Bonanno boss, over a debt Rastelli said was owed him. "You got nothing coming. I'm going to war tomorrow if you want," Sciascia bluntly told Rastelli.

Sciascia wasn't endearing himself to anybody, and his assertiveness was making Massino think he had designs on challenging his power. It was during an interlude at the twenty-fifth wedding anniversary party for some relatives of Vitale that Massino pulled him aside and told his brother-in-law "George has got to go." Massino said that he had already spoken to DeFilippo, his main captain in the Bronx, that it was his call as to how Sciascia was to be taken care of, and that Vitale was to oversee things. Then, to create an alibi, Massino left the next day for a vacation with his wife, Josephine, in Cancun, Mexico.

According to Vitale, DeFilippo worked out a plan in which one of his associates, John "Johnny Joe" Spirito, got a car and picked up Sciascia. The pretext for the rendezvous was to take Sciascia to a meeting over some fabricated dispute. Vitale provided the gun.

Conspicuously absent from all the planning and preparation was Basciano. Since he was friendly with Sciascia, it would have been a bad idea to involve him in the plot. But while he undoubtedly knew of what was going to happen to his friend, Basciano didn't intervene or break mob security to tip Sciascia off. Another old saying goes that when it comes to the mob, only your friends can hurt you. The Bronx boys showed how true that could be.

Police found Gerlando Sciascia's body on a Bronx road on March 18, 1999. The disposition of the corpse purposely gave the impression to Sciascia's Canadian buddies that he died as a result of a problem with a drug deal. Drugs had long fallen into the wheelhouse of the Canadian wing of the family, and all the members knew the inherent risks in plying that trade. The necropsy recovered six .25 mm rounds too deformed for the NYPD crime scene unit to use for ballistics comparison. It took years for cops to sort out the murder.

To further throw suspicion that the Bonanno family had killed one of its own, Massino ordered many of his captains to attend the funeral. He also had them make inquiries about what had happened, another feint to keep attention away from the borgata and which also kept most of the captains in the dark about what had really happened.

"I asked every captain in the family," Vitale recalled later. "I said, 'The administration had nothing to do with his murder. He was like a brother to us. We want to know what is going on. If you find anything out, bring it to our attention.'"

But the tactic didn't fool everyone. Baldassare Amato, one of Sciascia's compadres, had his suspicions because Massino had already had another Canadian gangster killed, Cesare Bonventre. First Cesare, now George, Amato said pointedly to Vitale, who played dumb and insisted that he had no idea what had happened to Sciascia.

The wake for Sciascia was well attended by the Bonanno family—except for Massino. Vitale showed up, as did an emissary from Canada. Patrick DeFilippo made an appearance. FBI surveillance records also show that Vincent Basciano attended. While the deception may not have tricked some in the mob, it kept the FBI puzzled for years.

Although Basciano played no direct role in the killing of Sciascia, the murder made the Bronx crew under DeFilippo more valuable to Massino. It wasn't just because guys like Spirito did some of the dirty work on the hit. Sciascia's killing drove a wedge between the Canadian wing of the Bonanno family and Massino's leadership. As noted by authors Lee Lamothe and Adrian Humphreys in *The Sixth Family: The Collapse of the New York Mafia and the Rise of Vito Rizzuto,* Massino's attempt to make Rizzuto a captain in charge of Canada met with indifference and hostility. Rizzuto, angry about not being informed of Sciascia's killing, said as much to Vitale when he visited Canada sometime in late 1999 or 2000. Rizzuto also suggested that he was as powerful—if not more so—as Massino.

But money really showed the way that Montreal's connection to New York was fraying. Lamothe and Humphreys reported that a secret Royal Canadian Mounted Police report on the problems in the Bonanno family suggested that the payment of tribute to New York by the Canadians "ended with Massino's sneak attack on Montreal's man in New York," an apparent reference to Sciascia.

If Montreal cut off Massino, then the boss would have to rely more and more on his homegrown soldiers for power and support. That state of affairs made people like Basciano more valuable. Vinny Gorgeous had a knack for making money. He wasn't some brokester who always had to hustle to make a living with an illegal racket, like so many of the older mobsters in the family. He still had his gambling operations, but he was also stepping out and creating new companies and creating a real estate empire. Always a big tipper in restaurants, he also kept doing the right thing by the Bonanno bosses. When Christmas came, Basciano gave Vitale about $5,000 along with a basket of goodies that cost around $400. We can only guess what Massino was getting.

7

Joe Massino's Casablanca Restaurant on Fresh Ponds Road in Queens wasn't a very grand establishment. Located in the Maspeth, a working- and middle-class area, it had none of the frills or ambience of a fancy Manhattan restaurant. Its exterior was drab painted stucco. Its interior decor played up the connection to the Bogart and Bergman movie with a full-size statue of Bogart by the entrance and photos from the film on the walls. Pictures of Bogart and Bergman marked the doors of the gender-appropriate restrooms.

With Massino as the behind-the-scenes owner, the cuisine was Italian with lots of dishes with red sauces. Bonanno members were expected to stop by once every week or two to pay their respects to the boss and boost profits, some of which Massino skimmed for walking-around money.

Some nights, after the place closed, regular patrons long gone, Massino and some of his captains sat around talking. Those who knew Massino discreetly knocked on the door to be let in, much like at the old speakeasies of years gone by. The restaurant featured a singing guitarist, who stayed on and played as Massino and the others fed him some cash. The chats sometimes went on late into the night.

Vincent Basciano came to Casablanca on occasion. But according to Richard Cantarella, one of Massino's favorite captains, the crime boss often absented himself when Basciano was expected. Basciano made Massino uncomfortable. Aside from Vinny's reputation for being trigger happy, Massino didn't understand how the Bronx soldier made his money.

Yet it wasn't much of a secret that Basciano worked the legitimate world as well as he did everything else.

As a businessman, Basciano didn't let anything stand still. After exiting the video store business and starting the Hello Gorgeous beauty salon, he tried his hand at being a restaurateur, florist, and trucker. In the mid-1990s, Angela Basciano and Anthony Donato were listed as incorporators of Villa Developers, a company that constructed a few two-story homes in the Bronx.

But the big construction business turned out to be Burke & Grace Avenue Corp. What made Burke & Grace different from the other Basciano family business ventures was that it paired up with Robert Van Zandt, a well-known Bronx tax preparer. Angela Basciano had an interest in the company and is listed as a principal in corporate and court records. Van Zandt and his wife, Kim, worked with a network of accountants and financial sources who, according to records, provided capitalization for Burke & Grace business deals.

With sound financial backing, Burke & Grace in 2001 began to take a role in numerous real estate deals in the Bronx, notably in the Throgs Neck area where the Basciano family was living. A signature project was a major town house development on the water by the Bronx end of the Throgs Neck Bridge. The Schurz Avenue location commanded a dramatic view of the East River and provided brilliant sunrises and sunsets. The development took up an increasing amount of Basciano's time and was the project on which Randy Pizzolo was working when he was murdered.

The death of Pizzolo, as it turned out, didn't impact Burke & Grace's planned developments. The company produced a spate of one-, two-, and three-family homes as well as a number of condominium conversions. Basciano project-managed some of them, while his wife also did some work planning interiors.

The most ambitious project Burke & Grace took on was the purchase of a tract of land in upstate Bethel. The two-hundred-plus-acre site, once a golf course, became the proposed home of a large housing project for anywhere between 165 and 200 town houses. The project also involved a Bronx attorney by the name of Thomas Lee, a criminal and real estate lawyer who had a fascination with mobsters. Lee at times represented some of the workers in Basciano's gambling stores when they were arrested and eventually started passing and receiving messages for Massino in jail when the crime boss was arrested in early 2003.

Involved in so many real estate projects and other dealings, Basciano was making a comfortable living and amassing sizable wealth. To be closer to the center of his construction operations—and to be nearer to his in-laws—Basciano and his wife purchased a large home at the south end of Revere Avenue, literally doors away from where Angela had grown up. A 1994 mortgage of $145,000 bought the new property close to a secluded section of the Bronx waterfront known as Silver Beach.

But while Basciano seemed to have enough to keep him occupied legitimately, he couldn't stay off the radar of law enforcement, even after such a close call in the Blue Thunder case. He was, after all, a gangster, and gangsters get into trouble. This time the problem didn't involve the Bronx but had its roots instead in Belize, a nation with which American investigators were becoming well acquainted for a variety of reasons.

With the spread of the Internet, gambling operators realized that they could establish a booming business, relatively immune from law enforcement, with offshore employees in Central American countries like Belize and Costa Rica. Customers could place bets by telephone through an 800-number to a wire room in one of those countries. The calls would go through Venezuela and then on to Central America. Employees of the gambling operation in New York City could accept payments from the bettors and pay them any winnings.

In March 2000, a longtime confidential informant for the Queens County District Attorney's Office tipped his handlers about a bookmaking operation allegedly run by one Taylor Breton, a round-faced, bald man who resembled Curley from the original Three Stooges comedy team. Law enforcement officials knew Breton to be an associate of the Gambino crime family, and he had a gambling record as far back as 1978. By reputation and behavior, Breton was a big roller, knocking up losses said to be as much as $16 million on one occasion. Officially a resident of Connecticut, the forty-eight-year-old moved around a lot, residing at various times in Florida, New York, and apparently New Jersey.

The informant had enough specific information that detectives in Queens put wiretaps on a number of telephones, including those of Breton and a number of associates such as Frank Rizzo, another Connecticut resident. The taps were attempting to ascertain how the gambling operation was being run, who was involved, and how much money was going through the business. Wiretaps had been gathering information for a few months when investigators discovered the source of the financing for Breton's gambling business: Vincent Basciano.

"It became clear from the conversations and surveillance that Basciano is providing financial backing to the operation and that Breton has recently become associated with Basciano," a Queens assistant district attorney stated in an affidavit used to get a judge to extend the original wiretap order. "Furthermore, several intercepted and recorded calls over the last month indicate that Basciano is using a cellular telephone . . . to control the gambling operation."

The taps often didn't pick up Basciano saying anything very descriptive. But in one call on November 28, 2000, Basciano told Breton that he would meet him at the St. Regis Hotel in Manhattan's Midtown. Breton, Basciano, and Bruno Indelicato all went into the hotel and had a thirty-minute conversation. Police don't know what the three men discussed, but Indelicato's presence later caused him a great deal of trouble. A federal felon on parole, Indelicato wasn't supposed to be consorting with another felon or members of organized crime. Basciano fit both categories, so in his presence Indelicato was doubly guilty of violating the terms of his parole.

Wiretap records show that Breton understandably disliked that Basciano and the Bonanno family had taken over the rights to his gambling operation. While Breton originally was an associate of the Gambino family, his main contact with that borgata recently had been convicted and sent away to prison. Exactly how the Bonannos took over remains unclear, but Basciano became the new overseer the previous August according to the wiretap records.

What particularly angered Breton was that he had to share his earnings with Basciano, who also wanted to have a copy of records showing which bettors owed the ring money. Sharing that with the Bonanno family would lose him even more money, Breton complained in a wiretapped conversation in late 2000. "I don't know what I'm gonna have left anymore," he said, dispirited.

Seven months later, Breton found out just how much more he was going to lose when a Queens grand jury indicted him and four others, including Frank Rizzo, on charges of running a multimillion-dollar money-laundering and gambling operation in six states as well as Belize and Costa Rica. Indelicato was also charged with violating his federal parole.

Again conspicuous by his absence in the indictment was Vincent Basciano, who continued to lead a charmed life. The grand jury didn't have enough to charge him. Some of the available wiretap evidence showed that while his conversations were enough to get court orders extending the surveillance, they didn't rise to the level of indictable offense. Even Breton was vague in his recorded conversations, but without more evidence Basciano couldn't be a part of the Queens case.

The New York gambling charges added to a growing number of setbacks for Breton. Three months before the state indictment, New Jersey gaming officials moved to have him barred from Atlantic City casinos. New Jersey authorities also brought charges against him for gambling, racketeering, and other offenses. He pleaded guilty to a single charge of promoting gambling in late November 2001 and received a three-year prison sentence. In the Queens case, Breton also pleaded guilty that month to one count of money laundering and received up to three years in prison, said officials in New York.

Though Basciano wasn't being indicted for gambling, the activity was still getting him into deep financial trouble. He had a gambling habit, and it was known among the Bonanno family that he borrowed a lot of money from the mob to finance visits to the Atlantic City casinos. Basciano may have won some money, but he also went into a lot of debt with the casinos. All that time at the gaming tables resulted in lawsuits filed by the casinos against Basciano, apparently to recoup money he owed them.

Bronx state court records showed that in one case Resorts International won a default judgment against Basciano for over $98,000. In another, Trump Taj Mahal Casino got a judgment against him for over $106,000. In the latter case, when the casino wanted information about Basciano's income, assets, and finances, his old attorney, Benjamin Brafman, wrote to lawyers for the casino to put them on notice that the Bronx gangster wasn't going to disclose that information easily.

Basciano did "indeed have a good faith basis to invoke his Fifth Amendment privilege" with any questions about his money, Brafman said in a letter dated May 25, 2000, and filed with the court. Given what was taking shape, Basciano had every reason to keep his financial affairs secret.

8

In its day, the Manhattan Grille on First Avenue on Manhattan's Upper East Side made for a plush steak house with a nice, nostalgic setting. The bar, with mahogany and oak trim dating back to 1904, had been salvaged from the old Astor Hotel when it was demolished. It felt like something from the Roaring Twenties. Steaks were the main attraction. It also made a good place for drinks and, in the case of Vincent Basciano, a classy venue for what amounted to a casting call for the mob.

One night in December 1999, Basciano joined three other men for martinis at the restaurant: his old friend Bruno Indelicato and a man from the Bronx named Peter Cicale, who had driven into Manhattan with his nephew, Dominick. A handsome, strapping young man just out of prison for a drug conviction in Florida, Dominick Cicale had been called to the meeting by Indelicato, whom he had met while they had spent time in a federal prison in Pennsylvania. Both men had stayed in touch, and when Cicale needed work he looked up Indelicato.

Knowing Cicale's past, Indelicato saw that he had potential for the world of organized crime. Eager to please, Cicale, like so many of the young Italian men whose families had mob roots—with relatives blooded to various New York crime families—had a fascination with the hoodlum life style. Cicale seemed fearless and ready to take care of himself in a tough spot. He had been convicted of manslaughter in Florida after slaying a man in a motel room whom he believed was plotting to kill him. For that he received a ten-year prison sentence but got out in only seventeen months for good behavior.

As a young man, Cicale never had good male role models in his life for very long. His father had gone to jail, allegedly became a junkie, and left the family to marry another woman, said Cicale. His godfather Peter, his father's uncle, had done time for heroin trafficking and hung around with the Lucchese crime family. An aunt and his grandmother were largely responsible for raising him. He had no stand-out father figure in his family. Only the mob played that role.

Cicale's youth consisted of street fights, pistol whippings, car robberies, and drug deals for dime bags of marijuana and kilos of cocaine. Illegal gun possession was almost a given, and there were plenty of arrests for that. Tattoos were the mark of a tough guy, and Cicale had plenty of those, too. They weren't subtle works of skin art, though. The devil with an ax graced his upper right arm; a Mach 10 handgun with silencer on his right forearm; a panther on his chest; a dragon on his upper back; and a parrot on his right calf. His left bicep featured an executioner with the caption "Who's next?" and his left forearm hosted the Grim Reaper.

At the Manhattan Grille, Basciano liked what he saw of the young Bronx man seated across the table. Cicale's rugged masculinity, his poise, the machismo that he exuded all mirrored Basciano's self-image. Unlike Basciano, though, Cicale was rough around the edges and uneducated, having dropped out of high school in the tenth grade. Basciano hadn't done much better, but he still graduated. Yet

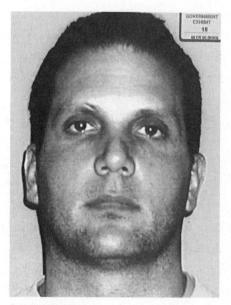

Dominick Cicale

the youthful ex-con and the mobster seemed cut from the same block of stone. Basciano questioned the young man about his arrests and time in jail. In fact, he questioned Cicale a number of times about his days behind bars, more than any other item on his mob resume, as if weighing the youngster's credentials and ability to take care of himself. Basciano asked if he was associated with anyone in organized crime, and Cicale truthfully could say that he wasn't.

Drinks at the Manhattan Grille led to more martinis later that same night in a visit to Rao's Restaurant in East Harlem. On parole, Cicale shouldn't have gone to Rao's, but that didn't stop him. Basciano got upset when he saw Cicale walk into Rao's that night because of the parole issue, but after scolding the young man's uncle, he ordered more drinks anyway.

Rao's, tucked discreetly at the south end of Pleasant Avenue in East Harlem, wasn't the sort of establishment where just anyone could walk in off the street and get a table. Reservations had to be booked well in advance. To be invited by an established patron meant you were worth special consideration. A seat in Rao's didn't go to just anyone. By that time in the evening, Cicale's mother, his aunt, and his ex-wife joined the party. As the group knocked back drinks in the intimate confines, Indelicato found a moment to pull the young Cicale aside. The two men already had a close relationship, and in Cicale's mind Indelicato, son of a slain mob captain, had a distinct mob family lineage.

Basciano liked him, Cicale heard, liked the way he handled himself. He had passed the audition. Would Cicale like to be "around" Indelicato? he was asked. Being around an already established member of a borgata was a crucial first step to being connected to the mob. Cicale of course said yes. Indelicato wrote on a slip of paper the number of a prepaid cell phone that Cicale could use to contact him. There was one more thing, Indelicato told him. Always make that call from a pay phone.

So it was on a winter's night that Dominick Cicale, amid the chandeliers of the Manhattan Grille and the tightly packed tables of Rao's, gained his entree to the Bonanno crime family. If Cicale needed help with any problems, Indelicato could deal with it. He was a soldier in a major crime family, so no one could give Cicale grief without consequences. Such were the benefits of being associated with a made man. "I was happy," Cicale said years later about the arrangement.

The not-so-secret reality of organized crime is that at its core it's a moneymaking operation. In his first attempt to bring in cash in early 2000, Cicale brought fraudulent checks ranging between $175,000 and $500,000 to Indelicato at his office in a New Jersey trucking company. The Bonanno soldier had a no-show job there to prove to his probation officer that he had gainful employment. Could anything be done with the checks? Indelicato took them and, as Cicale remembered, showed them to Basciano, who quickly realized that attempts to cash them could only spell trouble. Indelicato gave the checks back to Cicale.

Vinny Basciano, left, and Dominick Cicale, right, at the christening of Cicale's daughter Angelina around 2001

Throughout 2000, Cicale socialized with Indelicato and Basciano. He always took care when he traveled to drive circuitous routes and scrupulously check his rearview mirrors to make sure he wasn't being followed. He also used a prepaid telephone card for calls. If law enforcement ever got wind that Cicale and Indelicato were consorting, both of them could have their probation status revoked, and it would be back to prison for either or both of them.

Basciano, who liked control and to be sure of those around him, had no use for devious or disloyal people. He also didn't like those who couldn't hold their alcohol and did stupid things. The mob had plenty of them, the meatheads who shot off their mouths, got into fights, or otherwise called unnecessary attention to themselves—as the unfortunate Pizzolo found out. If the Manhattan Grille and Rao's had been casting calls for Cicale, another night of drinks at a restaurant in Forest Hills served as the audition. It wasn't so much a test of Cicale's ability to commit crimes—which he already had shown that he could do—but more of an integrity check.

The drinks flowed freely at Bartini's one night as Basciano, Indelicato, and Cicale drank the ubiquitous martinis. A fourth person joined the group: Debra "Shorty" Kalb was Basciano's girlfriend and an erstwhile employee of Hello Gorgeous. A petite woman with dirty blonde hair, Kalb proved her usefulness to Basciano in many ways. On this particular evening, she administered a crucial test of loyalty. As Cicale remembered years later, the diminutive woman, seated next to him, began rubbing her leg against his. These weren't accidental jostles under the table but more seductive caresses, meant to give the impression that she might be available on the sneak. If Cicale entertained any ideas that Kalb was coming on to him, he did nothing about it and let the moment pass. It was the right thing to do. Basciano told Cicale that he purposely had Kalb carry on that way to see if he would make any moves on her.

Having proved his trustworthiness, even with Basciano's girlfriend, Cicale received more introductions around town. There was high-rolling gambler Taylor Breton as well as other numbers guys giving Basciano as much as $25,000 in tribute at Christmas time, money that Cicale collected on occasion. Gambling, particularly with sports, provided a mainstay for the Bonanno family, and Cicale proved his usefulness by gathering collections from bettors and finding new customers. At times he traveled to check in on sports betting operations. For a man who grew up in modest single-family homes in the Bronx, Cicale found himself in a new world. A trip to an apartment of one gambler on Ocean Drive in Miami Cicale found particularly impressive.

"When we pulled up, it was like pulling into a hotel," Cicale recalled. "It was very elegant. They had a doorman out there, valet parking. When we arrived on the floor to the apartment, there was only two apartments on that floor."

For years the Bonanno family had been in the drug racket, but over time its connections with the Canadian faction had withered. But when Cicale came on the scene, a concerted push to revive that line of business was taking shape, even if the old Bonanno members from Canada had left the picture. Basciano, who had already gone through the ordeal of the Blue Thunder trial, saw Cicale as a useful front man.

"He trusted me," Cicale remembered when asked why Basciano wanted him involved.

The new sources for marijuana were three men from Canada whom Cicale met at a Ramada Inn in New Rochelle. As payment, Cicale gave the men $25,000, money that he said had been owed to the suppliers by Basciano from a previous deal. A shipment of about 250 pounds of weed would come down in a couple of weeks, the Canadians said. But officials arrested the suppliers a few weeks later, costing Basciano and the Bonanno family not only the $25,000 but also the pipeline from the north itself, according to Cicale. There was talk about sending family member Sal "The Iron Worker" Montagna, who had Montreal connections, back to Canada to try to revive the marijuana connection with borrowed funding.

When Montagna, Italian by birth, finally did make it back to Canada it was because the US government expelled him over a rather low-level felony that cut against his immigration status. The Iron Worker—so named because of his metal fabrication business in Brooklyn—couldn't stay out of trouble in Canada, either. In a crime for which the motive remained unclear, Montagna was murdered on what was the US Thanksgiving Day 2011, on the snowy banks of L'Assumption River by the Ile Vaudry, in Quebec province. Police think he was shot multiple times when he fled the house of a convicted drug dealer on the island and tried to swim to the mainland.

Meanwhile Cicale's ties to Basciano strengthened as the mobster began using him for various missions around New York City. He sent him on gambling collections, trips out of town, and to the casinos. When Cicale needed an apartment, he rented one within walking distance of Basciano's house on Schurz Avenue in a home owned by Basciano's mother-in-law. Cicale's tile business got a boost when men whom Basciano used for electrical work in gambling locations got him work at the Hunts Point Market doing tile installation.

A person's usefulness to the mob is measured by what he can do competently for the bosses. Some men become members, so it goes, because they can cook a good dish of spaghetti or mix a drink. Others are earners, valued because of the money they can make, sometimes legitimately, often criminally. That latter category fit Basciano. Then there are those who do another kind of work.

In February 2001 Cicale received a call from the prepaid cell phone number that Indelicato had given him about a year earlier at Rao's. Indelicato called to tell him that a situation had developed where Basciano needed help. It might involve hurting somebody. It seems that some guy from the Bronx was trying to kidnap one of Basciano's sons. Was Cicale interested? Certainly—anything he could do to help a friend.

9

FRANK AND MARIA SANTORO EACH HAD RESPONSIBILITIES IN THE household. Blonde and pretty, Maria worked at a real estate company in Manhattan and took care of the cooking. Frank walked the dog.

They had been married for twenty-one years, and it hadn't been the easiest of marriages. Maria worked to keep the household finances on an even keel, although the family seemed to be doing reasonably well. Frank had tough luck keeping a job, and when he did try to work at his own cabinet business, it often ran into trouble. He also had a tendency to get arrested. Cops had nabbed him as far back as 1993 for gambling, resisting arrest, possessing marijuana in a public place, and petty larceny. That last one came right after the new year in 2001.

But for all his faults, Frank Santoro made the time to be home for dinner with his wife and son, as he planned to do the evening of February 15, 2001. Maria prepared the loin of pork. The recipe came from her mother-in-law, whom she called as Frank Santoro leashed up the Doberman pinscher and stepped out into the chilly night.

The area of Throgs Neck where the Santoro family lived took its name from British settler John Throckmorton, although George Washington bastardized the pronunciation as "Frogs Neck" in one of his Revolutionary War journals. The neighborhood lies on a slice of land that juts out into Long Island Sound, a setting that once made it a desirable place for the summer homes of city dwellers. Over time, the neighborhood of estates and farms evolved into a middle-class neighborhood. Modern one- and two-family homes line streets like Pennyfield Avenue, much of

Frank Santoro in one of his better moments in life at a birthday party for his son, also named Frank

it renovated or new construction. The community consisted of a mix of Italian, Irish, and Greek immigrant families.

Frank Santoro decided to walk the Doberman down Pennyfield. The street sits next to the busy highway leading over the Throgs Neck Bridge, which connects the Bronx with Queens. Truck traffic—and a lot of it crossed the bridge—could be particularly noisy.

As man and dog circuited back along Pennyfield, a neighbor happened by. They stopped briefly to chat. Both men had talked earlier about a car that the neighbor wanted to sell. But tonight the conversation was short. The neighbor always felt a bit uncomfortable around Santoro, so he said, because he always seemed high on something. The small talk over, Santoro continued on his walk and made the turn back to his house and past a car parked a short distance away. Home and the pork loin dinner lay just steps away.

"Excuse me," said a man's voice from behind Santoro.

Back at the house, flanked with two sculpted lions guarding the front walk, Maria Santoro was getting ready to serve dinner and noticed that the evening dog walk was taking longer than usual. She bundled up and went outside, walking past the lions and turning to the left. The service road near where they lived ran past an undeveloped tract of land not far from the house and had a small indentation in the curb. At the curb cut, Maria saw her husband but not the dog.

The driver of the Bronx number 8 bus had driven his regular circuit from the Williamsbridge neighborhood in the northern part of the borough and gone south about six miles to make the turn on to Pennyfield at about 9:30 p.m. In another couple of blocks, he would make the loop back up north. But before he did, he noticed a woman standing by the side of the road, yelling. He stopped the bus and opened the door.

"Get up, Frankie!" she screamed.

The driver saw the body of a man lying in the street. He stayed by the corpse as Maria Santoro ran back to the house to get a phone. Had he looked closely—that is, if he really wanted to look closely—he would have seen white flecks around Frank Santoro's head. They were what was left of his brain.

When police from the 45th Precinct arrived, Maria Santoro was standing over her husband's body and talking into her cell phone. "He took too long, he was walking the dog," the cops heard her say. Although the officers tried to talk with her, Maria, too distraught to answer, kept repeating: "I'm in shock—my son, my son." The news was going to devastate the child.

Cops noticed a dark-haired man, about forty years old, dressed in a white T-shirt and black leather jacket, observing the bloody scene. He came closer, looked at Santoro's body, and then walked away. Two officers, their interest piqued, followed him. The man in the leather jacket noticed

The Frank Santoro murder scene near Pennyfield Avenue in the Throgs Neck neighborhood of the Bronx

them and quickened his pace. Jumping into a dark-colored car, the man sped in reverse and then, without the headlights on, drove away from them toward East Tremont Avenue. It all happened so fast that no one could get a plate number from the vehicle.

The body of Frank Santoro was taken to the medical examiners' office, and the cause of death was quickly noted as a homicide. "Victim was shot multiple times about the upper torso and head with shotgun, by unknown perps for unknown reasons," was the descriptive notation on the police report. The medical examiner went into more clinical depth, listing the cause as "partial avulsion of brain and perforations of liver, lung, kidney and small bowel due to shotgun wounds of head and torso." In other words, someone had blown his brains out.

In a different Bronx neighborhood, about four miles from where medical examiners had inspected Santoro's body on the street, another group of people was gathering in a different surrounding and for a much different reason. The men inside the bathroom of the house on 106th Street in the Pelham Bay section had used it before for discussions that the lady of the house, Debra Kalb, wasn't supposed to hear. Women like Kalb, close to mobsters, shouldn't be involved in what the menfolk were doing. That was a mob rule for as long as anyone could remember.

Behind closed doors by the toilet and bathtub, three men wore a look of celebration. They had hidden their weapons elsewhere, so there was no risk if police happened to come inside. Two of the men hugged and kissed Dominick Cicale like gleeful parents.

"Congratulations, you have just done your first piece of work," they told him.

Cicale had just shown the two most important men in his life—Vincent Basciano and Bruno Indelicato—that he could be trusted. He had also proved the depth of his loyalty.

The year 2001 saw 960 reported homicides hit the books in New York City. The death of Frank Santoro, on the ides of February, received relatively prompt attention from the police. That didn't mean the detectives from the 45th Precinct would solve the case quickly, however. From interviews and canvassing the neighborhood, they quickly got the sense that Santoro's life led to the possibility that any number of people could have wanted to do him harm. The toxicology report from the autopsy alone hinted at the darker corners of Santoro's life: traces of opiates, methadone, marijuana, and cocaine.

One friend of the Santoro family told detectives that Frank mused about how crazy his life had become. During the day he worked on cabinets, and at night he said he had to travel to Little Italy to talk with mobsters about "business." He was also wheeling and dealing. The cops heard that he bought lights, seeds, and other accoutrements for the hydroponic growing of marijuana. But apparently Santoro had planned to rip off the harvest, cheating his other two business partners in the venture. In the end, Santoro took control of the plants and then said that his conspirators had broken in and stolen the crop. Santoro also had bookmaking connections. A witness told detectives that Santoro was tasked with getting $300,000 from a deadbeat bettor, with the promise of receiving half if he collected.

"Frankie was into all kinds of stuff," the witness told police. "He always had to deal somebody out of something. He had a lot of enemies in the neighborhood."

The police didn't pick up on everything about the death of Frank Santoro, though. With a mob hit, a lot stays secret. Rumors on the street said that Santoro was kidnapping jewelers and doing the same with drug dealers. Eventually detectives learned of Santoro's arrest record with one Dominick Cicale of the Bronx, both found carrying a large amount of marijuana in the trunk of a car in Kansas. Court records didn't reveal any disposition on the case.

At the time of Santoro's death, Cicale was fifty-seven years old and had a son with the same first name. The younger Dominick wasn't even thirty years old when his father was arrested with Santoro in Kansas. The boy had no idea what Santoro looked like when he helped kill him.

10

It took cops and federal agents a few years to crack the Santoro murder case. But word on the street about who and what lay behind the killing had begun to circulate quickly in the Bonanno crime family. By March 2001, Joseph Massino knew the whole story because Vincent Basciano told him, said the younger Cicale.

Massino didn't earn the nickname "The Ear" for nothing. He might not have involved himself in everything his captains were doing on the street, but he was boss, so all he had to do was call somebody for a full report. He also kept his ears tuned for rumors, and what he heard about the demise of Santoro bothered him. Vitale was the first to bring the story about the Bronx murder to Massino's attention. Massino called Basciano to see him, a request honored with no questions asked.

As Cicale later recalled for the FBI, about a month after Santoro died on the street Basciano related how he had told Massino about what had happened. The crime boss had inquired about the incident, and Basciano told him about the murder and how he, Cicale, and Indelicato were involved, according to Cicale. The conversation gave Basciano the opportunity to showcase his loyalty to mob life to Massino and stress his status as a protégé, Cicale said.

This was the second time Massino had heard a story about Basciano murdering someone. Although Basciano claimed that he had informed his captain, Patty DeFilippo, about the Santoro incident, DeFilippo denied it, recalled Sal Vitale in one of his many FBI debriefings. In mob life, an unapproved murder can pose a serious infraction. The transgressor can lose rank—stripped from captain back down to soldier—or, if the victim was another made man, the murderer could also be killed. Neither Santoro nor the man Basciano allegedly killed some years earlier in a social club were made members of organized crime. But when Massino remarked to a trusted captain in his restaurant a few months later that he was unsure about Basciano, the two killings surely were weighing on his mind.

"Joe Massino was always leery of Vinny," Richard Cantarella said years later. "Too quick, too hard-headed—he stayed an arm's distance from Vinny."

Basciano also allegedly requested permission from Massino to kill others. One request involved an Albanian gang associate who had beaten up a member of the Colombo crime family. Basciano, who knew a lot of the Albanian players, wanted to retaliate and kill the man, but Massino told him to mind his own business, according to Cantarella. What had happened didn't involve the Bonanno family. Massino may have killed during his rise to the top of the family, but as he was consolidating his power, he relied less and less on murder as a way of policing his subordinates. In fact, when Massino later went on trial for racketeering, his supporters and attorneys noted that since he left prison in 1992, he had only the killing of George Sciascia in 1999 to his credit.

Although Massino, Basciano, and the rest of the Bonanno captains always assumed the FBI was targeting them, in 2001 they had no idea of the depth of the forensic accounting investigation under way that later—through a series of fortuitous breaks—changed the face of the mob forever. But before that happened, the FBI Bonanno squad in New York had begun the tedious task of wading through records to find the weak link in Massino's armor, which the bureau hoped would bring down a large part of the crime family. John Stubing, a career agent who had started out in the FBI in 1977 as a file clerk and began agent training in 1984, organized the task. After arriving on assignment to New York in 1986, Stubing received an appointment to the Bonanno crime family squad, rising to the head of the squad in 1995. Over a period of about five years, he focused his effort on Massino by bringing in Jeff Sallett and Kimberly McCaffrey, two fresh-faced special agents right out of the FBI Academy. Both were certified public accountants.

Sallett always wanted to be a G-man, while McCaffrey, who had a promising career as a gymnast until she hurt her knee during a floor exercise, settled on accounting as a career and then the FBI on the recommendation of one of her college professors in Maryland. Traditional investigative methods like surveillances and wiretaps only go so far. The business paper trail, which leads investigations to new, unknown evidence, sometimes provides the best means for a sneak attack into a crime family.

In an office at FBI headquarters at 26 Federal Plaza in the Civic Center area of New York City, Sallett and McCaffrey sifted through years of FBI surveillance photos. Dating from the 1970s, the images looked crude by modern digital photographic standards: fuzzy, underexposed, and quickly shot outside mob social clubs in Manhattan and elsewhere. But for the two young agents the photos served as a tutorial into the history of the Bonanno family. Old underboss Nicholas "Nicky Eye Glasses" Marangello and captains like the late Al Embarrato and Frank Lino showed up, as did a slimmer and younger Massino. Images captured a jaunty Vitale walking with another powerful Brooklyn captain, Anthony Spero, and Vincent Aloi, at one time acting boss of the Colombo family.

But the devil is always in the details. Sallett and McCaffrey noticed that Massino's wife, Josephine, had an interest in a number of parking lots in lower Manhattan—an unusual investment for a woman who had lived most of her life as a housewife in Howard Beach. Records showed that Josephine Massino had business dealings with her brother Salvatore and Loretta Castelli, the wife of Cantarella. Sallett and McCaffrey probed, but they didn't find anything illegal with the finances of the company.

Yet a name kept appearing on checks drawn on the various company accounts, that of Barry Weinberg, a chain-smoking Queens businessman who also had interests in a number of parking lots around the city. Sallett and McCaffrey uncovered checks each for almost $17,000. Clearly Weinberg warranted further attention. The two agents found through surveillance that Cantarella and Weinberg were meeting regularly in restaurants in Little Italy. On the surface nothing about the relationship between the two seemed suspicious. But as Sallett and McCaffrey analyzed Weinberg's tax returns, they discovered evidence of evasion. Weinberg had an income of millions of dollars over several years, and the evasion of tax on that income appeared substantial.

They had found the weak link. In early January 2001, just over a month before Santoro was murdered, Weinberg was arrested and brought to a small federal office where Sallett and McCaffrey laid out the incriminating evidence against him, which amounted to a federal loss of over $1 million. Weinberg puffed his way through innumerable cigarettes as he listened to the poor prognosis of his future. Tax evasion on that scale meant years in jail, he heard. If he worked undercover for the FBI and taped his conversations with Cantarella and others, Weinberg could escape jail. It was no contest. Weinberg immediately decided to cooperate and over the course of nearly ten months secretly recorded conversations that had repercussions that neither Sallett, McCaffrey, nor anyone else in law enforcement could have predicted.

The tapes Weinberg made showed that Cantarella and another captain named Frank Coppa, involved in parking lot deals, were shaking Weinberg down for hundreds of thousands of dollars. In one instance, Cantarella slugged Weinberg. When the businessman complained to other gangsters about such treatment, he got squeezed for more money. The tapes were damaging to Cantarella and Coppa—though not harmful to Massino—and provided the ammunition that the government needed to start tipping the dominoes within the Bonanno family.

The FBI was also picking up some troubling intelligence indicating that Cantarella was growing suspicious of Weinberg. Cantarella expressed his feelings to Massino in one of his regular meetings with the boss at Casablanca. Massino was prepared to have Weinberg killed. In the end, though, Cantarella told Weinberg to stay away from him, to avoid coming to the restaurants—a sure sign to Sallett and McCaffrey that Weinberg's string as an informant was coming to an end.

With Weinberg no longer viable, Sallett and McCaffrey turned to another helpful source. Agostino Scozzari had a successful scaffolding business in Europe but wanted a change. He sold his company and packed up his Persian wife and her kids to make it in New York. With about $4 million in assets from the sale of his company, Scozzari bought a house in New Jersey and sank some money into a couple of restaurant ventures in lower Manhattan, one in Little Italy. These forays into the restaurant business connected Scozzari with Weinberg. As author Selwyn Raab notes in *Five Families*, Scozzari had developed a fascination with the mob and agreed to Weinberg's offer to introduce him to Cantarella. Scozzari steadily entered the mob's sphere of influence.

When Weinberg disappeared into the witness protection program, Sallett and McCaffrey approached Scozzari and convinced him to tape Cantarella. Weinberg had implicated the Italian in money-laundering activity, giving the agents the bargaining tool that they needed, reported Raab. Anxious to stay out of trouble, Scozzari made more secret recordings of Cantarella from about December 2001 until August 2002.

The Weinberg-Scozzari period of secret taping—extremely fruitful in terms of the evidence collected—also occurred around one of the most tumultuous and wrenching events in US history: September 11, 2001. In New York, agents working on organized crime cases were suddenly dragooned into rescue and recovery work at Ground Zero. McCaffrey and Sallett sifted through the smoldering debris of the Twin Towers to try to find the black box recorders from American Airlines Flight 11 and United Flight 175. After working at Ground Zero, Sallett was detailed to Washington, D.C., to work on the follow-up investigations into the terrorists' financing network. Meanwhile, McCaffrey stayed in New York, keeping the Bonanno crime family investigation alive.

The Bonanno squad of the FBI was interested in more than just Massino, although he was the holy grail of their investigation. Another team headed by Special Agent Michael Breslin was focusing on the regimes of Basciano and DeFilippo, among the two most prominent elements of the crime family in the Bronx. That particular investigation had a rather circuitous history. Basciano and DeFilippo had been on the radar of law enforcement, particularly the NYPD, since about 1994, when the Blue Thunder trial ended, Breslin recalled in an interview. By 2000 Breslin left the Bonanno squad of the FBI in Manhattan, transferred to the agency office in Westchester County, where he worked in the organized crime section. The resulting investigation netted a few Bonanno associates but didn't do much with Basciano. It took until 2002—when Breslin transferred back to the Bonanno squad, known as C-10—for Basciano to become more of a focus.

Meanwhile, McCaffrey was tending the Bonanno family investigation while the rest of her squad was dealing with the fallout from September 11. To let the mob know that they were being watched, federal prosecutors used evidence obtained by the FBI's Bonanno squad to target Vitale. While Massino's nominal underboss, Vitale was coming into growing disfavor with his brother-in-law because he was alienating some of the crime family captains and raised suspicions with Massino that he might have been moving to take over the family. Vitale also had okayed a few murders while Massino was in prison in the early 1990s of which the boss didn't approve.

Still, Massino allowed Vitale to keep watch over his crime family. Frank Coppa later told the FBI that in the late 1990s he and Vitale divided up the captains between them for periodic visits as Massino had wanted. As a way of insulating himself from the rest of the family, Massino also created a ruling council at that time, which changed in composition over the years. But eventually Massino kept Vitale from interacting with those captains in such a way that he denied him a cut of profits from illegal activities.

As described in *Five Families,* Vitale also took part in a particularly ingenious racket involving the branch of a bank on Long Island, a scheme that turned the branch into a serious player as a mob money-laundering and loan-sharking office. A Brooklyn federal grand jury indicted Vitale and others in 2001 on charges they structured currency deposits. This meant that the defendants made deposits of just under the $10,000 threshold for filing currency transaction reports—CTRs as they're known in the banking industry. Court records showed a large number of the cash deposits made at the bank's branch in Melville, New York, in central Long Island. In another strange twist, Vitale's men used an office inside the branch to threaten loan shark and gambling customers. A former bank manager cooperated with the FBI, and, without letting too much time pass, Vitale and the others decided to plea bargain. The Bonanno underboss admitted guilt to a charge of racketeering, for which he received a forty-five-month prison sentence in upstate New York and a $15,000 fine and had to make restitution of $40,000.

Despite the prison sentence, Vitale didn't cooperate as a witness. But that didn't stop Massino from suspecting his brother-in-law had flipped into the government's camp. The sentence he received just wasn't severe enough. As a precaution, Massino held a meeting with some of his trusted captains, among them Cantarella and Coppa, and told them that if he should ever be arrested that Vitale should be taken down. In the lingo of La Cosa Nostra, he meant that Vitale should either be killed or removed as underboss. Killing Vitale wasn't a simple move for Massino. Vitale was his wife's brother, so murdering him would have created major tensions within Massino's home.

The palace intrigue within the Bonanno crime family continued as Massino, trying to anticipate the FBI, made a key decision by 2002 about who should run the family if he did go to prison. If he had any doubts about Basciano's temperament or reputation for volatility, Massino put them aside. In late 2002, possibly in November or December, Massino started making moves. With Coppa and Cantarella locked up and Sciascia dead, the crime family needed new captains. During a meeting at Danny's, a popular Chinese restaurant in Howard Beach, Massino promoted Basciano to captain, according to a source familiar with Bonanno family operations. Massino told Basciano that he had become part of the crime family administration, answerable directly to the boss.

"Take it easy, go slow," Massino told his newly anointed captain.

According to Massino, he picked a triumvirate of men to run operations: captains Joseph "Joe Saunders" Cammarano, Anthony "Tony Green" Urso, and Peter "Peter Rabbit" Calabrese. But a Bonanno crime family member later confided to acquaintances that Basciano started helping the ruling panel when Calabrese had to deal with problems at home. Basciano gave this assistance without Massino's knowledge or approval.

No matter his shortcomings, Basciano had the energy, drive, command, and ruthlessness to help hold the family together. Massino knew this. Cammarano and Urso—older than Basciano—had the seasoning and diplomacy that come with being veterans. They could counteract Basciano's reputation for aggressiveness and hold him in check, or so Massino thought.

Yet for all his planning, Massino was making misjudgments that became apparent down the road. By keeping Vitale on a short leash, cutting him off from illicit income and emasculating him in the eyes of the crime family, Massino was undercutting any of his brother-in-law's remaining loyalty. After all, Massino had orchestrated six or seven homicides that had involved Vitale in some way. The FBI would find a treasure trove of information in Vitale if he ever decided to become a cooperating witness.

By 2002 Massino, Vitale, and the rest of the crime family knew that the FBI, specifically Sallett and McCaffrey, were zeroing in on them. To further armor himself, Massino allowed the initiations of sons of some members into the family. The theory was that by ensnaring the sons or other relatives in the family business, the fathers would be less inclined to cooperate. So the sons of Cantarella and Coppa became soldiers, as did those of five other captains.

Yet as crafty as Massino thought he was in recruiting the sons of some of his trusted captains into the fold, he was actually creating a Trojan horse that provided the FBI with a way of penetrating the crime family in ways that investigators had never seen before. In October 2002, armed with secret tapes made by Weinberg and Scozzari, federal prosecutors in Brooklyn indicted Coppa; Cantarella, his wife, and son; and other Bonannos, including Anthony Graziano. Two months earlier the FBI had searched Cantarella's Staten Island home, hauling away boxes of financial records and other documents, including a list of various crew members, as well as telephone numbers for Massino and Vitale. Cantarella had to be expecting the knock on his front door when Sallett and McCaffrey arrested him.

Cantarella faced not only extortion charges but also a racketeering charge involving the disappearance and murder of *New York Post* supervisor Perrino, who left his home in May 1992, never to be seen again. The murder charge carried a maximum life sentence. Coppa also had a serious predicament. He was already saddled with a seven-year prison term for a stock fraud conviction handed down in July 2002. If Coppa was convicted on the new racketeering charges, the portly sixty-one-year-old with a heart condition wouldn't get out of prison until he was well into his eighties. Coppa already knew the taste of prison life from the 1990s. He had cried then because he missed his family. No hard-as-nails gangster, Coppa, an aging grandfather, hated the idea of dying in prison. He became the first made member of the Bonanno family to cooperate with federal prosecutors.

By doing so, Coppa was violating all the Mafia tenets that he had sworn to uphold. During his original induction ceremony, Coppa, like the other initiates, had to denounce God and swear by the rules that directed them all to answer only to the family boss. They couldn't date the wives, girlfriends, or daughters of other members, and they learned of the all-important issue of paying tribute up the chain of command. There was no leaving the mob except by death. Nor could they discuss family business with law enforcement. If a mob member talked about murder, then the crime family would "put your lights out," Coppa explained to the agents.

Cantarella had problems similar to Coppa's, but he struggled with the added dimension that his wife and son had also been charged. Once one of Massino's closest captains, Cantarella knew that his future didn't lie with the Mafia anymore, to which he had belonged since 1990. There was only one option to save himself. "In my mind I knew I was cooperating," remembered Cantarella. Both his wife and son, Paul, accused of working as an enforcer for his father, also decided to cooperate and worked out separate deals with the government.

To the surprise of the FBI and Brooklyn federal prosecutors, two senior members of the crime family capitulated within a few weeks and became cooperating witnesses. The classic code of silence in the mob meant little to Cantarella and Coppa—and for good reason. In this new reality, the government held all the cards. Massino couldn't do anything to help them. Their only hope to see daylight in what was left of their lives was to tell the FBI everything they knew and hope for a reduced sentence. In the past, Massino always wanted copies of plea agreements sent to him for inspection whenever anybody in the family wanted to plead guilty. There was no way that was going to happen now.

Coppa underwent extensive debriefings by the FBI first and provided agents like McCaffrey and Sallett with an insight into the Bonanno family that held them rapt in attention. Coppa knew so much because he was one of the old-timers, introduced to Massino in 1977 at the Parakeet, an eatery in the Fulton Fish Market, by Matteo "Little Moe" Valvo, then Massino's captain. Not paying much heed to Massino at the time, Coppa soon learned that the stocky Queens mobster had carried out the order to murder Carmine Galante, the pretender to the title of family boss, in July 1979. The order had come from imprisoned Bonanno boss Philip Rastelli. After that, Massino became a rising star and orchestrated the murder of the Three Captains to solidify his power. Seeing how the hierarchy was shifting, Coppa began paying tribute to Massino of about $1,000 a month.

Coppa told the agents about a wide assortment of crimes, some tied to Massino, others implicating Vitale and other family members. There were numerous murders, including seven that directly implicated Massino: the Three Captains (Indelicato, Trinchera, and Giaccone), Dominick "Sonny Black" Napolitano, Anthony Mirra, Gabe Infanti, and Gerlando Sciascia. Coppa painted Massino as a greedy leader, who reportedly received as much as $250,000 in tribute at a crack from just one captain. Coppa also helped the agents compile a list of the Bonanno family members, a group that Massino had said totaled around 160. Coppa also identified the various captains and—to the extent he knew—the identities of the men who served under each of them. The names of Vincent Basciano, as well as the aging Patrick DeFilippo, naturally came up.

Coppa recalled that he had first met Basciano when Vitale introduced him during a trip to Atlantic City in the late 1980s. Both Vitale and Basciano had won about $15,000 on the trip. Basciano liked to gamble, and Massino tipped off Coppa that Vinny from the Bronx, as he was still known then, liked to borrow a lot of money to feed his gambling habit. Coppa told the agents that at one point he loaned $15,000 to Basciano. But aside from Basciano's gambling and his Joker Poker machines around town, Coppa didn't have much to tell the agents that incriminated the Bronx mobster.

In his debriefings, Cantarella gave more insight into Basciano's questionable dealings. In his talks with Massino at Casablanca Restaurant, Cantarella learned about Basciano's links to the Albanians and the requests he had made—which Massino turned down—to kill those who had disrespected the Italian mob. Basciano was rumored to be into drugs, not a surprise to the FBI, and "quick with a gun," said Cantarella. Basciano had floated a construction business idea with Massino, but the boss remained leery because there were "unknowns"—which Cantarella didn't explain but possibly related to the crime boss's inability to figure out how Basciano made his money.

By early January 2003, Massino, always aware of law enforcement activity, was becoming ever more conscious of the FBI's increasing surveillance of him. At one point, he remarked to his daughter Joanne on shopping trips that he saw the government cars. With the feds breathing down his neck, Massino took preemptive action. Around January 7 he summoned Basciano and Indelicato for a chat at a diner on Rockaway Boulevard. In the event of his arrest, Massino told them that if anybody had to be killed that they should get a message to him with the code word "jocko" before the intended victim's name. Massino would then let them know if he approved.

Everything came to a head on January 9, 2003, the day before Massino's birthday. At around 6:00 a.m., Sallett and McCaffrey, wearing FBI-emblazoned raid jackets, walked up to the front door of Massino's nicely appointed Georgian-style house and knocked. Massino, dressed in black, opened up and with a smile said, "I was expecting you yesterday." Bidding his wife, Josephine, good-bye, Massino exited the palatial foyer, escorted into a waiting government sedan.

Massino had always been respectful to law enforcement officials, and during the ride he was both calm and courteous. Massino told the agents that he had heard their names around town. The amicable chitchat in the vehicle along the Brooklyn Belt parkway invariably turned to food, Massino's favorite subject. He could find the best pizza at Casablanca, Massino told Sallett. The sauce there was incomparable.

By now Massino knew well that Coppa had turned. Although Sallett and McCaffrey said nothing to confirm that, the crime boss knew enough to sense that he was falling into serious trouble. Coppa had been privy to the details of many of the Bonanno family homicides. McCaffrey mentioned that Massino was going to be charged with the killing of the Three Captains—one of the events about which Coppa had information although no personal involvement.

On the day of the slaughter of the three men at a club in the Bay Ridge section of Brooklyn—May 3, 1981—Frank Lino, who had accompanied the victims to the location, escaped the gunfire and ran out the door. Lino ultimately fled to Coppa's home for protection, revealing who had been present during the gunfire. Lino identified Massino. After some intervention by Gambino underboss Aniello Dellacroce, Lino visited Massino at his home, accompanied by Coppa. During that discussion, Massino indicated that he knew what had happened and feared that Bruno Indelicato, son of one of the victims, would seek to avenge his father's death. Ultimately, Massino told Lino that he had nothing to fear and eventually made him an acting captain, placing under him some of the men who had been working with the Three Captains. Among the latter was Bruno Indelicato, who by this time also had nothing to fear from the rest of the Bonanno family.

During the ride to FBI offices, Massino's mind churned. The list of those who could betray him ran long. His thoughts also went to his brother-in-law Vitale. He asked McCaffrey if he had been arrested too. He had, she responded. McCaffrey thought it curious that Massino would ask about Vitale in particular.

Massino and Vitale had shared much over the years. His brother-in-law had acted as his surrogate, so the crime boss knew what information his underboss possessed. If he weakened, Vitale could implicate Massino in a number of crimes, particularly the Three Captains murders. Would he weaken? Massino had given Vitale a lot of reasons to become a turncoat: the lost income, the humiliation of not being able to act like a true underboss, the personal slights over the years. Once the closest of friends—Massino, a strapping athletic young man, even teaching Vitale to swim as a teenager—their relationship had withered into contempt.

"Sal is going to rat on every-fucking-body," Anthony Urso had said just three weeks earlier.

Sallett and McCaffrey didn't expect any trouble from Massino during his arrest, and he didn't give them any. It was too early in their relationship to say that the drive provided a bonding experience among the two agents and Massino, but they treated him with dignity, thereby laying the groundwork for a relationship that took years to play out. To spare Massino the ordeal of going through a "perp walk" after his routine arrest processing at FBI headquarters in Manhattan, Sallett and McCaffrey brought him into the building through an underground garage, avoiding the media horde that, alerted to his arrest, had been assembling.

11

THE ARREST PROCESSING OF JOSEPH MASSINO AND SALVATORE VITALE went quickly. The booking photographs taken at the FBI offices depicted both men staring expressionless at the camera. Massino looked inscrutable. Whatever his thoughts, Massino's countenance betrayed nothing. Vitale, appearing puffy-faced, also showed no emotion. But look at Vitale's deeply set eyes and tight lips, and you could easily understand that he was a fearful man. A once handsome and dark-haired man of Sicilian ancestry who bore the moniker "Good Looking Sal," Vitale now looked old. Concern visibly weighed him down.

Both men appeared before magistrate-judge Joan Azrack in Brooklyn federal court, arraigned just after noon. Not a regular federal district judge, Azrack was an appointed magistrate, which gave her the ability to handle arraignments and take guilty pleas when necessary. Through his defense attorney for the arraignment, Matthew Mari, Massino pleaded not guilty. Attorneys John Mitchell and Sheldon Eisenberger represented Vitale, who spoke on his own behalf and also pleaded not guilty when asked by Azrack.

Faced with numerous charges of racketeering, with the added factor of being boss of the Bonanno family, Massino wasn't going to get bail. The same held true for Vitale, who faced the same indictment. The prosecutor, the driven and dogged assistant US attorney Greg Andres, was meeting Massino in court for the first time. A lean man with flinty eyes, Andres had proved himself a wunderkind of the Brooklyn US Attorney's Office in its investigation of the Bonanno family. Andres argued against bail for both men. Massino in particular faced the prospect of indictments on additional murders based on what a secret witness had told the government. As expected, Azrack ordered both Massino and Vitale held without bail. The defense attorneys knew there was no use in arguing.

By the time Massino and Vitale were arraigned, news of their arrests had plastered the news. From Bay Ridge in Brooklyn to Baychester in the Bronx, the various Bonanno captains heard the development. It shocked none of them. They had expected something like this ever since Coppa and Cantarella were picked up three months earlier. The triumvirate of captains whom Massino had selected—Calabrese, Urso, and Cammarano—checked in with the other captains, finding out what was going on and keeping matters on the street on as even a keel as possible. Massino was still the boss and would get his cut of rackets

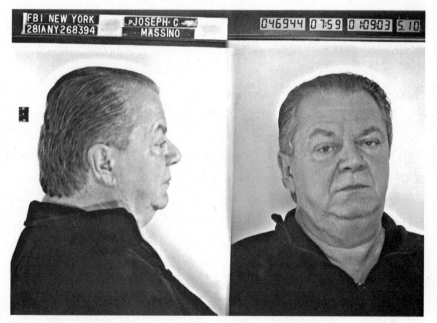

Massino's mug shots, taken at FBI headquarters in Manhattan, on January 9, 2003

despite being in jail. In another deft planning move, Massino had set up a special legal fund fed by monthly contributions from crime family members to pay for his legal expenses. A wealthy boss, he had millions of dollars squirreled away in hard cash and gold coins, so Massino wasn't feeling any immediate financial pinch. But other members had to rely on the fund, which had been paying out tens of thousands of dollars.

On February 28, 2003, it became clear that Vitale, long abused by Massino, had become a cooperating witness. He dismissed his attorney with a curtly worded fax from his new counsel, a former federal prosecutor known to represent cooperating witnesses. Massino now had had *three* people turn against him in a matter of a few months. He knew he was in deeper trouble. What investigators expected to be a long investigation suddenly turned into a treasure of witnesses against the last major Mafia boss to rule in New York City.

———

"Louie, meet Vinny. Vinny's a captain in the Massino family. Vinny, meet Louie. Louie's a captain with the Massino family."

Anthony Urso made the matching introductions. Urso was the new elder member of the ruling committee of the Bonanno family that Massino tried to rebrand in his own image. Massino didn't like that the elder Joseph Bonanno had written a book and given a *60 Minutes* interview about the mob some years back, an act that many old-timers thought an unpardonable breach of Mafia secrecy.

"Louie" was James Tartaglione, a Bonanno member who had moved from New York to Florida. With one federal conviction under his belt and weary of the mob life, Tartaglione wanted to retire in the Sunshine State, where the weather suited him. His deep tan impressed even Basciano.

Tartaglione was also preoccupied with the health of his daughter, who had a cancer scare. Massino implored him to move back to

New York, but Tartaglione resisted. He was also on parole. If the FBI observed him consorting with organized crime figures—much like what had happened to Bruno Indelicato in 2001—he would go back to prison. But he agreed to keep in touch with the crime family, and on December 17, 2003, he made an appointment to talk with Urso and Basciano at the Sea Crest Diner off Guinea Woods Road in Old Westbury on Long Island.

Despite his earlier reservations about parole violations, Tartaglione had gone back and forth from Florida in the fall of 2003 for meetings with Urso and Joe Cammarano Sr., one of the other members of the ruling committee. On one of his trips to New York in September, Tartaglione joined Urso and Cammarano in bemoaning how informants had riddled the family. Urso said that he never did like the turncoat Vitale and recalled that Vitale had tried to get him killed. The three men gossiped about the other cooperators, retelling a story about Cantarella attempting to commit suicide three times and how the crime family members were all paranoid.

About two months later, Tartaglione showed up at a second meeting, according to an FBI report known as a Form 302, which discussed intelligence about the Santoro homicide some twenty months earlier. Agents compile the Form 302 after debriefing an informant. Normally they don't disseminate it beyond the FBI, but once an indictment is filed, a defendant and defense attorneys have the right to get copies if they relate to a witness expected to testify in the case. The forms can give crucial insight about what evidence the FBI has on a variety of crimes.

Basciano wasn't around the first time that they discussed the Form 302, so the group agreed to a follow-up meeting at the Sea Crest Diner. Urso ordered coffee and french toast. By Massino's earlier decree, he had become acting boss of the crime family. He also served on the special triumvirate of captains with Basciano and Cammarano, overseeing all operations with Massino in jail. The introductory chitchat covered the weather, old friends, and the joys of living in Florida. Basciano hadn't seen Tartaglione in a few years. They talked about getting old and gray, trying to figure out who looked the best for their age. They sounded like retirees meeting for a daily coffee break.

"Lots of luck my pal, lots of luck," Tartaglione said when he learned that Basciano had been promoted to captain.

"We could all need it," replied Basciano. "Well, we all need it."

"We're in trouble. We're in trouble," said Tartaglione twice for emphasis.

A waitress who didn't seem very busy doted on the three men, telling them that they could stay as long as they wanted—all day in fact. It was Basciano who finally brought up what each of them had been pondering for months: Vitale becoming a turncoat.

"Do you believe this guy over here?" Basciano said incredulously. "Do you believe this? Do you believe what happened to us over here?"

They had known for a few months that Vitale had become a government witness. As a result, they had begun searching their pasts for crimes they might have committed with the old underboss, acts that could come back to haunt them. Basciano had made some gambling trips with Vitale to Las Vegas and Atlantic City—but Basciano's gambling was an old story. Apart from that, they hadn't done anything together.

"I got news for you, Lou, he doesn't know anything that I did," Basciano said confidently.

"Well, I don't know," said Tartaglione, sliding the Form 302 across the table to Basciano, who had heard from Urso generally what it contained.

Basciano looked at the document and started reading from it to himself, talking softly. On the surface it seemed to be a statement that Vitale had given to the FBI, recounting a discussion he had had with Basciano about the Santoro murder. But something didn't seem right.

"I never talked to this guy," Basciano said after reading the material. "I never talked to this guy. I took three trips with this guy, I never talked about anything illegal."

Basciano had gone gambling with Vitale, but their relationship wasn't close, certainly not as close as his ties to people like Cicale or Indelicato, both of whom knew Basciano's secrets. Vitale never even asked him to do anything illegal.

"They're trying to put something together on me," concluded Basciano, referring to the FBI. "You see what they're trying to do?"

Basciano didn't seem worried, however. He knew his way around the criminal justice system, and, knowing the rules of evidence, he didn't see how anything could tie him to the Santoro murder.

"They're gonna be tough to pinch me on this," said Basciano. "You wanna know why? They got no forensics. They have no guns. They have no nothing. Forget about the fact that I didn't do it anyway. Okay? I had nothing to do with it. But if I did, there's no guns, there's no cars, there's no eyewitnesses, there's no rats. How are they going to pinch me on this?"

For a man who professed no involvement in the murder, Basciano seemed to know a lot about what evidence the cops had or didn't have in the case. Given the current environment in the crime family with informants, Basciano really couldn't be certain that someone wasn't telling the FBI that he was involved. But he didn't seem concerned.

Tartaglione said that perhaps the FBI was putting the material out as a way of fouling the water, painting Basciano in a bad light with the murder allegation in the hopes that if he ever was indicted that his guilt on other charges would create a vortex that would suck Basciano in and saddle him with a conviction on the murder as well.

Basciano laughed.

The trio sat at the diner for about two hours, nursing their coffees, not rushed for time. They talked openly about a wide variety of topics that in retrospect didn't seem prudent for such a public place. Basciano in particular raved about his new acting captain, Cicale, whom he called a "hoodlum" as a compliment. He also lamented that loyalty, a quality which Basciano held dear, was sorely lacking now in the mob. Massino was his boss, and only he deserved his fealty, said Basciano.

"I got 100 percent faith in him," Basciano said. "If I'm your fucking guy, if I'm gonna walk on hot coals, if I gotta fucking jump in the ocean, let me do it for one guy." Divided loyalty only makes you a whore, he added. "I got faith in one guy. And that is where my allegiance is always gonna be, for one fucking guy. That's it, I'm living and dying with one guy," he concluded.

"And that's a good position," Tartaglione said in agreement.

They also talked about girlfriends: Urso didn't want to marry his longtime lady. Tartaglione was married. Basciano said that Angela hated him and loved him in alternating cycles, depending on his behavior. Rumors had started that Basciano had a child with another woman, and he deflected Angela's suspicions by saying the stories were nuts.

"So I denied everything, and I'm still married, I'm not divorced. She's crazy about me, I'm crazy about her," Basciano explained about his marital situation. Looking to the future, Basciano said that legitimacy—or at least "legitimate rackets"—was the way to go. Have a legal business, and maybe skim some money or evade taxes. Crimes that wouldn't lead to much prison time—that was the way Basciano wanted to live. When it was time to go, the three captains said their gracious good-byes.

"First of all, have a nice, have a happy New Year," Tartaglione told Basciano.

"It was a pleasure seeing you," answered Basciano. "A real, real pleasure seeing you."

"Tony, happy holidays. Everybody, send everybody, everybody my love," Tartaglione told Urso.

"Nice seeing you, Lou," Basciano closed.

All three men went their separate ways at around 11:30 a.m. Each had come to the diner in a different car. It took Tartaglione about a minute to start up his vehicle, turn on the radio, and make the call.

"Hi Joe, I'm in the area," said Tartaglione. His words, like virtually all the others spoken in the diner rendezvous, rang unmistakably clear.

The final comment heard on the tape came not from Tartaglione but from another man. "This is Special Agent Joseph R. Bonavolonta. The date is December 21, 2003. The time is approximately 11:30 a.m. We are retrieving the recording device from the CW [confidential witness], and I'm going to deactivate it."

12

IT ALL SEEMED VERY SUSPICIOUS.

For months, James Tartaglione had avoided coming back to New York City as Joe Massino had wanted. Tartaglione feared that he might violate his parole if he returned to the Big Apple to socialize with his old associates. But suddenly he reversed himself. He made regular trips up the coast from Florida. What's more, he was meeting regularly with the Bonanno crowd. It gave Vincent Basciano an uncomfortable feeling. Not quite suspicion, but it seemed like a sign that maybe old Big Louie had become an informant. He wasn't certain, but Tartaglione didn't seem worried about getting caught on a parole violation. What else could explain that?

"It was strange. All of a sudden, out of the clear blue Big Lou wanted to come around and start running the Bonanno crime family," Dominick Cicale later remembered.

Basciano wanted him to take a little extra precaution for the next meeting at the Seacrest Diner, Cicale recalled. "Vinny Basciano wanted me to conduct a countersurveillance on the diner."

On the cold and rainy morning of January 18, 2004, around 9:30 a.m., the four men arrived and sat down at the diner. Meeting with Tartaglione, who was wearing a secret recording device, were Basciano, Urso, and Cammarano Sr. To the uninitiated, it looked like nothing more than four middle-aged men having coffee. But, Tartaglione aside, the group represented the ruling committee of the Bonanno crime family. The conversation started with a bit of male vanity. Tartaglione looked like he got a sunburn in Florida, which Urso thought looked good. Basciano had just returned from a skiing trip and had his own dose of rays.

"Hey, you got some nice tan, " Tartaglione told Basciano. "You're not afraid to go skiing?"

"Big slopes, forget about it. I love it. I love it," answered Basciano.

When the conversation shifted to food, Tartaglione recalled seeing an old gangster known as Matty the Horse dining on octopus in Howard Beach. Meanwhile, Urso had remarked that he liked the cold weather in New York. Outside the diner, in that cold weather with slushy snow on the ground, Cicale was trying to seem unobtrusive. His job was to watch the area and see if he noticed any law enforcement surveillance. If he spotted anything, he would page Basciano the code "5050."

The FBI made it easy. Cicale quickly noticed a number of cars circling the diner. But amid the slush of winter roads in the area, the vehicles all looked clean and devoid of road salt and splatter, as if they had been garaged. The cars also had tinted windows. The diner clearly was under surveillance. He went next door to a service station. Using a pay phone, Cicale called Basciano's pager number and transmitted the code before walking back to his car to wait.

At the table, Basciano brought up the subject of the FBI reports that Tartaglione had showed him previously. Suspecting that he was talking to a government informant, Basciano had to profess ignorance and not compromise himself.

"The whole thing don't make sense," said Basciano. "Both of those pieces of paper that you gave me, I don't even know what they are talking about, Lou."

A waitress came up to the table and poured Tartaglione some more coffee. She offered some to Urso, who politely declined: He only drank one cup in the morning.

"What's this?" continued Basciano, not talking about coffee but one of the documents. There was a name on it he didn't recognize.

"I have no idea, I just thought I would do you a favor," Tartaglione replied.

The FBI's plan was to use the documents to tickle Basciano, make him say something incriminating about the Santoro homicide. At the first meeting just before Christmas, Basciano made intriguing remarks that Breslin and other agents thought signaled that Vinny from the Bronx had taken part in what had happened to Santoro. On the tape Tartaglione made, Basciano seemed sarcastic and calculating. On the one hand, he denied involvement in the killing, but in the next breath, sounding like O. J. Simpson, Basciano proffered that if he did do it there wasn't any evidence to convict him. Hardly the words of an innocent man, the agents thought.

But if Basciano seemed to take the bait on December 21, this time he was backing away. Tartaglione sensed his shift, the obfuscation. When Tartaglione asked if he remembered a character named Junkyard Richie, Basciano demurred. "I don't know him, Lou, I don't know the guy, I don't know who he is."

The waitress stopped by the table and took Tartaglione's order for tea with milk. The other two men asked only for water. Basciano wasn't in the mood for anything else. He steered the conversation again to the FBI documents. By now he must have received the message from Cicale outside and believed he was being taped.

"I got news for you, Louie," Basciano said. "You know something, the paper. The only thing that puzzled me the last time we spoke, every single thing on that paperwork was bullshit. I went through, the everything. It don't even make sense to me. . . . The whole thing don't make sense. Both of those pieces of paper that you gave me last time, I don't even know what they are talking about, Lou."

Basciano excused himself to go to the bathroom. By the time he returned to the table, a hungry Cammarano had arrived, ready to eat breakfast. He ordered scrambled eggs with home fries and whole wheat toast.

"Hey, Lou, let me ask you a question," interrupted Basciano, whose suspicion was steadily rising. "Is it possible the way you are getting this information, and they're baiting you?"

It was a perceptive observation. Basciano was showing a canny knack for not trusting the source. It was almost as if he had read the FBI playbook. The documents had been provocative. The writers of the material, federal agents, believed Basciano had something to do with the murder, and he thought it possible that the material was meant to rattle him—or worse.

"Well, they're feeding him," chirped Cammarano after listening to the discussion.

"They might be feeding you, Louie," Basciano agreed.

Tartaglione was sliding on a slippery slope now. He couldn't try to vouch for the materials, which would only raise more suspicion than apparent at that point in the conversation. In fact, there was a lot of suspicion about Tartaglione and his documents.

"Did you talk to him yet?" Cammarano asked Basciano and Urso.

"No, I didn't say nothing. I waited for you," Urso answered.

"All right," Cammarano said, looking at Tartaglione. "What we would like you to do, stay in Florida until your probation is finished. After your probation is done, you can come back and get your guys back."

"Okay," said Tartaglione. He seemed calm, considering that the ruling committee of the Bonanno family was putting him on the shelf, scotching any plans he had to come back and be an active captain in the borgata. It also effectively killed his usefulness as an informant.

Cammarano said the committee wasn't worried only about Tartaglione getting into trouble, but they had heard reports of another crime family member going over to the government. When Tartaglione asked who it was, Cammarano said he couldn't say because it didn't concern him.

"How could you say no?" asked Tartaglione, his anger steadily rising.

"But this guy doesn't concern you, all right?" Cammarano shot back. "He's got nothing to do with you."

"Now, for you not to tell me, you might be saying to me, maybe you are a rat," said Tartaglione, trying a new gambit.

The three other captains reassured him that wasn't the case, although Tartaglione, evincing staged anger, continued to vent. In decades past, in the wild days of La Cosa Nostra, a suspected informant like Big Louie might have been shot or stabbed dead on the spot. But the three captains couldn't take such a risk in so public a place. They also had reason to suspect that Tartaglione was recording them with a special transmitter broadcasting to nearby FBI cars. There wouldn't be any violence. Instead, the group continued their cat-and-mouse game of deception. Tartaglione continued to show anger.

Finally, Basciano told Tartaglione that this wasn't the old days of the mob. "The times today, the times we are going through today, okay, make Joey and make Tony take certain precautions that normally they wouldn't take. Okay, you cannot be offended."

"I am offended," replied Tartaglione.

Nagged by Tartaglione and his staged anger, Cammarano finally relented and told him that the suspected government informant was an old Bonanno soldier known as Mickey Bats. But Tartaglione, skeptical, accused Cammarano of lying. Cammarano stuck to his guns, though, and insisted Mickey Bats was the suspect.

Then—in a twist that no one expected—Tartaglione turned from anger to saying that he had some jewelry and Krugerrands stolen from Connecticut that he wanted to unload. The total stash was worth about $1 million, but all Tartaglione wanted was $75,000.

"I ain't doing nothing illegal no more," said Basciano dishonestly, holding his hands up, palms out. "Nah, if it is hot, why do I get involved. I'm doing too many nice things, Louie."

Basciano's problem was that he was always the happy-go-lucky man who everybody thought had lots of money but not a care in the world. The reality, he said, was much different. "You know my problem is that for many, many years everybody thought I had tons and tons and tons of fucking money. I'm always a clown in the circus, I am always a clown in the circus. You know. But I put myself in the position that I'd rather do things on the straight and narrow."

Basciano was staying legal, using lawyers and accounts, because he believed that the FBI would never stop targeting him. The documents that Tartaglione had showed him clearly indicated that he remained on the federal government's list of high-value Mafia targets.

"They're gonna try to pin something on me sooner or later," he said.

While the conversation lightened up with talk about an upcoming football game and the point spread, there was no denying that the atmosphere had tightened at the table. The Bonanno bosses essentially had chased Tartaglione out of New York for the duration of his parole, and he had made a very audible stink about it. On top of that, Basciano, Cammarano, and Urso all viewed the FBI documents as possible plants in some kind of government entrapment scheme.

It was time for Tartaglione to leave.

"Everything said, we all done here?" he asked.

"Yup," answered Urso.

"Have a good day gentlemen," Tartaglione said tersely.

Five minutes later, with the music playing on his car radio, Tartaglione contacted his FBI handlers, Joe Bonavolonta and Greg Massa. About fifteen minutes after that, Tartaglione met them at the rendezvous point, where Bonavolonta retrieved the tape as well as the unused diamonds and Krugerrands in the trunk of the witness's car.

Tartaglione couldn't be used any more for these meetings with the high-ranked Bonanno people, but that didn't mean that what he had done was useless. He had done a pretty good job of pretending to be angry when told that he had to stay in Florida. Before he decided to cooperate, Tartaglione risked being indicted for his supporting role in the Three Captains murder. He also had pulled another squirming, mortally wounded Mafioso out of a car to be finished off. But Tartaglione had no more fears about being implicated in any new indictments because he remembered the compassion shown him by a prosecutor back in Brooklyn.

Ruth Nordenbrook, an assistant US attorney, had a reputation for being a tough investigator and attorney, particularly when it came to the mob. A woman who preferred to dress in black, Nordenbrook earned the distaste of a number of mob men because she had pushed to indict their wives, usually for tax crimes. She didn't always win those battles, but she knew how to mix in a little kindness. Which is what happened when Tartaglione, under indictment in 2001, let Nordenbrook know that his daughter might have breast cancer. Luckily, the younger woman was okay, but Nordenbrook had taken the time to find and give him the name of a cancer specialist.

When indictments started to rain down on the crime family, Tartaglione sought her out. He wanted to start cooperating *before* he was indicted, which allowed him a freer hand to come back to New York, under FBI control, as a captain in the Bonanno family and make a collection of what turned out to be scores of recordings. He still had to plead guilty to some crimes, but, with that kind of cooperation under his belt, Tartaglione would have a life outside of a prison cell.

Basciano didn't know the story about Nordenbrook, nor would he have cared. All he knew when he left the Seacrest Diner that day in January was that Tartaglione was cooperating. Cicale met with Basciano after the meeting and heard what had happened. The hot diamonds and Krugerrands out of the blue said it all. Big Lou had gone over to the other side.

13

TWO DAYS AFTER HIS BREAKFAST OF SCRAMBLED EGGS AT THE SEACREST Diner, Joseph Cammarano Sr. learned that for the foreseeable future he would be drinking his coffee courtesy of the federal government. On January 20, 2004, a grand jury in Brooklyn federal court indicted Cammarano, Urso, and several others on racketeering charges. They were promptly arrested. Another defendant grabbing headlines was Vito Rizzuto of Canada, charged with playing a role in the infamous Three Captains murder.

When the tally of defendants added up, the new indictment listed eight captains or acting captains, over a dozen soldiers, and four associates of the Bonanno crime family. In a news release, the Brooklyn US Attorney's Office noted that in almost two years virtually the entire leadership of the crime family had been arrested or indicted, "with only a few family captains remaining unindicted." One of those was Vincent Basciano.

With so much success under his belt, the law office of Benjamin Brafman had moved to larger quarters on Third Avenue in Manhattan, one block south of the well-known Smith & Wollensky steakhouse. The photos and memorabilia on the walls of his office spoke volumes about the type of clientele that had gravitated to Brafman since the Blue Thunder case. Success often breeds success, and in the legal business you can measure that in a lot of ways.

In 1999 rapper Jay-Z was arrested on charges that he assaulted a producer at the Kit Kat Club in Manhattan. Brafman negotiated a plea deal that gave the singer three years probation and no jail time. In 2001 Brafman won an acquittal in state court for another rapper, Sean Combs, known then as Puff Daddy, on weapons charges stemming from a shooting in a Manhattan nightclub. At the time, Combs was dating singer-actress Jennifer Lopez, also detained and questioned by police but never arrested. A signed photo of Lopez hangs prominently in Brafman's office.

Brafman's white-collar defense work also attracted a high-end group of defendants. He had kept true to his promise to steer away from mob defendants. Clients like French politician Dominique Strauss-Kahn and pro-footballer Plaxico Burress still lay years in the future for Brafman when in 2004, not long after the Urso-Cammarano indictments, an old client whom he had hoped never to see again walked through the door.

Basciano knew it was just a matter of time before FBI agents presented him with handcuffs. He had maintained a good relationship with Brafman after the acquittal in the Blue Thunder case. On Jewish holidays, Basciano sent Brafman and his family a giant basket of fruit and food—all Kosher—the biggest that the lawyer's family had ever seen. Basciano's request to Brafman now was vague but simple: Things were happening; if he should get indicted, the now famous attorney who had won him an amazing acquittal ten years earlier, would be his lawyer, right?

No, Brafman answered. He would not.

Brafman explained that not only was he through dealing with violent racketeering cases, but one of the victims of the Bonanno crime family killings had been an old client. Gerlando Sciascia, who had died at Massino's instigation, was dumped like a dog on the street. Brafman previously had won an acquittal for the murder victim on a federal heroin case. True, Basciano hadn't been charged in the Sciascia murder and wasn't involved. But the potential existed for a conflict of interest if

Brafman let himself become ensnared with a defendant in a Bonanno crime family prosecution.

"He was very upset," recalled Brafman about Basciano's response. "He was very upset. . . . He was very angry with me. We discussed it. He pleaded. I stood fast."

Since Basciano hadn't been arrested yet, Brafman didn't know what kind of case might be coming down the road. But to commit to what likely would be a major racketeering case, given the demands of Brafman's law practice, would have proved foolhardy.

"I said, 'I hope you are wrong and not in trouble. I don't know what you have been up to, but I really don't want to do this. I can't commit to representing you, and don't rely on me to represent you,'" Brafman said. In the end, Brafman believed that Basciano, despite his unhappiness, respected his decision to steer clear of the case—in part to avoid getting too close to any of his clients. Getting too close to a client can put you in a position where he can compromise you, the lawyer explained. "The one thing I have done throughout my life, regardless of who the client is, I generally keep my distance from him, so they are never in a position to say, 'Hey you are my friend, you can't abandon [me].'"

Brafman graciously showed Basciano the door.

Up in the Bronx on Morris Park Avenue—in a neighborhood markedly different than the Turtle Bay area of Manhattan where Brafman had his offices—lawyer Tommy Lee did things differently. Brafman kept his professional distance from his clients, but Lee wanted to be their friend and business partner. With a booming high-end law practice, Brafman had a stable of famous clients in the business and arts world; Lee took on gambling cases and scratched out a living with relatively small real estate deals. Brafman avoided anything even seemingly inappropriate for a lawyer; Lee did just the opposite, particularly where it concerned the mob. The Bronx counselor evolved into a glorified errand boy for Massino, passing messages that ultimately devastated his legal career.

Lee grew up in the Pelham Bay area of the Bronx, a product of the city's school system. After attending Fordham University, Lee graduated from Seton Hall University Law School in New Jersey, working summers at Murray Richman's firm. While doing criminal work in Richman's firm, Lee met Basciano, whom he found likable and charismatic. After finishing law school in 1992, Lee opened his own law office in the professional building that Richman owned. In time, Lee began doing small legal work for members of Basciano's immediate family, such as real estate closings, hoping to break into some of the big mob cases later.

From the 1980s through the 1990s, organized crime cases kept many lawyers busy. But as the FBI succeeded in its pursuit of the Gambino, Lucchese, and Colombo families, the pickings were slimming. Some of the low-level defendants were so stretched for funds that the courts often had to appoint counsel to represent them. The skein of high-profile prosecutions involving the late John Gotti and his ilk had ended—although his son, John Junior, still interested prosecutors. Probes of the Genovese and Bonanno families remained, and lawyers were competing vigorously to represent the cases evolving from those probes.

As it turned out, Lee had a slight advantage in getting Bonanno family business. As he later told the FBI, Basciano turned over a lot of the gambling defense work to him, effectively making Lee house counsel to the numbers operation. Basciano wanted to keep a distance from the gambling operation, so Lee told investigators that he worked with Anthony Donato, one of Basciano's closest associates. According to Lee, Donato contacted him whenever a gambling location worker got arrested, and the attorney appeared at the arraignment and arranged for bail. Usually the cases ended with a plea bargain that required paying a fine. Either Donato or Basciano paid Lee for his legal services.

But the gambling cases were small stuff. What made Lee more valuable as an attorney was his willingness in late 2003 and early 2004 to meet with the jailed Massino and become a messenger for him, a vital prospect for the crime boss's ability to maintain control of the organization while incarcerated. With Urso, the acting street boss, arrested in January 2004, Massino groped around for a new one. He settled on Basciano and started preparing his captain for the job.

At first, Massino used Lee to pass mundanities to Basciano like friendly greetings and good wishes. Then during one meeting, Massino told Lee that he really liked Basciano, a big boost to the already large ego of Vinny from the Bronx. As time went on, Massino confided in Lee that he really trusted Basciano, who should "take the rein," which Lee promptly reported to his law client. It sounded like a battlefield promotion, but the gratified Basciano wasn't sure what the crime boss really meant. It was also unclear how others in the Bonanno family would react to Basciano as street boss.

In the parking lot of an International House of Pancakes near New Rochelle, not far from where Lee and Basciano both lived, both men met again to clear up any ambiguity. With the words, "Don't worry about it," Massino, with Lee as intermediary, told Basciano not to fret over what others in the family thought. It was time to take charge. Basciano reacted like a "giddy school girl," Lee remembered.

So Vincent Basciano, forty-four years old, had gone from grinning young man who hung out with mobsters to the acting boss of one of New York's five families. It was the pinnacle of achievement. Basciano had relished the gangster life; "I'm a hoodlum through and through," he once said. He may never have aspired to being a boss, but, with so much of the family under siege, Basciano was one of the few good men Massino had left. Basciano had the right to pick whom he wanted as an underboss and consiglieri. He settled on Michael Mancuso for his second in command and Anthony "Fat Anthony" Rabito, an aging, obese gambler from Queens, for the role of counselor. Massino wouldn't have picked them for himself, but he let Basciano do what he wanted. The promotions were temporary anyway.

With Basciano as his surrogate on the street, Massino continued to use Lee as an intermediary. It was a cumbersome but necessary arrangement. Massino was coming up for trial in May 2004 and needed to control what was left of the crime family. He also needed to get his share of monies owed him, using Basciano for that purpose, Lee recalled. When one old Bonanno captain hadn't paid the $200,000 that he owed Massino, Basciano paid his son a visit and worked out a deal to pay off the amount in $4,000 installments, Lee later told the FBI. The greedy Massino didn't like the deal: He wanted the entire amount up front—but there was little he could do about it now.

Some bosses work smoothly, building allegiances and working political angles skillfully. The problem with Basciano, Lee remembered in his discussions with the FBI, was that Massino didn't have the time to groom him for the job of acting boss. He had only on-the-job training, and his supervisor, Massino, wasn't accessible. That left Basciano having to relay questions through Lee to Massino about how to conduct family business. The unavoidable game of telephone invariably led to delays, and Basciano, either overzealous or unable to get immediate feedback from Massino, ran into difficulties.

Basciano ruled by fear. To test loyalty, he called people for meetings at odd times and demanded that they show. Lee claimed that members of the family who didn't comply were dealt with harshly, one actually receiving a beating.

Massino soon realized that Basciano wasn't being a diplomatic manager. Massino essentially had centered his operations in Queens, but Basciano shifted them to the Bronx. That wasn't necessarily bad, but Basciano didn't stop there. Lee told the FBI that when Basciano called captains to the Bronx for a meeting he had them all strip to check for surveillance devices. Given the atmosphere within the family and the incident with Tartaglione, it was a prudent move. But even the idea of older, overweight Mafiosi pulling down their pants before they could talk to Basciano angered many. Basciano didn't relent, though, telling the captains that he was acting boss until Massino told him otherwise—or until someone killed him, said Lee.

Cicale remembered one meeting in particular in the summer of 2004 in the dining area of an apartment on Fish Avenue in the Bronx. Basciano had called a number of captains to attend, including Mancuso and Rabito. Each stripped as directed, then removed jewelry and cell phones, the latter kept in the basement.

"Joe Massino was still our boss in the Bonanno crime family," Cicale remembered the street boss telling the captains, "and if Joe Massino wanted somebody else to run the Bonanno crime family, Vinny Basciano would step down and support that other person."

Family loyalty remained with Massino, with Basciano basically a caretaker, albeit a powerful one. He was running a tight ship and wanted to know everything that everyone was doing. There might be more informants in the family, and, if somebody like Basciano kept abreast of things, the traitors could be filtered out.

Cicale also remembered that Basciano, who always believed that in the end everybody would get arrested, said that he wanted to have money available to retain a lawyer. For that, Cicale said, Robert Van Zandt Jr., Basciano's partner in some construction projects, was approached to stock the war chest. The way things were going, it was wise that Basciano get his hands on the money sooner rather than later.

⸺ ⸺

The trial of Joseph Massino began on May 24, 2004, in Brooklyn federal district court at the foot of the Brooklyn Bridge. As mob trials went, Massino's ranked as most important in New York City since Gotti's conviction in 1992. Massino represented the last of the old-style bosses: crafty, intelligent, politically astute in his world, and ruthless when he had to be. The indictment accused Massino of orchestrating or taking part in the murder of seven mobsters: Philip Giaccone, Dominick Trinchera, Alphonse Indelicato, Dominick Napolitano, Cesare Bonventre, Anthony Mirra, and Gabriel Infanti. A hefty array of racketeering charges also covered gambling, arson, loan-sharking, and extortion.

While one major turncoat, Salvatore "Sammy the Bull" Gravano, testified against Gotti, Massino had *seven:* Frank Coppa, Frank Lino, Joseph D'Amico, Duane Leisenheimer, Richard Cantarella, James Tartaglione, and Salvatore Vitale. For a crime family once touted as never having produced a single cooperating witness, prosecutors had amassed a stunning array of cooperating witnesses against Massino. Each had served as a trusted aide or associate and knew many of Massino's dark secrets. Vitale, in particular, had acted as aide-de-camp to Massino for decades and could provide prosecutors with a virtual road map through the crime boss's reign.

Against such an arsenal, Massino's defense attorneys, David Breitbart and Flora Edwards, knew it was useless to argue that he wasn't involved in the mob. In their opening statement, they conceded that point. Instead, Breitbart argued that each of the witnesses had a motive to lie: If he helped secure Massino's conviction, each would get out of prison in return for his cooperation.

The lead prosecutor in the trial, assistant US attorney Greg Andres, had lived with the Bonanno investigation for years. Andres already had helped put much of the Bonanno crime family behind bars. But Massino represented the ultimate prize. Two other prosecutors, Robert Henoch and Mitra Hormozi, shared the trial duties. Also sitting at the prosecution table were two faces very familiar to Massino: FBI agents Kimberly McCaffrey and Jeff Sallett.

After a bumpy start with a witness who had been a mob associate, the prosecution started its avalanche of evidence by calling Frank Lino as its first key witness. Lino was crucial because he had accompanied the Three Captains—Giaccone, Indelicato, and Trinchera—to the social club in Bay Ridge, Brooklyn, to what they thought was a meeting to settle a power struggle with Massino's faction over control of the Bonanno family. Instead, Lino testified, they walked into a slaughterhouse. Masked men jumped into the room and began shooting at the Three Captains. A shotgun blast struck Trinchera, who weighed nearly three hundred pounds, in the stomach, which one mobster later said must have taken fifty pounds off him. The gunmen cut down Giaccone and Indelicato as well.

Lino had the good sense to dash out an unguarded door and fled through the neighborhood, eventually taking refuge in a nearby home and contacting Coppa. The testimony in the hushed courtroom was gripping. At one point, describing how Trinchera had charged his assailants before being shot, Lino choked up and almost broke down. Fleeing the scene spared him the sight of blood and viscera on the floor and the bizarre quiet after the shooting ended. Eventually the bodies were taken in a van to Howard Beach and given to a crew of Gotti's men, who buried them in a desolate lot near Ozone Park.

In the Mafia, *omertà* bars members from discussing what happens in the organization. Each man swears to honor it and accepts that he will die if he betrays the code of silence. But the Massino trial provided solid proof that omertà meant nothing like it did in ages past. Those who cooperated against Massino weren't old Sicilian immigrants bonded to one another by family and village ties as the forebears of the Bonanno family had been. No, these were middle-class men—wealthy from lives of crime to be sure—who had grown comfortable. They were also middle-aged and didn't want to die in prison, away from family and friends. Criminals at heart, they had come together to make money. Loyalty among Mafiosi who shared no blood ties, bound only by a capitalist imperative, proved flimsy at best. Massino gave lip service to loyalty, but he certainly didn't engender it among his followers.

Coppa, D'Amico, Leisenheimer, Tartaglione, Cantarella, and Vitale all provided damning evidence. Sometimes they testified about similar events consistently, while on other matters they provided testimony unique to their own experiences with Massino. Vitale of course had the fullest picture of the family boss. He told the jury about years of carrying out Massino's orders for murder, while admitting that he had ordered a few himself without Massino's approval. It quickly became clear that Massino and his brother-in-law had a strained relationship and some crime family members had been prepared to kill Vitale, thinking he had designs to take over the family. Embittered by years of insults and diminished income, Vitale knew on his arrest that he was going to cooperate.

"He don't deserve the respect and honor with me sitting next to him," Vitale said.

The jury deliberated for four days in the Massino trial and on July 30 came back with a verdict sweeping in its reach: guilty on all counts, including the six homicides as racketeering acts. Massino showed hardly any emotion and just shrugged when he looked at his wife, Josephine, seated with their daughter Adeline in the courtroom. The jury broke for lunch after Judge Nicholas Garaufis told them to return for the next phase of the case, a hearing on how much money Massino had to forfeit to the government for his years of illegal activity. The government estimated that amount at over $10 million.

But Joseph Massino had ideas of his own.

With the courtroom cleared, Massino asked one of the courtroom marshals to tell FBI agent Sallett that he wanted to speak with him in private. The two men had always had a cordial relationship, even in the adversarial position in which they found themselves. Sallett, as well as McCaffrey, had a strange bond with Massino from the day they arrested him. During the two-month trial, Sallett in particular had some light-hearted conversations with Massino, mostly about food. That kind of human contact when a life is on the line can lead to the unexpected.

What happened next shook not only the courthouse but the whole history of the mob in New York City. With the courtroom sealed and other doorways on the floor also closed, Massino was led into Garaufis's chambers. To protect the record and himself, the judge had a court stenographer record the conversation. The newly convicted Massino had run out of options—save one. Massino told Garaufis that he wanted a new lawyer so that he could consider cooperating with the government. Joe Massino wanted to join Team America.

14

As the case against Joseph Massino had been building with the help of FBI agents Jeff Sallett and Kim McCaffrey, a second team led by Michael Breslin was getting into higher gear on the Basciano investigation. After the earlier investigation in 2001 didn't bear much fruit, Breslin decided that the better approach would take a historical look instead of trying to rely solely on wiretaps that might not detect anything incriminating.

Plenty of rumors and gossip about Vinny Gorgeous had been swirling. "We heard he was a suspect in multiple homicides," said Breslin, referring in particular to the Santoro case. "We wanted to do a comprehensive look at his entire history."

Using the same long-term look that Sallett and McCaffrey had used in the larger Massino probe, Breslin went back into old surveillance photographs and tapes. Many of those had captured Basciano and DeFilippo together at various social clubs and on the street. At times the photographers couldn't resist snapping photos of a lithe Angela Basciano as she walked en route to meet her husband.

Breslin also mined the case files from the old Bronx prosecution of Basciano in the attempted murder of David Nunez, a couple of gambling cases from the past, as well as intelligence reports that Basciano had connected with Anthony Colangelo's bookmaking operation. Nor did Breslin overlook Basciano's ties to Alfred Bottone Sr.'s numbers operation, as conceded in the Blue Thunder case.

Although the Nunez attempted murder had resulted only in a plea for Basciano to a gun possession charge, a dropped state murder case or even an acquittal doesn't destroy the usefulness of that evidence in a later federal prosecution. Under federal law, prosecutors can use allegations from state prosecutions as racketeering acts in a federal indictment. So pulling together evidence from the state cases allowed Breslin and prosecutors in the Brooklyn US Attorney's Office to structure a racketeering case. Then, when Vitale turned cooperating witness, the situation suddenly improved for the FBI.

Mainly useful as a witness against Massino, Vitale also had information that implicated other Bonanno members in a number of homicides, among them the slaying of Canadian captain Gerlando Sciascia in the Bronx in 1999. Vitale's debriefings in May 2003 on the Sciascia murder were brutal as far as they concerned DeFilippo. In various sessions with the FBI, Vitale stated how Massino, during an anniversary party at the Amici Restaurant on Long Island, set the wheels in motion to have Sciascia killed.

According to Vitale, Massino wanted to "take care" of Sciascia and had already spoken to DeFilippo about the plan. Massino instructed that a gun with a silencer be secured from Anthony Urso. Vitale said that Massino gave him the overall responsibility of making sure the hit took place and then promptly left the next day with his wife for a vacation in Cancun.

At a later meeting in Manhattan, DeFilippo acknowledged that he had received the contract and said he planned to have one of his trusted Bronx men, Johnny Joe Spirito, pick up Sciascia in a white van, according to Vitale. To make sure the murder weapon was working properly, DeFilippo attached the silencer and fired a test shot through the open moon roof of the van. When the murder took place, Vitale told investigators that he spoke with DeFilippo, who acknowledged that it was "all done." A newspaper story the next day reported Sciascia's bullet-ridden body found on a Bronx street.

The detailed information from Vitale gave federal prosecutors enough to charge Massino, DeFilippo, and Spirito with the Sciascia murder in a separate racketeering indictment in August 2003. For those men, the news came with the added menace that it potentially carried the death penalty under federal law. It had been seen rarely if ever in mob cases since World War II, and it added a twist to the case that later wound down a path filled with surprises.

By arresting DeFilippo, the FBI may have done him an enormous favor, however. After Massino's arrest in January 2003, agents were gathering information that Basciano not only didn't like his old mentor but thought him a rival who was going to try to seize more power in the crime family. An FBI informant said that Basciano devised a plan to use a fake police car as a ruse to pull DeFilippo over while driving and have him shot. Basciano and others, including Cicale, actually had a Chevy Impala fixed up to look like a law enforcement vehicle and kept it in reserve, according to government documents.

With the conviction of Massino, Basciano remained the most important Bonanno family member on the street, and he was a busy man. In the summer of 2004, his legitimate construction businesses had heavy commitments in the Bronx. A project on Weiner Avenue pushed ahead, as did another on Westchester Avenue with Basciano's financial friend and suspected con artist Robert Van Zandt Jr. On both, Randolph Pizzolo took care of excavation work and laid the footings and foundations for the buildings. Pizzolo's work wasn't good, Cicale later told the FBI. Basciano later confided to acquaintances that Pizzolo actually didn't do a bad job, but one way or the other Pizzolo was flying on Basciano's radar.

Then things got complicated. In October 2004, a drunken reputed associate of the Genovese family named Joey Bonelli allegedly drove up to a house in Queens, fired shots, and yelled out insults, impugning the manhood of Nicky Santora, a man whom Basciano had tapped to become one of his acting captains. The verbal barrage also insulted the Bonanno crime family generally. This, according to Cicale, didn't sit well with Basciano, who ordered Joseph Cammarano Jr., the son of the highly regarded Bonanno captain, to take care of the transgressor.

Nothing ever happened to Bonelli. Cammarano said he couldn't find him. When badgered about it by Basciano, he said that nothing had been done about Pizzolo either. Then Cammarano mentioned the incident involving Pizzolo appearing at a Queens nightclub with a gun. The story waved a red flag in front of an already hopped-up Basciano, Cicale later recalled.

If Dominick Cicale is to be believed in his entirety—and some, notably Basciano, don't believe him—the nightclub incident prompted Vinny from the Bronx to decree that he wanted Pizzolo dead. Even when Cicale found out from Pizzolo the true story—that he had only interceded to protect a fellow mob associate possibly in danger—Basciano didn't relent.

"Basciano was just furious. He didn't want to listen anymore. He wanted Randy dead," Cicale said later.

Cicale could rely on Joey Gambina, a cousin of associate Anthony Aiello. Gambina, one of those dyed-in-the-wool Italian-American kids, grew up knowing nothing about the world but what the mobster life showed or provided. An army of young, uneducated men like him spread around the city in places like Howard Beach, Bensonhurst, and Bay Ridge. Gambina was just a teenager when his uncle Tony used him to take messages and money to the aging Philip Rastelli, the crime family boss in the years before Massino seized power. Rastelli was home

Joey Gambina, Bonanno associate

from prison, so he couldn't associate with felons. Gambina, a teenager with no criminal record, had no problem acting as the lawful conduit to the crime boss.

At the age of twelve or thirteen, Gambina ran card games at his uncle's cafe in Queens. When he left the cafe job, Gambina went into the pizza business and made money handling stolen credit cards, loan-sharking, and dealing heroin—the kind of career path open to a kid who had dropped out of school in the fifth grade and who looked to major drug dealers as his role models. When need arose, Gambina committed arson for cash. He never hurt anyone to any great degree, although he admitted to firing a gun to scare his intended targets.

The father of Gambina's cousin, Anthony "Ace" Aiello, sold heroin out of various Queens cafes. When caught, the elder Aiello went away for over twenty years. But that didn't deter his son from embracing the mob life. When a gambler known only as Eric failed to pay his $45,000 debt, Cicale took Gambina and Aiello to confront the errant bettor. On Cicale's orders, Aiello struck Eric with a hammer, sending him to the hospital. They sent him flowers while there, the note attached reading: "We still want our money," or words to that effect, recalled Cicale.

With that kind of loyalty, Gambina seemed a good man for Cicale to approach to take care of the beleaguered Pizzolo. A loyal dog like Aiello—who earned the nickname "Luca Brasi" after a character in *The Godfather*—also made a good choice. The perfect acolytes for a baptism of blood, both were young, ambitious, and eager to make their bones and become part of La Cosa Nostra.

15

BUT WHERE WAS BASCIANO?

On the morning of November 19, 2004, the retinue of FBI agents fanning out through the Bronx had a hard time locating him. Surveillance from recent days found that he had a set routine of showing up at his construction site on Schurz Avenue before or around 9:00 a.m., dressed in jeans, work boots, and at times a hard hat—quite a change from his usual fastidiousness.

The project was finishing a group of pricey town houses with a majestic view of the East River, and Basciano needed to be there. For that reason, Agent Michael Breslin was lurking with his team at the location near the Whitestone Bridge, ready to pounce. The nearly two-year investigation had come to a head. They were about to make the arrest. Basciano wasn't following his own script, however.

Less than a mile away, in the same government Buick sedan used almost two years earlier to arrest Massino, sat agents Sallett and McCaffrey. They were only providing backup this time, one of a number of arrest teams supporting Breslin. While Breslin lay in wait at Schurz Avenue, Sallett and McCaffrey were doing the same outside Basciano's home at the corner of Revere Avenue and Schurz. Down the street was the popular Marina del Rey banquet hall. Angela Basciano's mother lived a few doors away.

But Sallett's car wasn't the only vehicle circling the area. Angela Basciano noticed a lot of law enforcement activity around the house. She called Cicale at the Schurz Avenue job site and told him to tell her husband. Cicale went to a nearby pub and transmitted the code "911" to Basciano's pager, which meant that he should call back. He never did.

Sallett and McCaffrey didn't expect Basciano to show at his home instead of the job site—but that's precisely what he did. Driving up in his Lincoln, Basciano parked and started up the front steps. Sallett jumped out of the sedan.

"Mr. Basciano, we have a warrant for your arrest! Do not go inside the house!" Sallett yelled out as he approached.

At the top of the stairs, Basciano tossed his car keys into the foyer. Sallett handcuffed and walked him back to the government vehicle. Meanwhile, Breslin, alerted to the arrest, sped over with agent Michael Trombetta and took charge of his new prisoner.

"From what I read in the newspapers, you guys usually do this at 6:00 a.m.," said Basciano cheekily. At least the delay gave him time to get dolled up for his mug shot.

Breslin searched Basciano and removed some money he was carrying, a driver's license, and some business cards. He found the pager in Basciano's car. Breslin later checked the pager with a search warrant and noted that it contained a lot of three and four digit entries—all codes.

Following arrest protocol, Breslin read Basciano his Miranda rights. Still, the chatty Basciano wanted to know if he was being taken to the Eastern District courthouse in Brooklyn and what the charge was. The indictment was for a racketeering conspiracy.

"That is not real," Basciano said when told of the charges.

Basciano also wanted to know if his old friend Anthony Donato had been arrested too. Told that he was, Basciano asked if he was being charged with the same offense. That struck Breslin as odd. Was Donato somehow involved in the Santoro homicide?

During the drive back to Manhattan, Santoro's name came up in conversation. Basciano at first said that he didn't know him, but Breslin mentioned he had been shot while walking his dog. He had heard about that, said Basciano. The incident had appeared in the paperwork that the "rat" Tartaglione had showed him nearly a year ago.

In the few minutes it had taken Cicale to go to Charlie's Inn to contact Basciano by page and then return to the site, he learned from Al Perna, another worker at the site, that Basciano had just been arrested. Cicale knew that he, Basciano, Donato, and Bruno Indelicato had taken part in the Santoro murder. He tried calling Donato a couple of times and got no response. Indelicato was in jail for violating his probation. Cicale was verging on panic.

After paging Michael Mancuso, Cicale met him for a quick briefing. With Basciano now in custody, Mancuso became the highest-ranking member of the Bonanno crime family on the street. But even at age forty-nine, he didn't have much experience leading large groups of men. Mancuso told Cicale to find out what he could and then arranged to meet him later in the day in the Country Club section of the Bronx, an area of nice homes on Eastchester Bay.

By the time of the second meeting, Cicale had learned that Basciano and Donato had indeed been charged with the Santoro murder. Cicale had always believed that his participation in the Santoro hit was a closely held secret. But when Mancuso snickered and said, "You're lucky they didn't arrest you," Cicale knew that news of his involvement went beyond Basciano's tight circle. Cicale answered Mancuso that he didn't know what he was talking about.

Of course Cicale knew everything. But that didn't mean he wanted his business out there for everyone to know. Too much now was becoming known on the street. A few months earlier, Cicale and Basciano had gone to the office of lawyer Tom Lee to listen to the Big Louie Tartaglione recordings, which had become available in the normal course of trial preparation for a lot of the Bonanno family indictments. Basciano didn't like the way he sounded on tape because he said too much—particularly for a man who supposedly didn't do anything.

"He was shocked," Cicale later recalled about hearing the tapes.

But it disturbed Cicale more that Basciano had seemed almost flip about him when talking to Tartaglione, a man suspected of being an informant. Basciano had said Cicale was a hood and was his acting captain. The remarks stunned Cicale by their imprudence.

"I was shocked," Cicale remembered. "Vinny Basciano is meeting with someone he suspects is wearing a wire, and yet he is exposing me, and he is basically bragging about the Frank Santoro murder."

Basciano apologized to Cicale for his remarks, but the damage had been done. Law enforcement likely didn't even know until that point that Cicale was involved with the mob, let alone a member of any crime family. Cicale believed that he had been walking in the shadows under the FBI's radar. But thanks to Basciano, he had become a person of interest.

At FBI headquarters at 26 Federal Plaza in Manhattan, Basciano waited and then had his mug shots taken. Officials also fingerprinted him. With the administrative procedures out of the way, the agents drove Basciano and Donato about a mile over the Brooklyn Bridge to the federal court on Cadman Plaza in downtown Brooklyn for arraignment.

The indictment turned out to be an amendment of the earlier one that accused Massino of plotting the murder of Sciascia. The grand jury had merely added counts for Basciano and Donato on the Santoro murder. In total, with Massino, DeFilippo, and Spirito, the case involved seven defendants. All of them trooped into the jury box from their holding cells and sat down as Judge Garaufis took the bench. Seated next to Massino, a sullen Basciano, looking tan and well coiffed, sat back in his chair, hands folded in his lap.

While Ben Brafman didn't represent Basciano, as a favor to Angela he had arranged to send a colleague, Andrea Zellan, to handle legal matters temporarily. Basciano pleaded not guilty to the two charges against him. With no argument from the defense attorneys, magistrate-judge

Lois Bloom ordered Basciano and the others detained temporarily. She set November 23 as the date for a bail hearing. Massino, already convicted and facing a life term, had no argument to make. All the prisoners went back to the federal Metropolitan Detention Center.

Court appearances often reveal a great deal, but in the case of Basciano and the rest of the Bonanno family, the real action was taking place well away from public view. Some of it took place in jailhouse meeting rooms, when prisoners sat and talked privately, waiting for their attorneys. The rest took place back on the street in furtive conversations among those fortunate enough not to have been arrested. Talk often turned to money or who was going to die next.

With Basciano locked up, Dominick Cicale thought that Randy Pizzolo could live. Cicale never really wanted to harm the man anyway and had lobbied hard to have his life spared. With Basciano off the street, no one really knew about the target painted on Pizzolo's back. Even Mancuso, the new acting boss, didn't want anybody killed or hurt, and Cicale certainly didn't volunteer anything about Pizzolo.

But a few days after Basciano was arrested, Mancuso let Cicale know that Pizzolo was supposed to be killed and to get it done. "Nothing skips a beat," said Mancuso about the affairs of the crime family. Loyal to the mob code, Cicale knew that he had to plot the murder now. He turned to the two loyal associates for help.

Joey Gambina had enough on his résumé to make him a good candidate for mob membership. He had done arson for hire, beat up people, stolen cars, and lifted merchandise. But mob politics worked against him, and he was traded, so to speak, to Cicale's crew in early 2004. Cicale, acting captain on Basciano's behalf, believed in being a tough taskmaster, all the more to impress Basciano. He told Gambina that drugs were out and to keep his mouth shut in public about what went on within the family, including when he might get inducted. Beepers were the method of communication among crew members.

If life under former crew master and reputed Bonanno captain John Palazolla ran easy and loose, under Cicale it got serious and ugly. Cicale liked ordering beatings of all sorts of victims: old, young, men, and women. One of the first things Gambina remembered doing was accompanying Aiello to beat up an elderly man named Frank.

"There was no room to play," Gambina later recalled. "It was very strict. When he called, you had to be there. You always had to be alert. He would call you twenty-four hours a day if he had to."

Basciano wasn't warm and fuzzy, either. When Gambina met him for the first time at his social club in the Bronx, he gave the captain a kiss on both cheeks as a sign of respect, as he had seen in the days of John Gotti and the movies. Basciano rebuked him immediately: "We don't kiss in public no more." Wary of FBI surveillance, Basciano didn't want to be seen receiving deference that way. Agents could draw conclusions about the crime family structure.

One of Cicale's insistent calls came in November, a few days after Basciano's arrest. Aiello told Gambina that Cicale had called them to meet him in Manhattan. The subject of the meeting was no secret: They had to kill Pizzolo. Gambina didn't like the idea. For a start, despite his bravado and willingness to assault people, he hadn't ever murdered any-one. Sure, he had fired guns at people—but for show, to strike fear in their hearts. Something else also seemed wrong: Cicale might be setting both of them up. This call was coming too soon after Basciano's arrest for murder. It seemed suspicious. Under the FBI's onslaught, everyone in the crime family looked like a cooperator.

At the bar, the two cousins listened as Cicale outlined the murder plan. Gambina would drive Pizzolo to a house to wait for Joseph Bonelli, the man who allegedly insulted the Bonanno family, to come out and then be killed. Once Bonelli was dead, the two men would switch cars and pick up Aiello, who in turn would kill the unsuspecting Pizzolo. That was the plan—an ingenious and complicated maneuver.

Fearful that Cicale was wearing a wire, Gambina said later that he tried to say very little during the meeting, voicing neither agreement nor disagreement with the plan. Cicale dangled news that Gambina had been approved to be inducted into the Bonanno family, but Gambina still remained apprehensive.

On the drive back to Queens, Gambina told Aiello to pull the car over by Juniper Park, a green space near Maspeth. They had to talk. "It doesn't feel good, Anthony," Gambina told his cousin. It seemed like a setup, he said.

The next day, both cousins met again in the parking lot of a drugstore. More resolute this time, Gambina again said that he wasn't going to take part in the killing. He wasn't a made member of the mob, so Gambina thought that he had the leeway to refuse without suffering dire consequences. He wanted to talk with Cicale, but the new captain was out of town.

Within a day or two, the Thanksgiving holiday came, and Gambina sat down to dinner with his wife and family. Looking over the meal, Gambina reflected on how he had saved Pizzolo's life, giving him the chance to enjoy the holiday with his own family. *Pizzolo is living because of me, because I was nervous*, thought Gambina. Of course, Gambina knew he was now in trouble, and before the end of the holiday Cicale tried to reach him by beeper. Gambina didn't respond at first and instead called his cousin.

"Anthony, Dominick just beeped me," said Gambina.

"I was there when Dominick beeped you," replied Aiello.

The three men agreed to meet, and Gambina gave a rash of excuses about a bad back. While Cicale tried to convince him to join the murder plot, Gambina kept firm, even when Cicale said he had "rat potential." Seeing that Gambina wasn't going to kill Pizzolo, Cicale appeared to accept the fact and agreed to keep the associate in his crew. Later, Aiello told his cousin that if Cicale ever wanted to kill him, he would tip him off.

Hitting a brick wall with Gambina, Cicale told him to tell Aiello to go with the alternate plan. Gambina didn't know what that was—but his cousin did.

On December 3, 2004, Gambina brought his car to a carwash on Rockaway Boulevard. Feeling hungry, he went to a deli across the street and ordered a pastrami sandwich. Picking up one of the tabloids, he flipped through the pages. Then he stopped.

A photo showed a BMW found the previous night in Greenpoint, the motor running and the body of a man in the street nearby. At that point, Gambina knew that Cicale wasn't an informant. Randy Pizzolo was dead.

16

ANYONE OUTSIDE A JAIL CELL WHO PICKED UP A NEWSPAPER IN EARLY December 2004 could have read about the death of Randy Pizzolo. But Joseph Massino wasn't getting a lot of information from the street in a timely fashion. He certainly didn't have subscriptions to the tabloids, either. When he tried to get messages back and forth from the outside, the stupidity of those on whom he relied vexed him. But he did get news in jail.

Since Massino's pending racketeering case involved multiple defendants, the law allowed them to meet together, with their attorneys, to plot a common defense strategy. These codefendant meetings took place with regularity. But at times, when attorneys stepped away or their attention went elsewhere, Massino and his cohorts could converse, sometimes sotto voce, in the meeting room. Prior to their arraignment on the new case, Massino and Basciano also could talk quietly to each other in the bullpen.

Usually what defendants say among themselves remains secret. But sometimes notes are made. In this case, private records examined by the author indicate that in one of those bullpen sessions on the day of their arraignment, Massino had asked Basciano in hushed tones about how things were going and reiterated that he wanted to know about everything. Other crime family members were complaining about Basciano's heavy-handed methods of control, Massino whispered, although the crime boss was sticking up for him. Another issue was the trouble that prosecutor Greg Andres supposedly was causing his wife, Josephine, presumably over legal forfeiture issues. Massino groused about money as usual and said that his heart was really broken by the way old friends had cooperated against him.

A few days later, Massino, Basciano, and some of their other codefendants met for a strategy meeting at the Metropolitan Detention Center in Brooklyn. The lawyers weren't in the room at one point, and someone whispered to Massino that Pizzolo had been killed. According to a private summary of the meeting, Massino looked at Basciano, who nodded his head. Lucky for other people it wasn't them, Massino said.

Massino had a distinct advantage over any of the other defendants. He had a secret that none of the other mobsters knew. Ever since he walked into chambers in July, Massino was trying to prove his worth to the government as a cooperating witness. Although not officially a cooperator, Massino, unknown to his regular attorney, Flora Lewis, had received a shadow counsel assigned by the judge. This secret lawyer, former federal prosecutor Edward McDonald, shepherded Massino through the process of cooperation and protected his legal interests.

At first the FBI professed skepticism of Massino's value as an informant. It wasn't clear in the summer of 2004 what he could offer in terms of a high-value target to the government. John Gotti Sr. was dead, and Vincent "The Chin" Gigante, head of the Genovese crime family, was already in jail. Most of Massino's top captains had been indicted or convicted. Anxious to prove his worth, Massino tipped off the FBI that the Three Captains, slaughtered in May 1981, lay buried in the same lot in a desolate area of Queens. Police had found one of the bodies, Alphonse Indelicato, right after the killings, but they didn't dig deep enough. Go further, Massino told investigators. After several days of excavation, the remains of Dominick Trinchera and Philip Giaccone came to light.

The unearthing of the remains solved a longstanding mob mystery and might prove useful in developing a future criminal case against members of Gotti's old regime already in prison. But what Massino provided didn't really amount to much. He was also facing another problem. In November 2004, US attorney general John Ashcroft had announced that the government would seek the death penalty against Massino for the murder of Sciascia. His codefendants, Johnny Joe Spirito and Patty DeFilippo, were getting a pass, however, and faced only imprisonment if convicted. Massino really needed to prove his worth as a witness if he was going to avoid the risk of a capital punishment trial. He had to give prosecutors something solid, something big, something they could use in court.

After the early meetings among the defendants in jail, it became apparent to the FBI that Basciano was a more important target. He had intimated to Massino that he knew about the Pizzolo homicide—perhaps even ordered it—and was receiving all sorts of messages from the street about crime family business. There had also been talk, cryptic and ambiguous perhaps, about harming prosecutor Andres. The problem was that whatever the FBI was getting from Massino while he was working as a jailhouse spy filtered through him, uncorroborated. Investigators needed something stronger. For that, the FBI came up with the "dirty team" to start secret surveillance aided by Massino.

Because jailhouse conversations between Massino and Basciano might deal with legitimate legal strategy, prosecutors in the Santoro case couldn't know anything from the tapes made of the conversations of both prisoners.

A bureaucratic Chinese Wall shielded this group of prosecutors and FBI agents—kept pristine as a "clean team"—from knowledge of the fruits of the surveillance. For the taping and handling of Massino, the FBI assigned agents Jeff Sallett and James DeStefano as the "dirty team," tasked with uncovering new evidence of crimes committed by Basciano. Anything Sallett and DeStefano uncovered went to a separate team of prosecutors not handling the current Massino-Basciano indictment.

Officials had to come up with a series of convincing moves inside the jail to get the crime boss and Basciano together so that the taping could take place. First, on November 29, the FBI and Bureau of Prisons had Massino moved out of his current MDC cell into a segregated housing unit (SHU), commonly known as solitary. The ostensible reason, according to court records, was that Massino was found with a newspaper article discussing his case. On December 29, Massino's attorney of record learned that prosecutors were recommending that he not be allowed to attend codefendant meetings. Prosecutors also told Flora Lewis that Massino was going in solitary because that was standard practice for death penalty prisoners. These measures amounted to a significant change in Massino's incarceration and separated him from normal jailhouse interaction with his codefendants, including Basciano.

So how would Massino and Basciano get to converse so that secret tapes could be made? According to additional private notes made available to the author, Basciano also went into the SHU with a few other inmates in late December. Both men were now in solitary, although in physically close proximity. They even were placed in adjacent recreation cells for part of the day so that they could talk, the notes indicated.

The stage was set.

On January 3, 2005, an official crime boss wore a surveillance device to gather evidence for the first time. Although nervous, Massino sounded like a seasoned spy as he tried to reconstruct old conversations that he and Basciano had weeks earlier. Still, it wasn't clear which of the two mobsters originally raised the subject of killing Andres. Had it been Massino as a way of priming the pump and getting Basciano to say something incriminating? Or had it been angry, hot-headed Basciano, who was trying to impress his boss? A source close to Basciano indicated that he claimed he had been joking when he originally raised the issue and that Massino was serious and wanted to think about it. Of course, under FBI control and in jail, Massino had no real desire to kill

Andres. Yet that wasn't going to stop him from rethreading that conversation for the recording. Basciano's response, "No, forget about it," indicated that talk had taken place about the subject of harming Andres, but the context remained unclear.

The Pizzolo murder was burning a hole in the FBI's pocket. The Bonanno squad had to solve it. By lashing out at the dead mobster, Basciano clearly showed to Sallett and DeStefano that he hated the man. On tape, Basciano alternately said that he ordered the murder, then backtracked, saying that he hadn't done so but knew about the hit: more ambiguity but enough for the FBI to target Basciano as the number one suspect—thanks to Joseph Massino.

Four days later, on January 7, Massino and Basciano again came together in the exercise cells of the MDC. The conversation dealt with many of the same topics, but Massino complained about Michael Mancuso, who took over as acting boss when Basciano was arrested. He also fished around about Cicale and his involvement in the death of Pizzolo. Massino feigned concern about being brought into an indictment for the murder if Cicale weakened.

"Dominick, you trust him," Massino asked.

"A thousand percent," answered Basciano, then paused. "Two thousand percent."

New York in December was hot for Dominick Cicale—too hot. After Pizzolo was killed, he became increasingly uncomfortable with the law enforcement surveillance and fled to warmth of a different kind: Myrtle Beach, South Carolina. Both he and Aiello picked up an SUV rented through a friend to make the drive. They met up with one familiar person at least, Lenny Caspar, a man Cicale knew from his days running a sports betting operation. Years earlier, Cicale sometimes threatened people who owed Caspar money.

There's only so much to do in Myrtle Beach in the dead of winter, so, New York born and bred, Cicale and Aiello came back to town in early January 2005. With Basciano in jail, Cicale had lost his main protector on the street. Mancuso was becoming something of a tyrant as acting boss, squeezing Cicale for information about what he was doing and how people were making money. Cicale resisted Mancuso's leadership but felt increasingly adrift. Using intermediaries, Cicale sent a message to Basciano in jail, saying he felt like a sitting duck on the street.

The message that came back to Cicale was simple: Don't feel like a sitting duck. If you have to do something, do it. Cicale interpreted that as license to kill Mancuso if necessary. He assembled a hit team, which increased his confidence and his chances of survival. The night of January 26, a friend told Cicale that he didn't think Cicale would be arrested.

The next morning, at his home in the Bronx, Cicale was arrested. The main racketeering charges involved the murder of Randy Pizzolo. Basciano appeared as a codefendant in the case, his second indictment in as many months. Based on Cicale's record of homicide and violence, the FBI had a SWAT team make a breach entry of the home while agents Jeff Sallett and James DeStefano waited outside. Inside, Cicale seemed more concerned about the welfare of his dog than of his pregnant girlfriend. Sallett and DeStefano came in and rounded up cell phones and documents before making the drive with Cicale in tow to 26 Federal Plaza to process their new prisoner.

DeStefano, a muscular agent who worked out, had his arm in a sling from a recent sports injury, and Cicale seemed to take a liking to him. The two men talked most of the day about sports. Cicale explained that as a young man in prison he was vulnerable and took to working out to build himself up.

DeStefano had a particular question for him. "Dominick, you are a very tough guy and have gone through some experiences. What is a lot of time in jail for a guy like you?"

Cicale thought for a moment. He glanced down at his shoes and then looked up. "One day."

DeStefano instantly realized that he had a shot at making Cicale see the light and begin cooperating—but not quite yet.

17

IT WASN'T SO MUCH THAT BASCIANO AND CICALE HAD BEEN INDICTED for the murder of Pizzolo. What stunned La Cosa Nostra—and the rest of the world for that matter—was that none other than Joseph Massino had implicated both men. The indictment didn't mention his name, but on January 27, 2005, news reporters, tipped off by the wording in charges of a "high-ranking member of the Bonanno crime family incarcerated" at the Metropolitan Detention Center, quickly zeroed in on Massino.

The staggering news spread like wildfire. Massino's daughters made statements distancing themselves from him. The irony of the situation was astonishing and lost on no one. A man who had bragged that his crime family—by whatever name—had never had a turncoat was switching sides, joining the small army of cooperating witnesses that the borgata had spawned. It looked like he had planned the switch for some time. Following his racketeering conviction—hit with an order to forfeit $10 million, which included his interest in homes in which his wife and mother lived—Massino was playing the one card he had left, and he was playing it well.

Basciano and Cicale were falling deep into trouble. Massino's jail-house tapes teemed with references about the Pizzolo murder. Arguably ambiguous perhaps, but Basciano had implicated Cicale as a member of organized crime, a fact previously unknown to anyone but his closest mob friends.

Attorney Tom Lee was also facing problems. Massino readily gave him up to the FBI, and Agent Sallett began another investigation into how Lee, disregarding his oath as an officer of the court, had been playing messenger for Massino. As soon as Lee found out that Massino had been cooperating, he had to withdraw his representation in a major criminal case involving reputed Albanian organized crime figures. Lee knew an indictment was coming.

Although not arrested, Aiello's days were numbered. The odd man out, he had talked so much that his involvement in the Pizzolo murder was widely known. His cousin Joey Gambina told him flat out to get out of town and stop playing around with the mob. Through an intermediary, Gambina gave him around $8,000 so he could get away. On January 30, Mike Breslin and other FBI agents went to Aiello's apartment in Middle Village, Queens—but they were too late. Aiello was in the wind. The agents rounded up documents and other papers, including a sticky note containing a telephone number.

Aiello had gone upstate, but he needed to get out of the country. Other relatives asked Gambina for money to fund his cousin's exit from the United States, but Gambina refused. Too many people were involved, and Gambina himself feared criminal charges if he helped Aiello flee.

By fleeing, Aiello was taking a page from the playbook of his father, Antonino, a major New York City heroin dealer in the 1980s. The elder Aiello, who owned a string of pizzerias, escaped capture in 1984 when he went on the lam after the FBI raided his Middle Village, Queens, home and found guns and cash. Antonino hid for two years. He dyed his hair, changed his name, and moved to Patchogue on Long Island. But in November 1986 federal agents arrested him. After his inevitable conviction, he began serving what amounts to a life sentence in federal prison for heroin dealing.

The younger Aiello didn't fare as well as a fugitive, however. Federal agents caught up with him in upstate New York near Syracuse in March 2005 after not quite two months on the run. He agreed to be brought back to Brooklyn, where Agent Sallett had sworn out a criminal complaint accusing Aiello of taking part in the murder of Pizzolo.

The document quoted liberally from the tapes that Massino had made of Basciano in jail. In one particularly incriminating passage recorded on January 3, 2005, Basciano said he believed "Dominick and Ace" had been used in the Pizzolo hit.

"'Ace' Aiello is like a Luca Brasi, he's your Luca Brasi," Basciano said on the tape. He was praising Aiello's loyalty to Massino, but the comment also sealed Aiello's fate.

With Massino now a cooperating witness, he moved from the MDC into the witness security program and a special prison facility, likely one in southern New Jersey. Massino was now in a different place psychologically as well. When he came up for sentencing later in 2005, a life sentence hung over him, and a trial on the Sciascia murder charge held the prospect of the death penalty.

Always a gambler, Massino made moves that began to pay off. Because of his secret recordings, the FBI made arrests for the Pizzolo murder. That Basciano and Massino had talked about killing Andres added a new element to the prosecution's profile of Basciano as a dangerous man. For the government, Massino clearly had value as a witness, so they moved to have the death penalty authorization against him rescinded, the motion completed successfully in May 2005.

Basciano needed a new attorney and fast. True to his promise not to get involved in another large racketeering case, Brafman was pulling out as soon as a replacement could be found. Several attorneys had been involved in the various Bonanno cases over the past few years, and one of them, Barry Levin, a Long Island–based practitioner, had handled the defense of Alphonse "Allie Boy" Persico, son of the legendary and imprisoned Colombo crime family boss Carmine "The Snake" Persico. By his own count, Levin had won acquittals in fifteen out of twenty-one criminal trials he handled. One of the Bonanno defendants whose wife knew Angela Basciano mentioned Levin as a possible lawyer. Angela convinced Levin to pay her husband a visit in jail.

"Vinny Basciano liked me," remembered Levin, a former high school and college boxer not easily intimidated either in the ring or in the courtroom. Their styles clicked.

Basciano authorized his cousin Stephen DiCarmine, an attorney at a prestigious Manhattan law firm, to give Levin an initial retainer. With that, he had a new lawyer. But Basciano was going to have to come up with a *lot* of cash to fund his defense over the long haul. If he went to trial on both the Santoro and Pizzolo murder cases, the defense likely would cost a minimum of $500,000. To raise money, Basciano sold the house on Revere Avenue. Angela, a partner in the Burke & Grace real estate firm, agreed to fund her husband's defense as well.

Levin's timing proved fortuitous. The situation for Basciano was going from bad to worse. By March 2005, he had been put into tough segregated housing in the federal lockup, kept in a cell for twenty-three hours a day with no telephone privileges, unable to watch television or listen to the radio. On top of that, he couldn't have reading or writing materials in his cell. Then he was moved from the Brooklyn jail to the federal facility in Manhattan, which had solitary accommodations rated worse by some lawyers than those in the other borough.

Prosecutors asked for the harsher incarceration because they alleged that Basciano had been passing messages to the outside in an effort to continue running the crime family and to have street boss Mancuso killed. Then there was the accusation of having threatened Andres's life during the taped conversations with Massino. Levin found the conditions onerous, however, and argued they were unconstitutional. Judge Garaufis agreed with Levin and on May 5 ordered that Basciano be allowed back in the general population at the Manhattan federal jail. He was also allowed to attend codefendant meetings at the jail again.

But Levin wasn't the only lawyer defending Basciano. With the prospect of the death penalty looming in the Pizzolo murder case—but not for the first trial on the Santoro murder—the court appointed a so-called learned counsel to help defend the capital punishment element should the need arise. Federal death cases actually consist of two trials in one: the guilt phase and the penalty phase. The penalty phase only takes place in the event of a conviction obviously and represents a moral battle over whether a defendant's life is worth sparing. In Basciano's case, the court appointed Ephraim Savitt as learned counsel, with assistance from Ying Stafford. Veteran criminal lawyer Peter Quijano also came aboard.

Savitt, a former federal prosecutor in Brooklyn, was in many ways the opposite of Levin. While Levin, sometimes combative, had high energy, Savitt, deliberative and low-key in court, had a reputation for being gregarious. Prior experience in federal capital cases earned him the designation of learned counsel, and he was of course against the death penalty. He had defended Ronell Wilson, a young man who killed two undercover NYPD narcotics officers, in an earlier capital trial. An observant Jew born in Paris, the child of Holocaust survivors, Savitt often received accommodation from judges who adjourned cases early on the Friday run-up to the Sabbath so that he could make it to synagogue on time.

A slender, dark-haired woman, Stafford had worked on a number of capital cases—although relatively new to the legal profession—and had been carving a niche in the specialty of death penalty law. She had assisted other learned counsel on the case of Ronald Mallay and Richard James, two Guyanese immigrants who faced the death penalty for running a scheme in which other Guyanese were killed for insurance money. The jury voted to spare them in favor of life in prison.

With four lawyers working for him, Basciano began the grind of getting ready for trial. Most defendants take part in their own defense, but Basciano seemed to want to take charge. Reviewing past testimony from the Massino case, Basciano typed out detailed annotations by way of telling Levin and the others what to ask or to give his theory about why a witness was lying. For instance, when Vitale characterized Massino as

"Machiavellian," Basciano noted that if the old crime boss was such a calculating man, he might have fabricated evidence against him. He also made notations about mob life, saying for example that an underboss would never talk with a soldier: "Fuhgeddaboudit!" Basciano didn't just suggest how Levin should manage the case, he dictated what he should do, even writing out portions of summations.

The attorney wanted none of it.

"At one point, Vinny told me and another attorney that this is how something would be done," remembered Levin. "We looked at each other and laughed."

"In almost every court appearance he always insisted that lawyers merely parrot what he wanted them to say," said Savitt. "He really wanted to get up there and do it himself."

Luckily for Basciano, Levin kept a tight grip on the case, with a number of tough legal issues to handle before trial. Also looming was the possibility that the government would get yet more cooperating witnesses. The weakest link in Basciano's group of friends had become Thomas Lee, whom Massino had implicated as his messenger. Sure enough, in June 2005 Brooklyn federal prosecutors announced the indictment of Lee on charges of racketeering, conspiracy to commit murder, and obstruction of justice. In a news release announcing Lee's arrest, prosecutors said Lee gave Massino a variety of messages from Basciano about numerous topics, including the induction of new members to the crime family and the various rackets. All of those charges covered the period when Basciano was free on the street as the acting family boss.

The most serious of the charges against Lee included his alleged ferrying of requests from Basciano to Massino for permission to kill the old Bronx captain Patty DeFilippo and the sons of cooperating witnesses. Other informants had told the FBI that Basciano feared that DeFilippo would make a power grab for control of the family. Both Lee and Basciano were charged with conspiracy to murder DeFilippo.

With his legal career in shambles, Lee had to post a $2 million bail and submit to house arrest at his spacious home in the Country Club section of the Bronx. His new arrangement gave him lots of time to think seriously about what he was going to do now that his days as a mob errand boy had ended. He had limited options.

Nor were matters going well for Basciano on the home front. For many months, his wife, Angela, had known that he had a relationship with the beautician Debra Kalb and had even heard rumors that he had had a child by her. Basciano denied it every way he could, convinced that she would stay with him. In the latter part of 2005, Angela likely considered the possibility of divorce, even while she made the effort— magnanimous under the circumstances—to raise money for Basciano's legal defense. The couple's son Stephen, then twenty-one, got into a fight with a neighbor in the Bronx and hit the man so hard that he broke bones in the man's face. Stephen was charged with assault. Then the tabloids reported that Basciano's eldest son, Vincent, had brawled with the son of reputed Genovese boss Dominick "Quiet Dom" Cirillo. The younger Cirillo disappeared two weeks after the fight, and soon the papers were running stories that investigators were eyeing the younger Vincent. (Basciano later told Massino Cirillo's disappearance had nothing to do with his son.)

Basciano's family troubles were distracting, but the federal case was also becoming complicated. Agent Sallett convinced Thomas Lee to cooperate almost immediately. Government records show that Lee started proffering to the government within days of his arrest, singing over a five-month period. He talked about everything from the start of his legal career in the Bronx to how he found ways to see Massino in jail, sometimes in codefendant meetings, at other times by pretending to be representing him. In one debriefing, Lee recounted how Massino appointed Basciano as acting boss. When Basciano found out, Lee said that the newly promoted mobster said: "I won't let him down."

Lee indicated to agents that Basciano may have used the code word "jocko" with Massino to indicate that he wanted to kill DeFilippo, but records show that Lee had no specific recollection of doing that. In context, the use of the word might have meant to demote a person rather than killing him. Lee had also done legal work for Basciano's family and gave investigators details about Robert Van Zandt Jr., suspected of financial fraud and doing shady real estate deals.

About two months after his arrest, Lee pleaded guilty, ending a modest legal career that led to much dishonor. His one hope of redemption lay in cooperation and testifying against Basciano. By September 2005, word hit the street that Lee had sold his Bronx home and fled with his wife and two kids to more secure settings.

Lee's cooperation meant another dose of bad news for Basciano. He saw the Massino betrayal as if his own father had turned against him. For months, Basciano wouldn't even mention Massino by name in codefendant meetings, referring to him instead as "Tessio," the character in *The Godfather* played by Abe Vigoda who turned against the Corleone family. Massino was bad enough, but Lee—who didn't have any firsthand knowledge of homicides—could corroborate what Massino had been telling prosecutors, including the passing of messages in jail. Basciano seethed at Lee, although he thought any testimony the latter gave wouldn't cause much damage.

"Vinny perceived Tommy Lee as a bullshit artist," Levin remembered of Basciano's overall reaction.

At this stage, the government was giving the impression that Massino could be its main witness against Basciano, particularly about his role in the Bonanno family. Although the Pizzolo murder didn't form a part of the indictment approaching trial, prosecutors would try to present evidence of the killing as proof of uncharged crimes, allowed under the federal rules of evidence. For that, Massino could be an important witness.

With Massino lurking in the wings, Levin and his legal team tried to attack Massino's usefulness as a witness by claiming he was acting as a government agent when he talked to Basciano. If Massino had such status, Levin argued, then the Bonanno chief had conducted an unlawful interrogation of Basciano without the presence of his lawyer. It was a significant argument, which Garaufis found compelling. The court believed that the use of the Massino tapes in Basciano's first trial would violate his Sixth Amendment right to counsel. The government decided not to push the issue, though, and said it had no plans to use the tapes in Basciano's trial, set to begin in early 2006.

Yet the Massino tapes presented another legal wrinkle. Patty DeFilippo was scheduled to be tried with Basciano. The most serious charge against DeFilippo held that he had played a role in the Sciascia murder. DeFilippo and his attorneys believed that portions of the Massino tapes could help his defense against the Sciascia murder charge. For instance, DeFilippo said that Basciano had the authority in 2003–2004 to order hits, although the Sciascia killing took place in 1999, well before Basciano made captain. The tapes also showed that Basciano trusted the alleged killer Johnny Joe Spirito more than DeFilippo did, according to court records. Judge Garaufis found both arguments weak and not worth the potential prejudice of allowing the tapes in their entirety.

But all of that still didn't mean the Massino tapes couldn't be used, said Garaufis. If Massino took the stand, as expected, then DeFilippo's lawyers might be able to use the tapes, with careful redactions, to show the crime boss's tendency toward untruthfulness. But then the government could use redacted portions of the tapes to show that Massino was a truthful witness. The tapes could cut both ways.

So much talk of Massino as a witness led reporters and the defense to believe that Basciano's trial would be a standing-room-only show, with Massino as the central witness for the prosecution. But another unexpected shift was happening. In early January 2006, defense attorney James

Froccaro, representing Cicale, suddenly couldn't find him. Prisoners don't just disappear from federal jail. Something dramatic had happened.

Cicale had been cooped up in a cell for about a year. He had already read volumes of legal documents, including the FBI reports of the various witnesses in the Massino case. His relationship with Basciano had more than frayed, particularly after learning that the Bonanno street boss allegedly wanted to kill Cicale's girlfriend for her indiscretion about Debra Kalb's child.

During codefendant meetings in early January 2006, Savitt noticed something strange. He spotted Basciano pulling Cicale off to the side to berate him. Savitt couldn't hear much of what was being said, but the conversation between the two men was animated. Basciano kept saying "this life, this life, in this life you have to do this" as if trying to remind Cicale of what he was expected to do in the mob, recalled Savitt.

The words echoed several phrases from *The Godfather II:* "This is the business we've chosen" and "If anything in this life is certain, if history has taught us anything, it is that you can kill anyone." The incident during the meeting may have been something Cicale later related to federal prosecutors: how Basciano allegedly wanted him to take the witness stand and perjure himself to discredit government witnesses. If Basciano was trying to remind Cicale of the importance of sticking with the mob code of conduct, it didn't work. By January 11, within days of Savitt's observation of the jailhouse conversation, Cicale signed his first agreement to provide information to the government. Records show that on that date he began talking in earnest to FBI agents about what he did with Basciano. It was all done in secret, and while Cicale had Froccaro as attorney of record, he too received a shadow counsel to help him navigate the legal waters of becoming a cooperating witness.

By January 19, word hit the street that Cicale was cooperating. Levin, Savitt, and Stafford made the trip to the federal jail on a weekend to tell their client the news. Once the lawyers had assembled in the jailhouse meeting room, Levin told Basciano that they had bad news. Basciano feared that something had happened to one of his children or Angela. Then Levin told him: Cicale was cooperating.

As Levin remembered, the room went dead still, and tears seemed to form in Basciano's eyes. Savitt also recalled Basciano tearing up, but didn't know whether from heartbreak or anger. Then Basciano launched a loud verbal barrage denouncing Cicale. The news came as a shattering blow. Basciano had felt like a brother to Cicale, whom he saw as a rougher, less sophisticated version of himself—but close.

"First my father and now the son," Basciano later lamented about how Massino and Cicale had turned on him. Loyalty in the mob had become a relic of the past.

The practical importance of what had happened was obvious. Cicale had cut a deal with the government or was about to cut one. He would be giving testimony about the Santoro homicide and many other crimes listed in the indictment against Basciano. Faced with such a setback, Basciano asked his attorneys to see if the government would make a plea bargain to avoid trial.

"Basciano didn't want to fight at that point," said Levin. "Vinny was prepared to plead out at that point."

Savitt approached Andres, the lead prosecutor, to see what kind of plea bargain they could strike. To Savitt's surprise, Andres refused. Whether Andres—allegedly the object of Basciano's solicitation to murder—should have remained on the case and made key decisions about the fate of the man who supposedly wanted him dead became a matter much discussed in the coming weeks and months. The defense argued that under the circumstances, Andres had a conflict of interest and should have recused himself. But Garaufis allowed him to stay.

As shattering as Cicale's change of sides had been, Basciano seemed to bounce back rather quickly. "He is like a prizefighter," Levin said later.

"You knock him down, and he comes back up. I saw him three days later. He had a smile on his face and said 'okay, lets go to work.'"

The case of Vincent Basciano and Patrick DeFilippo was set to go to trial on February 21, 2006. Basciano faced counts dealing with the Santoro murder as well as conspiracy to murder David Nunez and Dominick Martino, a reputed Genovese crime family associate who got into a fight with Donato. DeFilippo's most serious count dealt with the killing of Sciascia. They both faced extortion and gambling counts. But renowned mob investigator Kenneth McCabe died of cancer, delaying the start of the trial for a week because a number of government officials and agents had to attend the funeral.

The trial finally opened on February 27. Since the government alleged that Basciano at one point wanted to kill DeFilippo, the two men sat at opposite ends of the defense table. With Judge Garaufis presiding, prosecutor Amy Busa made the government's opening statement that Basciano, a cold-blooded killer, was a lifelong Mafia zealot. "When someone disrespected him or his family, he responds with murder," she said.

With so much evidence of mob association and so many cooperating witnesses who had dealings with Basciano set to take the stand, Levin made a tactical decision not to contest that his client was in the mob. "He is in the Bonanno crime family, we don't care," conceded Levin in his opening remarks to the jury. Pointing out a debonair Basciano, dressed on this particular day in an olive-colored suit, Levin said he liked to be noticed. "Look at him. He's well dressed. His hair's groomed, he plays the role, he plays it to the hilt."

With such a flamboyant opening and with Massino believed to be in the wings, the trial became a big draw, getting full coverage from the news reporters. But the media frenzy suddenly died down when Andres disclosed to the court that prosecutors had decided not to call Massino. Andres didn't elaborate, but it appeared that—at least in terms of making the case against Basciano for the Santoro murder—Massino wasn't essential. Massino also needed further investigating himself since he had failed two FBI-administered polygraph tests.

Sal Vitale was the first cooperator called to the stand. Despite getting Basciano's name wrong—calling him "Basamenti"—Vitale illuminated Basciano's stature in the Bonanno family for the jury. It was Vitale's second appearance as a witness in Brooklyn, and he seemed more at ease. He didn't have any firsthand knowledge of what Basciano had done, so his testimony wasn't that damaging. Yet he did recount something he had heard secondhand from Massino about the murder of Santoro. When Basciano jumped out of the car to shoot him, Santoro cried out "Oh, no!" according to Vitale. "Vinny said, 'Oh, yes!' and shot him," Vitale testified. Vitale also testified that Basciano had the reputation of being a "mad hatter," unpredictable and capable of doing anything at any time.

If Vitale didn't know much about Basciano's activities, Cicale told a different story. When he appeared in the courtroom for the first time, Cicale, a muscular man with a handsome Italian visage, seemed fidgety. He avoided looking at Basciano and spoke in a monotone, often referring in a stilted, formal way to the defendant by his full name. For his part, Basciano showed little emotion, watching his old protégé with dark eyes that betrayed little.

Cicale recounted for the jury that he had dropped out of high school in the tenth grade and gravitated toward a life of crime that included burglary, drug dealing, homicide, and other misdeeds. A couple of his business ventures failed. He first met Basciano in 1999, and there began the inexorable march from mob associate to made member of the Bonanno crime family, culminating in his rise to captain in 2004. But such a recitation of his criminal résumé made for a prelude to Cicale's main testimony about the demise of Frank Santoro on February 15, 2001.

The impetus for the killing came after Santoro had threatened to kidnap one of Basciano's sons, a "situation" as Cicale recalled. The report of the kidnap plot had come from a Bronx man who later denied saying as much when questioned by federal prosecutors years later. At first blush, Cicale thought that Santoro was supposed to be beaten up to teach him a lesson. Basciano said that Santoro was a junkie in the Bronx, and Cicale testified that the mob captain needed his help in trying to find out where the victim lived.

Trying to locate Santoro, Cicale contacted his own father, who believed that Santoro lived in the Pelham Bay section and had a dog. Meeting in the bathroom of the house of Basciano's girlfriend and speaking in whispers, Cicale, Basciano, and Indelicato discussed how they would drive around Pelham Bay looking for a man with a dog and, as Cicale told the jury, "leave him in the street" by killing him. It was a harebrained idea that amounted to nothing more than searching for the proverbial needle in a haystack. Armed with walkie-talkies, the group, which included Basciano's friend Anthony Donato, drove around the night of February 14 for a couple of hours and found nothing, Cicale remembered. Basciano called off the search and told everybody that he was going to find out where Santoro lived so that they all didn't waste time on such a wild goose chase, added Cicale.

The next night, Cicale testified, Indelicato called to summon him back from his home in New Jersey, where he had been preparing to take his wife out to dinner to make up for a cancellation the previous evening. A dutiful Cicale made the drive back to Kalb's house, where he said he met up again with Basciano, Donato, and Indelicato. Basciano, obviously irritated, said that Santoro didn't live in Pelham Bay but rather in Throgs Neck, just blocks away from where he himself lived. The group departed Kalb's home with the same guns from the previous night and drove south to the right neighborhood, said Cicale, both he and Basciano wearing all black.

According to Cicale, the group including Basciano and Donato drove in Donato's gold Acura while Indelicato and another man named John went in a red Honda, which served as a second escape vehicle. Once the group pulled off the expressway, they were driving on a service road that intersected with Pennyfield Avenue, very close to Santoro's house. The red Honda parked near some row houses while the other car circled the block a few times before pulling over to wait. A few minutes passed.

"'There goes Frank Santoro,'" Donato said suddenly, testified Cicale, recalling how they spotted the target talking to a neighbor.

Cicale told the jury that he was anxious and wanted to kill both men but that Basciano told them to wait. Donato wanted to abort the mission. Then something unexpected happened. Larry Weinstein, a gambling associate and friend of Basciano from the neighborhood, spotted him and came up to the car to say hello, said Cicale. Returning the greeting, Basciano told Weinstein very seriously to get away from the car.

Vincent Basciano, Anthony Donato, and Larry Weinstein captured in surveillance footage

In a few minutes, Santoro continued his walk with the dog. Basciano told Donato to make the turn down the street when the light turned green, said Cicale.

"My adrenaline was going," recalled Cicale.

Donato pulled the car over and slowed down. Cicale said he had the door of the vehicle open even before it stopped and then got Santoro's attention with two words: "Excuse me."

As he was getting out of the Acura, Cicale fired the first shot at Santoro's head and continued to shoot for a total of five times from a distance of about five to ten feet. Then, according to Cicale, he saw Basciano outside of the car firing the shotgun. With the shotgun rounds going off, Santoro fell to the ground. Basciano fired one final shot, testified Cicale.

"The last shot from Vinny Basciano's gun hit Frank Santoro when Frank Santoro was already on the ground," said Cicale.

While Cicale had a sharp recall of the incident, he wasn't a good shot. Autopsy results showed that Santoro sustained four shotgun wounds—but none from a revolver. One wound to the head pulled back some of the skull and exposed the brain, another to the shoulder fractured the humerus, and two more wounds in the body revealed damage to internal organs.

Donato quickly drove out of the area. Basciano told him to stop the car so he could get out with Cicale and get into Indelicato's truck, according to the testimony. Driving away in the truck, the trio—Donato in his own car—drove to a vacant lot on Schurz Avenue where Cicale said Basciano took his weapon, wrapped it in a rag, and got out of the vehicle. Basciano disappeared into some shrubbery and came back, apparently without the gun, according to Cicale. The group then drove about ten blocks to Basciano's house, where he got out of the car and hid the shotgun outside his home, recalled Cicale.

"He felt there would be no forensics with shotgun bullets," said Cicale, when asked why Basciano kept the shotgun.

The group drove back to Kalb's house and went back into the bathroom, where Cicale said there were hugs and kisses all around.

"'Congratulations, you just did your first piece of work,'" said Indelicato, according to Cicale.

Killing on behalf of made men signaled loyalty, and Dominick Cicale had proved himself a loyal dog. "I was happy," he remembered about having proved to Basciano he was a killer.

As he continued his narrative for the jury under questioning by the prosecution, Cicale noted that Basciano had told him and Indelicato in no uncertain terms never to discuss the killing. But when Massino a month later asked Basciano about it, he told the crime boss what had happened, which distressed Cicale. The secret had slipped out beyond the tight circle of the original conspiracy. Yet, under the code of La Cosa Nostra, Basciano had no choice but to tell Massino the truth, even though he left out the involvement of Donato and the man named John, said Cicale.

More evidence came of alleged extortion, gambling, and the attempted murder of Dominick Martino. Vitale also testified about events leading up to the murder of Sciascia and DeFilippo's involvement in it. But the most compelling testimony had come from Cicale on the Santoro homicide.

Basciano didn't like how the case had gone. When it came time for summations, Levin remembered that his client had become a bundle of nerves, trying once again to direct the attorney on how to give a summation. The trial had taken at least twice the time it should have, filled with constant courtroom sparring with prosecutor Andres. Levin didn't need more interference from his own client now. On the day of final arguments, Levin remembered going into the holding area of the courthouse to see Basciano and say good morning. Basciano immediately told Levin what to include in his summation. The lawyer couldn't take any more meddling. In the ensuing argument, after Basciano said he would punch out Levin, the lawyer angrily told the federal marshals to open the cell door.

"Take your best shot," Levin, the ex-boxer, remembered telling Basciano.

"I am betting on Levin," said one of the marshals.

The Bonanno captain put up his hands in mock surrender and said he had only been kidding.

As shocking and convincing as testimony about the murder of Santoro had been, the case wasn't a slam dunk for prosecutors. The jury deliberated for six days before announcing that it couldn't reach a verdict on the murder count. The panel had split 11–1 in favor of conviction for the killing, but the one holdout adamantly refused to credit the testimony of a cooperator like Cicale. As a result, on May 9, 2006, the jury convicted Basciano of racketeering but came to a mistrial on the Santoro homicide. The panel convicted Basciano of the racketeering conspiracy charge that he had run a gambling operation and had conspired to kill David Nunez back in 1985. But jurors cleared him of extortion and couldn't agree on a verdict for the conspiracy to murder Martino. DeFilippo, often overlooked in the trial coverage, was also convicted of racketeering conspiracy, gambling, and extortion, but the jury deadlocked on his involvement in the Sciascia murder.

Basciano still faced serious prison time as a result of the verdict, but he seemed all smiles when the deadlock was announced on the Santoro case, which would have earned him a life sentence upon conviction. Levin touted the result as a win of sorts. "He's in good spirits," he told the *New York Times* after the verdict. "He can see the light of day. What the jury said is, 'We don't believe the rats.'"

But prosecutors weren't done with Basciano—not by a long shot. They intended to retry him on the deadlocked Santoro murder count. They also were preparing for a trial on the second indictment for the Pizzolo murder. It wasn't going to be a quiet summer.

18

In Lewis Carroll's *Alice's Adventures in Wonderland*, the opening scenes have young Alice following a white rabbit, late for an appointment, hurrying down a rabbit-hole, which brings her to an alternate reality where nothing is certain. Over the years the phrase "down the rabbit-hole" has taken on a number of popular meanings, including starting an adventure or falling into a state of uncertainty and confusion. By any of those definitions, the case of Vincent Basciano jumped down the rabbit-hole in August 2006.

Mob cases generally follow a pattern: investigation, indictment, and either a plea bargain or trial. If convicted, the mobster is sentenced and, depending upon the severity of the charge, goes away for life or gets a set term of years in prison. Those who cooperate often find the government filing a laudatory letter known as a "5.K," referring to the relevant section of the federal sentencing guidelines, which tells the court why the individual deserves consideration for helping the government. Often these letters shave years from a cooperator's sentence, leading to freedom.

In Basciano's case, after the partial verdict in his 2006 trial, the expectation was that a new trial would be held on the deadlocked Santoro murder count before the trial on the Pizzolo homicide. Basciano was expecting to spend his days at the MDC awaiting retrial and taking visits from his family and lawyers. Levin had had more than enough with the first trial and decided against an encore. With what was left of his financial resources, Basciano hired James Kousouros, an experienced attorney from Queens who had represented a number of organized crime figures, including an Albanian gangster who had dealings with Basciano. As Kousouros remembered, one of his Albanian clients, Alex Rudaj, spoke with Basciano while both were awaiting court proceedings in prison and suggested the Bronx gangster consider hiring the lawyer. After meeting with Basciano in jail, Kourouros agreed to represent him on the retrial. Kousouros and his cocounsel, Stephanie Carvlin, a highly regarded appellate and criminal attorney, made regular visits to the MDC facility to discuss the case with Basciano.

But suddenly the lawyers faced the unexpected. On July 28, 2006, Basciano was moved from the general jail population back to the special housing unit—that is, solitary confinement. But Basciano hadn't seen restrictions like this before. He couldn't have contact with anyone, including his attorneys, investigators, or family members, nor could he access his own legal documents or even have a radio. No one knew what was going on.

Prison officials eventually allowed Basciano to see his lawyers—although they couldn't have physical contact with him. He eventually could have a radio in the cell as well as copies of his legal papers. But then officials moved Basciano to a cell where the previous inmate, who had psychological problems, had urinated and defecated around the tiny room. Prison orderlies cleaned up the mess, but Basciano had to sprinkle Comet cleanser around the floor by his bed to mask the lingering odors.

After Judge Garaufis prodded them to finish their investigation of the matter, Brooklyn federal prosecutors made an astonishing revelation. Another inmate had told investigators that Basciano had given him in jail a handwritten list of five people whom he wanted murdered. On the list were the names of Garaufis, Andres, Lee, Cicale, and Tartaglione.

In a carefully crafted letter to Garaufis, prosecutors alleged that Basciano had "indicated to the inmate, in sum and substance," that he was seeking to murder the people on the list. The letter didn't reveal the inmate's name. Apparently to embarrass Basciano, prosecutors disclosed a copy of a letter that he had written to his girlfriend, which they used to verify his handwriting. Basciano revealed in the note that Cicale's betrayal "broke my heart" and that the way things had turned out showed him that "all things I held sacred ... were a fraud." He reminded Kalb to send him her photograph, preferably in a G-string. But by then any salacious revelations about his relationship with Kalb couldn't make matters any worse for his family life. Court records show that Angela Basciano had filed for divorce in April 2006.

There was no denying that Basciano had prepared the list. But the explanation as to why he had done so took the case into a realm no one expected. At a hearing in August, Kousouros explained to Garaufis that the mysterious inmate in the case had approached Basciano to say that his mother was into voodoo and Santería, an Afro-Caribbean religion that mixes Yoruba, a West African creed, and Catholicism. The religion has a wide following in the immigrant communities of New York City.

"This inmate, the person we believe to be this inmate, is somebody who approached our client and told him that his mother is some priestess," said Kousouros. The inmate told Basciano "to make a list of everybody involved, put it in your right shoe, stamp five times a day during trial and it will help." The inmate set Basciano up by going to the authorities with the list, said Kousouros.

In an interview in November 2006, Angela Basciano noted that her husband did put stock in voodoo and black magic. A Roman Catholic and a disbeliever in such mysticism herself, she nonetheless sought out the mystery inmate's mother in the Bronx to find out how to cast a good spell. But the old woman wasn't home, and Angela talked with her own friend, a believer in Santería who said that the list could create good luck and positive energy. Prosecutors had interviewed Angela earlier and she said she told them the same story.

Not revealed at the time, according to court records Basciano had also crafted a weird letter that contained two lists, one in his handwriting and the other penned by a guard, with this preface: "I Vincent Basciano before the house of the judge, three dead men look out the window one having no tongue the other no lungs and the third was sick, blind and dumb." Following that statement came several names, including Garaufis, Andres, and Massino. Another list had even more names and included those of Agent Breslin and DeFilippo's attorney, Richard Levitt. The defense maintained that the letter and names proved that the so-called hit list was a prop for a Santería ritual.

The explanation didn't persuade the government. On September 21, federal prosecutors disclosed that the attorney general had authorized that "special administrative measures" be imposed on Basciano—in this case measures usually used against terrorism suspects. If solitary was tough, the SAM measures only made life worse. Basciano was isolated from other inmates, locked up for twenty-three hours a day, with one hour for exercise alone. He had no access to a radio or periodicals, and his cell was illuminated and videotaped twenty-four hours a day. He could have only one personal visit every two weeks, and his lawyers had to sign statements affirming that they wouldn't pass messages from Basciano to anyone else. Other lawyers couldn't have physical contact with Basciano and had to have a guard pass legal papers to him.

It took months for Basciano to determine why the SAM restrictions were imposed. In a filing with the court, prosecutors related how Cicale had alleged that Basciano sent messages from jail through former attorney Tom Lee seeking the killing of Michael Mancuso. Basciano also told Massino on tape that he intended to pass a message through his son, Vincent Jr. But two other reasons seemed questionable. Prosecutors claimed they had an informant who revealed that several inmates had plotted to harm a witness for the government on Basciano's behalf. Ultimately, prosecutors acknowledged they had no hard evidence linking Basciano directly to such a plot. Then there was the so-called "hit list," which the government insisted showed Basciano's desire to harm people.

The list had a strange life in the history of Basciano's various legal wars. On the one hand, government investigators believed it a credible and reliable indication of Basciano's plan to kill the five people whom it named. But Garaufis himself raised an alternative explanation, which undercut the efficacy of the list as a device to perpetrate harm. In responding to a motion by Basciano to have him replaced as the presiding judge in the case, Garaufis said that it appeared that one of the defendant's reasons for writing the hit list was to engineer recusals. Garaufis came to that conclusion after learning that Basciano, in a taped telephone conversation with Angela, said he was "going to try to get a different judge" and that to do so he had "to pull all the rabbits out of [his] hat." Garaufis concluded that the list, coupled with Basciano's attempt to get a new judge, represented a "thinly disguised effort to manipulate the judicial process." Garaufis denied the motion to have himself recused.

But which was it? Was it a true hit list, earmarking five people for death? Or was it a crafty invention to engineer a recusal of Garaufis? Garaufis cast doubt that the list had any deadly purpose. It also seemed strange that, after getting burned by so many informants and witnesses from his circle of mob friends, Basciano would then entrust a hit list to an inmate he barely knew. Yet the government continued to refer to the list in later proceedings as evidence of Basciano's dangerous tendencies.

In 1984 Congress crafted a new federal death penalty law able to withstand legal challenges. New York State briefly resurrected capital punishment between 1995 and 2004, when a court of appeals decision effectively struck it down. After the 2004 decision, if you committed a crime in New York, you ran the risk of execution only if the federal law covered the crime. Such was the case for certain murders committed in violation of the racketeering laws.

While the death penalty remains on the books for the federal system, to date it has led to only three executions nationwide. Juries around the country, faced with the prospect of deciding to kill a guilty defendant, often resist the possibility. Most federal death row inmates live in the South or Midwest. New York State has seen a number of death-eligible defendants over the years, mostly in Brooklyn federal court. But aside from Ronell Wilson, convicted in 2006 of killing two undercover police detectives, New York juries have rejected the death penalty, opting instead for life in prison without parole. In Wilson's case, a federal appeals court overturned the death penalty in 2010 because of prosecutorial missteps.

In Basciano's case, prosecutors in the Brooklyn US Attorney's Office didn't hide that they believed the murder of Randy Pizzolo merited the death penalty. But before the death penalty can even come to consideration at trial, the US Department of Justice has to authorize the case as one in which it will seek capital punishment. Before that decision takes place, the local US Attorney's Office and the defense have the opportunity to present their respective cases before a panel of officials during separate meetings in Washington, D.C.

It fell to Savitt, as appointed death penalty counsel, to make the trip to talk to the government committee on Basciano's behalf. His most important argument, Savitt recalled, was that Randolph Pizzolo—not someone who engendered much sympathy in the first place—had put his own life at risk generally by associating with the mob. If Pizzolo put himself in mortal danger, why execute Basciano?

Savitt didn't remember the names of the three panel members, though he characterized two as "southern boys." At least one panel member raised the issue of the so-called hit list. How to explain that? The list was a red herring, argued Savitt, that had nothing to do with any planned murders. Savitt also argued that Massino, who had admitted responsibility for numerous murders, was given a break when the death penalty was taken off the table in his case. The panel thanked Savitt and then heard the arguments of the Brooklyn federal prosecutors.

Since the list formed an important piece in the death penalty decision by the government, it had to be addressed. In a move of surprising hubris or bravery—possibly both—Basciano insisted that he take a lie detector test and have the results considered by the government panel. It backfired. The polygraphist's report said that Basciano had indicated deception or untruthfulness when asked if he had wanted to harm anyone with the list. But of course, as Savitt explained later, depending on how the question was asked, Basciano's physiological responses might have been recording his own confused reaction. After all, taken at face value, the list invoked mystical or spiritual harm but not physical harm to those named on it. The gambit failed, and the day after the test results came back, the Justice Department announced that it was authorizing the Brooklyn US Attorney's office to seek the death penalty in the Pizzolo murder case.

But the deadlocked Santoro murder case still had to have its day in court—again. The retrial on the remaining counts against Basciano took place in July 2007, much different in tenor than the first trial. Prosecutor Andres, another former college boxer who constantly locked horns with defense attorney Levin, no longer sat on the in-court trial team, moving on to other duties and cases in the office. This time assistant US attorneys John Buretta, Winston Chan, and Amy Busa represented the government in court. Kousouros, Carvlin, and Allan Brenner spearheaded the defense.

"It was the same testimony," remembered Levin, who wasn't involved in the retrial. Cicale took the stand again as the main witness, with more testimony by Vitale, by then a trial veteran. Tartaglione and disgraced former attorney Thomas Lee took the stand as well. Also appearing was the widowed Marie Santoro, the first government witness, who gave emotional testimony about finding her husband dead in the street.

Even though the testimony was much the same, reporters still found time to be amused. When the fastidious Basciano came to court one day without a proper dress shirt, Garaufis came to the rescue, loaning him a blue Brooks Brothers Oxford dress shirt and a yellow tie. Garaufis wasn't sure if the shirt would match Basciano's green sportcoat, but in the end he thought it would be acceptable.

"I would do my shopping here," Basciano joked as he went into a back room to change.

"We have limited availability," Garaufis retorted.

While Kourouros tried to paint Cicale as a "degenerate liar" who admittedly once tried to cheat his ninety-four-year-old grandmother, the evidence proved too overpowering. On July 31, 2007, the jury convicted Basciano of everything. They found him guilty not only of the Santoro murder and conspiracy to murder Dominick Martino but also of solicitation to murder Vitale, conspiracy to distribute marijuana, and assorted illegal gambling charges.

Basciano's face flushed as he heard the results. He shook his head in disbelief.

19

In 2008, Vincent Basciano was supposed to undergo the death penalty trial for the murder of Randolph Pizzolo. It didn't happen.

Then it was 2009. It didn't happen then, either.

Seasons of legal wrangling pushed the date to 2010. Basciano's case was turning into *Jarndyce vs. Jarndyce* in *Bleak House* by Charles Dickens, which became synonymous with endless legal proceedings. With so many delays, it was fair to ask if the case would ever go to trial. Perhaps a more important question was whether Joseph Massino, who had serious health issues, would live long enough to take the stand.

Basciano wasn't getting any younger, either. Arrested in 2004 at age forty-five, Basciano was now fifty-one and getting heavier himself. But to the amazement of many observers, he seemed to hold up well under the onerous confinement conditions. Prisoners subjected to isolation develop all kinds of psychological and emotional issues. But whenever Basciano met with his lawyers he seemed focused on the legal battle ahead of him. During court appearances he behaved jovially, flashing a smile to reporters in the courtroom and bantering with his attorneys. His now grayer hair always looked well coiffed. He also retained a tan that rumor ascribed to his use of crushed Cheez-Its or, more likely, blood pressure issues.

Attorneys did notice subtle changes in Basciano's persona, though. He sometimes focused too much on minutiae and thought Garaufis and the prosecutors were in league to do him in. Savitt remembered Basciano becoming more prone to depression. The isolation was also affecting his family. His sons had limited ability to see him, with Vincent Jr. prohibited from visits at all. He had served as a source of stability in their lives, but now contact with his sons was virtually cut off. Angela could make visits, but they were also limited.

Other problems revolved around Basciano's fifth son, the one with Kalb. The child, Anthony, a healthy dark-haired six-year-old, bore a striking resemblance to his father. According to a report filed with the court by a clinical psychologist, Anthony suffered from separation anxiety caused in part by Basciano's incarceration. Prior to his arrest, Basciano had spent most evenings and mornings interacting with Anthony. But as with other members of Basciano's family, contact with Anthony greatly abated after the SAM restrictions went into place. Anthony's total interaction with his father after that consisted of just two cards sent by mail.

This separation from his father, whom he called "Din," made Anthony fear that if something happened to his mother he would be alone in the world. When the psychologist asked Anthony what he worried about when his mother wasn't around, the child responded, "I'm afraid she will get dead," the report stated. The anxiety caused Anthony to cry, suffer from stomachaches, and fear being outside of his mother's presence— even if she was in the next room while he watched television, the psychologist noted.

Made aware of the difficulties that the SAM restrictions appeared to be causing the child, Garaufis facilitated in the courthouse a number of meetings between Basciano and his youngest son under the watchful eye of US marshals. The child had been led to believe that his father was in the Army and would eventually return home, a myth no doubt exposed as he grew older and learned of events surrounding his father from friends. A person familiar with the courthouse visits said that Basciano gushed over his son and that anyone watching the scene felt the emotion of the moment.

Garaufis was also clearly having enough of the government's attempt to push along with the death penalty case. Basciano had already received a life sentence for the conviction in the Santoro case. Spending so much time and effort, as well as millions of dollars, on another prosecution seemed misguided to Garaufis. So in May 2010 he wrote a letter to US Attorney General Eric Holder asking the government to reconsider the capital case, saying "current conditions require a candid reappraisal of whether the resources necessary for a death penalty prosecution should be devoted to this case."

Garaufis carefully phrased his argument in terms of money and judicial efficiency, but an unwritten fact lingered beneath his words. Juries in New York City, particularly in Brooklyn, remain hostile to the death penalty in racketeering prosecutions. Since the reinstitution of the federal death penalty in 1984, every attempt by Brooklyn prosecutors to use it had failed—with the exception of the Wilson case, where an appeal later overturned the death verdict. Jurors in the district always found just enough redeeming qualities in a defendant to spare his life.

Some federal judges in Brooklyn also opposed capital punishment. In one case, of drug dealer Kenneth McGriff in 2008, Judge Frederic Block saw the inequity of the government agreeing to a plea deal with some in order to get the conviction of McGriff for the same killings. As the trial progressed, Block believed that seeking the death penalty was wasting time and asked prosecutors to see if then–US Attorney General Alberto Gonzalez would take the capital punishment off the table. Gonzalez refused. The jury convicted McGriff but spared his life, giving him a life sentence instead. On the verdict sheet, some of the jurors pointed out that the favorable plea deals given to witnesses argued against the death penalty. Many on the panel believed that the victims contributed to their own deaths by engaging in violent crimes. Spurred by the burdens and costs of death penalty prosecutions, Block later wrote an op-ed piece on the subject for the *New York Times*.

The senior judge in the district, Jack B. Weinstein, held the death penalty in personal disfavor. When in 2008 he was handling the case of another murderous drug dealer, Humberto Pepin Taveras, Weinstein told the US Attorney's Office that its chances of getting a death verdict were "virtually nil." That jury convicted Taveras of chopping up the two victims, but they also spared his life.

Yet the Brooklyn US Attorney's Office persisted—against such a poor record—with the death penalty case against Basciano. So far the case had gone the government's way, with Basciano not only getting convicted but losing many post-trial motions. But in 2010 the Second Circuit Court of Appeals indicated that prosecutors had been piling on with Basciano. The court didn't use those exact words, but in a March 2010 opinion a three-judge panel of the appeals court found that certain charges of the pending indictment—that is, the Pizzolo murder—contained racketeering charges for which he had already been convicted in the earlier Santoro case. The principle of double jeopardy required dismissal of the charge, and the court ordered Garaufis to do so. Still, a substantial part of the case remained, including the Pizzolo homicide, and the government was bringing it to trial. With Joseph Massino preparing for the performance of his life, as well as Basciano's, it was going to be a moment not to be missed.

20

THE ROTUND JOSEPH MASSINO FINALLY APPEARED IN THE COURTROOM as the star witness in *U.S. v. Vincent Basciano,* case number 05-cr-60. Dressed casually in dark clothing, looking much larger since last he had appeared in public, Massino stood flanked by two US marshals as he waited for the jury to enter and sit. As a precaution against unauthorized taping or cell phone monitoring of Massino's testimony, Judge Garaufis had everyone shut off those devices and threatened that they would be confiscated if his order wasn't obeyed. The courtroom was dead silent. Even the sketch artists ceased their often audible scratching. Finally, Massino took his seat. It was just after noon on April 12, 2011.

"You may inquire," Garaufis said.

The job of questioning Massino fell to the very pregnant assistant US attorney Taryn Merkl. Her state added a note of contrast to the death penalty case: one life about to begin and another possibly coming to an end. The lead prosecutor, she headed the organized crime unit of the Brooklyn US Attorney's Office. A polished lawyer with good trial skills, she had done her share of mob cases, but questioning Bonanno boss Joe Massino in front of the world was going to be hard to top in anybody's career. The world had been waiting for this moment for six long years.

In the government's opening statement earlier that morning, prosecutor Nicole Argentieri had prepared the jury by saying that Massino had ruled the crime family for over twenty years. It was Massino, Argentieri said, who got Basciano to confess to Pizzolo's murder. Merkl quickly got to the main point of Massino's story. She asked him just a few minutes into the direct examination whether he had ever heard about Randy Pizzolo from anyone in the Bonanno family. Massino said he had and that Basciano was the one who told him while both were in the federal lockup.

"What did Vincent Basciano tell you about Randolph Pizzolo?" Merkl asked.

"He told me that he killed him," Massino answered.

It was a strong statement of fact that put Basciano in a hole from which he would have to work very hard to climb out during the rest of the trial. But it was still early, and any reasonable juror would want to know more. Through her questions, Merkl then marched jurors back in time, having Massino illuminate decades of a life of crime, which included stealing pigeons at the age of twelve to his conviction in 2004 for seven mob rub-outs. Massino's life had appeared in countless news articles and three books. Yet he broke new ground, answering questions about which cops and mob buffs had wondered for years.

When Vito Borelli was killed in the 1970s for making fun of the late Gambino boss Paul Castellano to his daughter, it was John Gotti Sr., then an acting captain, who shot Borelli, said Massino. When the Three Captains were slaughtered in a social club, Massino held on to the legs of Philip Giaccone as he tried desperately to flee the kill zone, allowing enough time for George Sciascia to pick up a handgun from the floor and pump some bullets into Giaccone's head. Months later, Sonny Napolitano was killed because he wanted to control the crime family—apparently not because of the earlier infiltration of the Bonanno family by undercover FBI agent Joseph Pistone working as wiseguy "Donnie Brasco."

Massino's retelling of mob history mesmerized the courtroom. His recollections seemed ironclad. Basciano's attorneys hardly made any objections as the crime boss went through his narrative. Running the crime family, even when on probation from an earlier federal conviction, was easy, said Massino. He relayed messages through Vitale and met people at a mansion on Long Island. After he became boss, Massino decreed that new members had to have parents both of Italian ancestry. He banned anyone from induction who had a drug conviction within the previous five years. He also ordered all mob social clubs in the crime family closed to make it more difficult for FBI surveillance.

"You could take one FBI agent and he could stand outside that club and watch fifty people go into that club. If you close that club you need fifty FBI agents to watch fifty people," explained Massino.

One new twist on mob history emerged when Massino explained why he had Sciascia killed in 1999. The conventional wisdom—as testified in earlier trials—held that Massino was angry with the too assertive Sciascia for calling Anthony Graziano a drug abuser. But according to Massino, Sciascia had committed the unpardonable sin of killing the son of another Bonanno gangster.

"I knew, once he did that, I was going to kill him," Massino told the jury. "I gave the contract to Patty DeFilippo in the Bronx." Massino left for vacation in St. Maartens and, ever conscious of wiretaps, had Vitale call him with instructions to use the code phrase "I picked up them dolls for the babies" to signify Sciascia's death. Soon enough, Vitale called and spoke the code. Sciascia's body was dumped in the street because normally the Bonanno family buries its victims, said Massino. "If you bury, right away they are going to surmise it came from the Bonanno family," he explained. "Throw him in the street."

Massino had made DeFilippo a captain because there hadn't been a Mafioso of that rank in the Bonanno family in the Bronx for nearly fifty years. But DeFilippo wasn't that effective at times. When he wanted Anthony Donato killed for bragging about a pair of murders he didn't commit, Massino ordered DeFilippo to get the deed done. But when nothing happened after a couple of weeks, Massino said that he called off the hit because "something stinks here."

Massino recalled that his first meeting with Basciano took place at the Casablanca Restaurant. DeFilippo walked up to Massino's table, where he had been dining with his wife, and said that Basciano really wanted to meet the boss. Always leery about meeting mobsters in public settings, Massino agreed to handle the introduction in the kitchen.

"'Joe, meet Vinny,'" said DeFilippo, according to Massino. "'Vinny is a friend of ours in the Bonanno family.'"

"I wished him good luck, and we went back inside," said Massino. DeFilippo later praised Basciano's abilities to the Bonanno boss, saying he was a good money earner and could be counted on to "do work"—mob shorthand for committing murder. "It takes all kinds of meat to make a good sauce," added Massino. "Not everybody is capable of killings."

But Basciano, to continue the food analogy, was tough to swallow and was giving Massino agita. Under Merkl's questioning, Massino brought up the Santoro murder and told how he called Basciano and Bruno Indelicato on the carpet for the killing. He met both men separately down by the "weeds," a section of marsh reeds at the south end of Howard Beach near Massino's house. Massino bridled at Basciano when they met and gave the young soldier a dressing down.

"'How do you kill somebody without getting an okay? You just do what you want to do?'" Massino recalled saying.

Aside from the unsanctioned killing, Massino said he was angry with Basciano for using Indelicato to drive one of the vehicles. A soldier in a different crew, Indelicato couldn't be used for anything without the permission of the family boss, Massino scolded. But for reasons only he knows, Massino simply told Basciano never to do it again. He said the same to Indelicato, adding "You could die for that."

Santoro's murder didn't have any lasting effects on Basciano's crime career, however, since Massino said that by late 2000 he agreed to make him a captain on Vitale's recommendation. Massino also agreed to make Donato a member of the family and put him in Basciano's crew. The Bronx now had two captains, which turned out to be a recipe for more trouble.

The mob existed for money, and Massino was swimming in it, taking cash tributes from people whose names he didn't even know. It came in batches of a few thousand dollars to as much as $30,000 for a cut from the San Gennaro feast or $160,000 at Christmas from the crime family captains. As boss, Massino knew a lot of people by their nicknames: Sal the Iron Worker, Petey Rabbit, Joe Stutters, Vinny Bionic, Bobby Bad Heart, Vinny the Die Maker, and Frank the Fireman. Often Massino didn't know their last names. Names didn't matter much. The money came to him all the same. He stuffed it into boxes in his basement and attic, hard cash totaling millions of dollars. Good thing he never had a fire in the house in Howard Beach.

One of the newer faces in the US Attorney's Office, Merkl had graduated from Columbia Law School, where she distinguished herself as an author of law review notes and articles. When she joined the office in 2002, she took an assignment in the business and securities crime section and got involved in some major fraud cases. By around 2007, the office had been seeing a lot of attrition, including the flight of top-line organized crime attorneys. Hiring was slow, and judges complained privately to reporters about a precipitous drop in indictments in the Brooklyn federal courthouse. By 2008 hiring ramped back up, and the office found its legs again, bringing more indictments, including big mob cases. Merkl formed part of that shift.

Walking Massino through his criminal résumé, she was doing what other prosecutors had only fantasized about. For the first time, an official boss of one of New York's major mob families—and the city really was the epicenter of the Mafia in America—was testifying in court as a government witness. True, other mobsters went public, like the legendary Joseph Valachi, who testified about the mob to Congress in 1962. California wiseguy James Fratianno also talked in and out of court in the 1980s. Acting boss of the Lucchese family, Anthony "Gaspipe" Casso, testified in the 1990s, as did Joseph DeFede in 2003, another acting Lucchese figurehead. But Massino was the biggest turncoat ever.

The story of Massino on the stand made front-page news all over the world. The New York tabloids ate it up, as did the British, Australian, and French news media. The crux of the government case rested on the tapes of Basciano that Massino secretly had made, spellbinding in their detail and stunning in the deception that they had embodied. The conversations, as far as Basciano was concerned, were confidential tête-a-têtes. Yet Massino, as puppet master, pulled the strings and induced Basciano to reveal details that the world was never supposed to hear.

On April 13, Merkl began playing for the jury the two crucial Massino tapes of January 3 and January 7, 2005. Not all parts of the recordings were played. Segments from the January 3 tape that contained comments about the alleged plot to kill prosecutor Andres were excised. After the appeals court ordered that some of the indictment violated protection against double jeopardy, prosecutors issued a new set of charges that didn't contain the Andres allegation. But by and large, the tapes ran as originally recorded. Playing various sections, one at a time, Merkl asked Massino to give his opinion about what he meant and what Basciano meant. Doing so, prosecutors hoped, gave the jury a road map to the case through the mind and the interpretation given by Massino.

Early in the recording of January 3, Massino asks Basciano, "you used, not Dominick, what's his name?"

"When you stated 'you used' what were you referring to?" Merkl asked Massino.

"Who clipped Randy Pizzolo," answered Massino.

A few moments later in the tape, after Massino asks Basciano if he used Cicale and Gambina to "clip" Pizzolo, Basciano states: "I don't know exactly what happened there. I am not sure exactly what happened there, but I gave the order."

Merkl zeroed in on that remark. "What did you understand Basciano to mean by that?"

Massino gave one of his devastating interpretations. "He doesn't know who did the shooting, but he gave the order to clip Randy Pizzolo."

In an effort to show Basciano as uncontrollable and unwilling to consult with other members of the Bonanno ruling committee, Massino said on the tape that the acting boss's failure to consult with his colleagues could lead to factions developing. "You can't kill nobody unless all threes they agree."

"But you know the bad thing about that, Joe? The only problem with that, you have to have faith in one guy . . . you have faith in me?" Basciano replies.

Asked about that exchange, Massino said that Basciano was saying, "He wanted me to have faith in him that he could do whatever he wants without checking with the panel."

In other segments where Basciano says that the order to kill Pizzolo didn't come from the crime family, Massino explained to the jury that Basciano was changing his tune and trying to placate him because Basciano saw how angry the crime boss was about the Pizzolo murder.

Throughout the recordings, Merkl asked Massino for his interpretations. Sometimes his comments proved humorous, as when he explained that a private investigator who had passed him incorrect messages was a "boob." But most of the time, Massino's spin on the words was that the power-hungry Basciano had more or less grabbed the reins of the crime family without his initial approval. Massino told the jury, in no uncertain terms, that Basciano had set up the Pizzolo murder, despite his obfuscations on the tapes to the contrary.

George Goltzer became the twelfth defense attorney to handle Basciano's line of cases. The court had appointed him to take over after Basciano and Savitt clashed so often and so strongly on tactics that an exasperated Garaufis removed the attorney, which the defendant didn't want. A middle-aged lawyer well respected among his colleagues, the silver-haired Goltzer had plenty of experience handling homicide cases, and he had served as president of the prestigious New York State Association of Criminal Defense Lawyers. Still, that didn't prevent Basciano, who prided himself on his own knowledge of the legal system, from disagreeing with him on legal tactics and strategy.

With the Massino tapes at the core of the government's case, Goltzer had to come up with a way of explaining what Basciano was saying to his crime boss when he made such incriminating remarks about Pizzolo. To do that, Goltzer stressed the deadly code of conduct in the mob for murders committed without boss approval. The defense essentially took the line that Basciano, by saying that he approved the killing of Pizzolo, was doing so to spare his good friend Cicale from Massino's wrath and possible deadly retribution. It was a fine line of a story but one that Goltzer stressed in his own opening statement.

"Why would Vincent Basciano say those things on tape if they weren't true?" Goltzer said to the jury. "It is simple. He did it to protect himself and his friend."

If Massino believed for a minute that Cicale had killed Pizzolo on his own, then as far as Basciano was concerned, Cicale was a dead man. If Cicale was a dead man, then Basciano's interests on the street weren't going to be protected, said Goltzer. "He was going to lose his money, and his loved ones wouldn't be supported."

The Massino recordings showed a lot of song and dance between the feared crime boss and Basciano that Goltzer had to admit was fascinating to hear. The defense also believed the tapes would show that Basciano didn't really know while he was in jail that Pizzolo was going to be killed.

It fell to attorney Richard Jasper, the death penalty counsel for Basciano, to flesh out the defense through a cross-examination of Massino that followed the nearly two days of questioning by the government. A tall black man with a thin moustache, Jasper belonged to a group of special lawyers versed in the federal capital punishment statute. He had worked earlier as learned counsel in the case of the Guyanese immigrants who, while convicted of murderous insurance fraud, were spared the death penalty. Jasper had a deliberative approach in court, starting slow in the way he questioned witnesses. Like a good poker player, he pursed his lips and creased his brow with a slight frown as he listened to witnesses, all the while shaping his next question.

Merkl had helped reveal a lot about Massino's criminal past, but Jasper fleshed it out even more, questioning Massino about his longevity in the mob at a time when so many other bosses had gone to jail or the morgue. Jasper drew him out on the details of old murders, showing how Massino had used his cunning and guile to set up victims and the way he coldly did nothing to prevent their deaths.

"When you walked into a room you knew you were powerful, correct?" asked Jasper.

"Correct," answered Massino.

"And you knew in your life what could happen if someone tried to take over a family?"

"Correct."

"You knew what happened to Lilo Galante, right?"

"Yes, I do."

Jasper recalled the classic news photograph of Galante, then acting boss of the Bonanno crime family, slain in the garden of Joe and Mary's Restaurant in Brooklyn, rivulets of blood flowing from his body, a cigar clamped in his jaws in the spasm of death.

"He got popped with a hit team and wound up with a cigar in his mouth on the front pages, right?" the attorney asked.

"Correct," said Massino.

Jasper wasn't trying to catch Massino in a lie but rather showing the depth of his life of crime and his acquiescence to Basciano's takeover as acting boss. Where the government had elided over this cooperation, Jasper pulled from Massino the secret machinations of how he tried to get into the FBI's good graces for months right after his conviction, which he admitted to considering privately for months.

Merkl didn't probe too deeply into the financial arrangements that Massino had with the government. Jasper took the opposite tack. Massino admitted to having about eight homes and pieces of real estate worth about $5 million, still in his family's possession, and which generated about $270,000 a year in rental income. While Massino claimed that he went backward financially after his 2004 conviction, he had to admit that, from his days as a lowly mob associate, he had done very well. True, he had to forfeit around $12 million in assets, mostly cash hidden in his house. But his wife and mother were spared a good deal of property under his deal with the government. Massino's deal also immunized his wife from any prosecution for money laundering or any other federal offenses.

It became clear as Massino testified under Jasper's cross-examination that Basciano had made a brash move by taking the reins of the Bonanno family the way he did. Under normal circumstances such a move could have gotten Basciano killed. In fact, the Genovese crime family, known in New York mob lingo as "the West Side," was prepared to do just that in early 2004 because of how Basciano was throwing his weight around and insulting the other captains. Other gangsters said that Basciano was dressing and acting like the late John Gotti, drawing comparisons to the way the latter mobster secretly engineered the assassination of Castellano in 1985, recalled Massino.

"I could have killed him," said Massino. "They wanted to kill him, and I gave him a pass. The west side come to me when I was on the floor [prison]. They said 'You need help? We'll get rid of him.' I said, 'Let him go. Let him run with it.'"

The overture to kill Basciano came at a point when Massino was already effectively cooperating, so he couldn't have allowed it in any case. But prior to that, Massino needed to keep stability in the crime family, and, despite Basciano throwing his weight around, Massino didn't clip his wings. Later in the taped conversation, Massino kept Basciano off balance, feigning anger over what he had done but letting him think he had some control while he milked him for information about the Pizzolo murder.

As damaging as the tapes had been for the defense, the cross-examination of Massino brought out that Basciano had told him that he had indeed killed Pizzolo. Massino said that it was during a codefendant meeting after Pizzolo was killed that John Spirito told him that the mob associate had been killed. The story had run in the newspapers, said Spirito. At that point, Basciano excused Spirito from the table, sat near Massino, and, according to the Bonanno boss, said he had killed Pizzolo.

Massino's recollection contradicted a version of the jailhouse meeting that Basciano had put forward, according to notes made available to the author. In that version, Basciano mentioned Spirito's remarks to Massino. But unlike Massino's testimony, Basciano made no mention about having killed Pizzolo. It was a major contradiction, but it couldn't be pointed out to the jury because the notes based on Basciano's recollection couldn't be used as evidence. The only way to get that version into the trial would have been to call Basciano as a witness, which wasn't going to happen.

Massino's four days on the witness stand became a watershed moment in the history of organized crime. He impressed many in the courtroom as being a very good witness, one with a solid memory not caught in any major discrepancies. Still, there were gaps in the proof. No tape recordings existed of the earlier conversation that Basciano and Massino had had during a crucial codefendant meeting. The jury had to take Massino's word about what had occurred.

But the prosecution had more than just Massino to parade before the jury. Cicale and Gambina, the man who refused to take part in the Pizzolo homicide, also proved crucial. Gambina had walked away from the plot and, fearful of his life, gladly became a cooperating witness for the FBI. On the witness stand, Gambina repeated the story he had told previously about being called to a Manhattan meeting with Cicale to discuss the murder of Pizzolo in November 2004.

"I didn't like the whole idea," Gambina said. "I thought Dominick was cooperating, they were all cooperating with the government."

The plan as hatched by Cicale was for Gambina to drive Pizzolo to a place where he was supposed to kill another mob associate for a different transgression. Then according to Gambina, he was to drive Pizzolo to a place where they were ostensibly to switch cars, during which Aiello would shoot him. As the plan was laid out, Gambina didn't say yes or no about whether he would participate. Later he told his cousin Aiello that he thought they were being set up and wouldn't do it. Over a period of days, despite requests by Cicale, Gambina said that he stalled about telling him whether he would take part in the hit, feigning a back injury and emotional problems. Cicale then told him to tell Aiello to go with the alternate plan, the details of which Gambina didn't know. The next Gambina heard about Pizzolo, he was dead.

For Basciano, the crucial part of Gambina's testimony was that he never mentioned the acting crime boss's name in the planning or preparation of the Pizzolo killing. It offered a significant contrast to Cicale's testimony. Gambina also said he never heard Cicale call off the murder following Basciano's arrest on November 19, which Cicale claimed that he did.

On May 2, Cicale took the stand to give his version both of his life of crime and the killing of Pizzolo. Much of his testimony repeated what he had said as a witness in Basciano's earlier trial. But to the new jury, it was all fresh. On the street, Cicale was a buff, handsome man. However, years in custody in the witness security program had changed him. Thinner and pale, Cicale had dwindled to a fraction of the imposing gangster he once had been. Yet he had a story to tell.

Under questioning by prosecutor Argentieri, Cicale recounted his miserable days as a child of a Bronx mob associate, his slide into a life of crime, which led to the homicide conviction in Florida, his induction into the Bonanno crime family, and his rise to the rank of captain. But before he could give many details, Argentieri cut to the chase and asked why he killed Pizzolo.

"Randy Pizzolo was killed on the orders of Vincent Basciano," answered Cicale.

While much of the Pizzolo murder had come out previously, this jury was hearing it for the first time. Cicale recounted how Pizzolo, who did well in the beginning, started to screw up in 2004 on construction projects given to him by Basciano. He was making the Bonanno acting boss angry. Added to that were stories coming back from various mobsters that Pizzolo's volatility was causing problems. He was becoming an embarrassment.

Cicale recalled for the jury how he tried to get Pizzolo another chance by having him move to Florida to handle a construction project. But Pizzolo rejected the idea of commuting back and forth from his New York home to the Sunshine State. When Basciano heard that over a meal in a diner, he flushed with anger. "He turned beet red," remembered Cicale, who recounted how he tried to defuse the situation by saying that Pizzolo was in fact going to make the move.

"'Well, he'd better fuckin' go,'" said Basciano, according to Cicale.

Matters kept getting worse, though, and after the incident at the Napa & Sonoma restaurant, where Pizzolo showed up with a gun, Basciano had enough and said the beleaguered mob associate was going to have to be killed, said Cicale.

"Vinny was adamant that Randy was going," testified Cicale. While Cicale tried to stick up for Pizzolo, Basciano wouldn't rescind the order to kill him. "'I don't want to hear it. This kid is going,'" said Basciano, according to Cicale.

Yet as fate had it, Basciano got arrested, and Cicale canceled the hit, sparing Pizzolo's life, at least for the moment. Mancuso was now acting boss and didn't know about the contract on Pizzolo, so Cicale said he lied when asked if there were any murders that had to be done.

"If he didn't know, I wasn't going to tell him, and I wanted to spare Randy's life," said Cicale.

But somehow Mancuso did find out about the previous order to whack Pizzolo—how he learned was never made clear—and told Cicale that the hit was on and to get it done.

"'If anybody has anything to say, I gave the order,'" said Mancuso, Cicale told the jury.

This on-again-off-again nature of the Pizzolo murder plot as described by Cicale became a point of defense for Basciano's attorneys. They tried in vain to get Garaufis to allow the jury to consider that there were actually two conspiracies to murder Pizzolo. Only one of the plots, the one put in motion by Mancuso, really counted, Goltzer insisted. But Garaufis wouldn't make that point later in his charge to the jury.

Aiello's murder of Pizzolo on Monitor Street took place on a cold, wet night when Cicale remembered he had planted plenty of alibis, including his attendance at the Nets game, to divert attention from himself. The day after the killing, Cicale said that he faked ignorance about Pizzolo's whereabouts, except with Aiello. It was at a Bronx body shop that Aiello described the dead man's last moments, including the way he extended his hand in friendship when his assassin approached him from behind the lumberyard and started shooting, testified Cicale.

Cicale said he kept up the pretense of shock over Pizzolo's death and ordered his crew to attend the funeral. He also spread the false rumor that the murder had taken place over a drug deal. Cicale went to the wake because not to do so would look bad, particularly since he had been asked to be the godfather to Pizzolo's child.

"I went and viewed the body. I felt bad, felt ashamed, and that was basically it," he told the jury.

Goltzer's cross-examination of Cicale didn't shake him on the basic story that Basciano initially had ordered Pizzolo's murder. But the defense attorney's questioning and the answers it elicited from the sometimes hostile and snippy witness brought out some major contradictions with what Gambina had said. Cicale claimed that Gambina had agreed to kill Pizzolo when Gambina had said in court that he was noncommittal and later told his cousin Aiello that he wouldn't take part in the hit. Pressed if he knew of any doubts that Gambina had expressed about the plan, Cicale answered: "It wasn't to my knowledge."

Another contradiction occurred over Gambina's claim that Cicale had told everyone in his crew to "strap up" and carry guns in case a war broke out among factions in the crime family. Cicale insisted that he never told Gambina that, especially after he didn't take part in Pizzolo's killing. There was also a question about Christmas money collected in late 2004. Gambina said Cicale asked him for $10,000 to be given to Massino. Cicale said the money was for Basciano.

The defense was trying to undermine Cicale about the allegation about a fake murder plot concocted to frame Basciano. According to court filings, Cicale allegedly tried to get another jail inmate to say that a guard tried to get an inmate to kill him as a favor for Basciano. Asked about the plot, Cicale responded sharply "Absolutely not, that is incorrect."

Goltzer ended his questioning of Cicale by bringing up an old story that the witness had been dogged early in his career by the allegation that he had a "bad wire" on him, mob talk for being an informant. Cicale admitted that was the case in 2000, that he had that reputation as he began to hang around with Basciano, but Vinny from the Bronx backed him, said Cicale.

"Vinny Basciano stood up for you?" Goltzer asked.

"After extensively checking into my background, yes, Vincent Basciano stood up for me," said Cicale.

"Obviously, he didn't check well enough," Goltzer remarked.

21

THE TRIAL OF VINCENT BASCIANO HAD LASTED NEARLY A MONTH. ON May 9, 2011, both sides made their summations for the jury. US attorney Stephen Frank gave the government's version, while Goltzer did the same for the defense. The summations went on for hours.

Frank noted that Basciano had already conceded that he belonged to the Bonanno crime family, having risen to the rank of acting boss. But while Basciano admitted on the Massino tapes to playing a role in the killing of Pizzolo, Basciano was making the improbable argument that what he was saying was all untrue, according to Frank. "He admits he played his role in the murder of Randolph Pizzolo to Joseph Massino but denies that he meant it when he said it. He admits what he can't deny. He denies the one thing he can't admit, the one thing that would make him guilty of the crimes for which he's charged today."

But it wasn't just the tapes that implicated Basciano in the hit. In early December 2004, after Pizzolo was dead, he made another damning admission during a codefendant meeting in the local federal jail. After John Spirito mentioned to Massino that the newspapers had carried a story about Pizzolo's murder, Basciano told Spirito to walk away and then told Massino that he had in fact ordered the killing of the mob associate and knew who made up the hit team, the prosecutor told the jury. "Why after Johnny Joe said they killed Randy Pizzolo would he [Basciano] immediately say he did it? And why if he didn't order that murder, how would he know who the original hit team was, including the member of that team who backed out, Joey Gambina?"

"The defendant's own words are devastating evidence, devastating evidence of his guilt," Frank told the jury. There was no other decision they could make but to find him guilty.

Goltzer addressed the jury for about three hours, just a little less than the prosecution, and he knew he had an uphill fight. He challenged the notion that Basciano had motive to kill Pizzolo. Far from a liability in the construction business, as Cicale had said, Pizzolo actually performed well for Basciano by meeting a critical deadline that allowed the condominium project on Schurz Avenue to complete fifteen town houses instead of eight, said Goltzer. Pizzolo also had put together a group of investors for more construction work.

"Everybody knew for years what Randy Pizzolo was about, and they also knew he had good connections. He could make you a lot of money," Goltzer argued.

But what about those tapes? Goltzer said they captured Basciano word-for-word as he spun a fake story about what had happened to Pizzolo. It was done, he said, to protect Cicale from Massino's wrath. "You cannot on this record discount the assertion that Vincent Basciano lied, combined truth with half truth, to take upon himself the justification for killing Randy to save Dominick Cicale." Goltzer asked the jurors to acquit Basciano of the charges.

The next day, May 10, Judge Garaufis charged the jury and sent them to begin deliberations. The first note they sent out asked for a replay of the Massino jailhouse tapes. The panel was focusing immediately on a key piece of evidence that either would sink Basciano or, as Goltzer had argued, show that he was lying about having ordered the murder to save Cicale.

When the late John Gotti had gone on trial in 1992 for racketeering, murder, and other crimes, his trial had lasted about six weeks and had plenty of tapes as well as a star witness in turncoat Sammy "The Bull" Gravano. The jury in that case stunned everyone by deliberating for only about thirteen hours before convicting Gotti on all counts. In Basciano's case, the jury mulled for three full days. Aside from a few notes about evidence and testimony, it was difficult to divine what was going on.

But privately the defense attorneys wondered whether they might have raised enough reasonable doubt about the Pizzolo murder. There was always a shot, despite the starkness of the Massino tapes, that the jury might find just enough ambiguity in what Basciano was caught saying to make the case that he really didn't give the order to kill Pizzolo. Vitale had once testified that when the mob set somebody up for a hit that a friend of the victim was often used. "Only your friend can hurt you," Vitale explained. Perhaps the government reliance on so many turncoats—men who had spent a lifetime deceiving their friends—had soured the jury.

On May 16, 2011, the jury finally sent out a note at around 2:30 in the afternoon saying that they had reached a unanimous verdict. The panel had adjourned the previous Friday, and each member had the weekend to think over the case. That kind of recess often brings news of a verdict during the next day of deliberations. Setting the beginning of deliberations at May 10, the jurors had spent about three and a half days considering Basciano's fate. The jury entered the courtroom at 2:48 p.m. The forewoman told Garaufis that they had reached a decision then gave the verdict sheet to courtroom deputy Joseph Reccoppa.

"On the charge of conspiracy to murder Randolph Pizzolo in aid of racketeering, how do you find the defendant, Vincent Basciano, guilty or not guilty?" Reccoppa asked the forewoman.

"Guilty," she replied.

Basciano didn't flinch, but his face again flushed, just as it had when he was convicted of murdering Santoro.

They announced the same verdict of guilt for the substantive murder charge as well as the use of a firearm. Including the quick polling of each juror to see if they all agreed, the whole process of taking the verdict took just four minutes. The jurors left the courtroom at 2:52 p.m. But they would return again soon to answer a question of life or death.

22

RICHARD JASPER NOW HAD HIS WORK CUT OUT FOR HIM.

The real battle in Vincent Basciano's case no longer revolved around innocence or guilt. Now the jury was going to grapple with the momentous question of whether he deserved to be executed for the murder of Randolph Pizzolo. As death penalty counsel, Jasper had to ensure that Basciano lived.

The last big-name mobster was executed in New York in 1944. Louis "Lepke" Buchalter was electrocuted to death at Sing Sing for the murder of a Brooklyn candy store owner. Actually, a total of three people were put to death for that crime, but Buchalter's name is most remembered.

Whether Basciano earned the dubious honor of following Buchalter to an executioner's room would play out in what amounted to a second trial. While the first fought over the facts, now the government and defense had to battle over where the balance of moral power lay in the case. Were there enough aggravating factors, including Basciano's possible future dangerousness even if in prison, that merited the death penalty? Or did mitigating factors exist—such as gangsters like Joseph Massino having body counts to their credit that dwarfed what Basciano had done—to push the pendulum to a life sentence without parole?

Under federal rules, all of the evidence from the guilt phase of the case—the murders of Pizzolo and Santoro, Basciano's alleged solicitations to murder Patty DeFilippo, Sal Vitale, and others—was admissible. Pizzolo's daughter Constance Cordero was going to testify about the impact of her father's death on her. There was also going to be one major addition.

The prosecution could put before the jury the allegations that Basciano had wanted to kill prosecutor Greg Andres. Kept out of the guilt phase of the case, that evidence now had relevance for the jury in considering the penalty that Basciano would face.

Under federal law in a death penalty case, the prosecution has the burden of proving all of the aggravating factors, including the alleged solicitation to murder Andres, beyond a reasonable doubt. The defense also had burden of proof, albeit less stringent. Basciano's lawyers had to show by a "preponderance of the evidence" that the mitigating elements, such as the value of his life to others, had been established. In other words, the factors had to be more likely true than not. Judge Garaufis also told the jury that their decision was to be an individual and moral one, not dictated by adding up the various aggravating and mitigating factors and seeing which were more numerous.

On May 25, 2011, assistant US attorney Jack Dennehy spoke briefly to the jurors and told them how Basciano had wanted to kill nine other people over the years, including the girlfriend of Dominick Cicale who blabbed to Basciano's wife about his child with Debra Kalb. That was enough, said Dennehy, for Basciano to receive the death penalty for the murder of Pizzolo. Prison wasn't a good enough punishment because Basciano passed messages to the outside world in an effort to run the Bonanno family, argued Dennehy.

When it came to his turn, Jasper said that prison would control Basciano just fine. His destination, the notorious federal supermax prison in Florence, Colorado, was the toughest, most secure facility around, said Jasper. "Life as he knows it, as a result of these conditions, is over. No suits, no shirts, no ties, no 'Vinny Gorgeous,' the rest of his life in a prison to be determined by the Bureau of Prisons and the attorney general."

There were also plenty of people equally culpable or more so in the death of Pizzolo than Basciano, argued Jasper, and they weren't facing the death penalty. Among them were Cicale and Aiello, he stressed.

It's always dangerous to blame the victim for his misfortune. But Jasper had to raise the touchy issue of whether Pizzolo bore some responsibility for his own death. Clearly, Pizzolo played the role of tough guy on the street and wanted to be a member of La Cosa Nostra. To become a part of the life, Pizzolo "willingly participated in dangerous and illegal activities," said Jasper.

"What I want to be real clear about, did Randy Pizzolo deserve to die? No, No, No. But you know what? He took actions that contributed to his death." That willingness of the victim was why Basciano should wake up in prison for the rest of his life until, as Jasper said, "he dies in God's time and not man's."

Joseph Massino, a man who orchestrated twelve murders, wasn't facing the death penalty either, and Jasper wasn't going to let the jury overlook that. In fact, Massino was hoping to see "the light at the end of the tunnel" and get out of prison while he still had time to enjoy life, the defense attorney added.

In jail when he was coaxing information from Basciano and taping it, Massino salted the conversations by saying how much he valued life. Basciano noted the hypocrisy, given the boss's record of homicide. Now Massino sat in a position to give evidence that could lead to his former underboss's execution.

When he took the stand again on May 25, Massino first testified about how he refused to give Basciano permission to kill a number of people, including DeFilippo, Vitale, the parents of witnesses like Joseph D'Amico as well as Lynette Ayuso, Cicale's girlfriend. The girlfriend issue sounded like something from a telenovela. Basciano supposedly told Massino that Angela had caught him walking out of Debra Kalb's house. According to Massino, Ayuso not only told Angela about little Anthony but even brought her to the girlfriend's house. It was Angela, according to Massino, who told her husband not to blame Ayuso.

"His wife told him, 'No, you can't kill her because it is your fault. You are wrong for doing what you did,'" said Massino, recalling Basciano's description of events.

"I thought he was crazy," Massino testified when asked how he reacted when Basciano asked for permission to kill Ayuso. "'Kill her for what? It is your fault.'"

Massino's main value to the government was his ability to flesh out evidence on the alleged plot to kill Andres. Evidence existed that Basciano broached the idea twice, once to Cicale while both were still out of jail, and then in late 2004 when Massino and Basciano met in jail. The first incident came, according to trial testimony, when Basciano said he thought Massino had sent him a message from jail to kill the prosecutor. Under questioning by Merkl, Massino said that it had been Basciano who had asked him during a meeting in the courthouse bullpen around November 23, 2004, for permission to kill Andres.

"We were talking about everything, and he said to me, 'Let me kill this guy when he comes out of the restaurant, Campagnola's,'" said Massino. "I said, 'Let me think about it.'"

By then, Massino secretly had been giving evidence to the FBI, and he testified that he immediately told the agents about what Basciano had said. The bullpen conversation wasn't recorded, but by early January 2005 Massino began taping Basciano to help establish a new indictment against him. The recordings never captured Basciano bluntly saying that he wanted to kill Andres. Instead, Massino got him to admit that the subject had come up in their earlier bullpen conversation. On tape, Basciano repeatedly says "Forget about it" when Massino presses the subject.

It never came out at trial, but records indicate that Basciano's recollection of the November 23 bullpen meeting closely matched Massino's—with one major exception. After Massino complained that Andres had embarrassed his wife, Josephine, by disclosing in court information about an old girlfriend, Basciano remarked, supposedly in jest, that "instead of killing all these guys you should have killed Greg Andres." Massino then replied, "Let me think about it," according to the records.

On cross-examination, Goltzer wanted to plant the seed of the idea with the jury that Massino anxiously wanted to deliver the best evidence he could to the FBI because he himself was hanging under the threat of the death penalty because of the Sciascia murder. "You knew at that point if you convince the prosecutors that if Basciano really wanted to kill a prosecutor, you might find a way out of the death penalty, right?" asked Goltzer.

"I didn't think about it," replied Massino.

Then, under questioning about whether the FBI initially doubted his claim that Basciano had talked about killing Andres, Massino seemed noticeably uncomfortable. "I don't recall," he said.

Moments later, Goltzer asked again about Massino's truthfulness on the death threat issue. "Did anybody tell you that you had to prove you were telling the truth?"

"Well, I failed two lie detector tests," Massino said, almost boasting.

The line stunned Goltzer, and total silence filled the room. The defense had just received a golden gift from the former mob boss. That Massino had failed two lie detector tests wasn't admissible in the case. But Massino had blurted it out, making the issue fair game.

Taking an instant to recover from Massino's gratuitous remark, Goltzer asked him to tell the jury when the lie detector failures had occurred. Some time around December 10, 2004, Massino replied. Goltzer asked Massino if the polygraph expert asked whether Basciano had suggested taking out Andres and he, Massino, had answered "yes" to the question. That was true, Massino said. Goltzer asked what the test showed. If he had been untruthful, it strongly suggested that Massino had lied. But the government objected to that last query on the grounds that it involved a legal conclusion that Massino couldn't make. Goltzer withdrew the question and moved on.

Yet Massino's admission had done damage. Lawyers in the court-room at the time said some jurors looked visibly surprised by Massino's statement. One even later told the defense lawyers that, had she known of the lie detector issue, she might have voted for an acquittal in the guilt phase.

Constance Pizzolo Cordero, a mother of two young daughters, tes-tified about the long-term effects of her father's murder. Although he was having major problems in his life, he always found time to talk with her each day, said Cordero. "It was a nice relationship we had."

Watching her younger daughter dance by standing on her husband's feet reminded her of how she used to do the same with her own dad. Both of Cordero's daughters never met their grandfather. But to make up for the loss, Cordero said that she keeps her father's picture around the house and took them to the cemetery. "We kind of camp out there sometimes so they know who Grandpa Randy is, and they say Grandpa Randy is in heaven."

Basciano's lawyers also called witnesses to show his good qualities. Hair colorist Damarys Mojica had worked in Basciano's salon Hello Gorgeous in the 1990s. When her son became ill and her husband lost his job, Mojica remembered that Basciano helped her financially. The money allowed her son to pull through a bout of mental illness and thrive as an adult, she said. "My question in my life is, did Vinny save my son's life? Did he save my marriage? I don't know. All I know is that, without bat-ting an eye, he was first" to help, she said.

Usually, family members of someone fighting the death penalty take the stand. But in Basciano's case he didn't want any of his sons—including Debra Kalb's little Anthony—or his ex-wife, Angela, to do that. He also flat-out refused to have his attorneys present information that he may have had an abusive childhood at the hands of his father, which Basciano said wasn't true. Basciano also didn't want his cousin, one of his best friends, to testify. But Stephen DiCarmine had his own ideas.

Angela Basciano and her four sons, from left to right: Michael, Joseph, Vincent Jr., and Stephen HANDOUT PHOTO

At the time he testified, DiCarmine was working as an attorney with the law firm of Dewey & LeBouf, which made international headlines for filing for bankruptcy in 2012. It was the kind of life that Basciano never experienced. DiCarmine said that he and Basciano grew up in Yonkers in a tight-knit family environment. Traditional Italian dinners took place on Friday nights and Sunday afternoons. When parents were playing cards in other parts of the apartments, DiCarmine, Basciano, and his two brothers horsed around the house.

"Vinny, how could I describe him? A bit of a daredevil for a kid," said DiCarmine. "He was the one that everybody followed."

At times Basciano and DiCarmine hung out down by the Hudson Line rail line and passed the time by placing coins on the tracks to watch passing trains flatten them. Basciano also jumped from a trestle onto the top of a train and then rolled off into the gravel rail bed, his cousin remembered. "That was Vinny," said his cousin. But regaling the jurors with tales of derring-do wasn't going to win much sympathy. To show more of Basciano's human side, DiCarmine recounted how he ministered to his dying mother and pitched in to help a female cousin find a home after she had a child out of wedlock and her parents threw her out of their house.

"I don't want to imagine a world where he doesn't exist," said DiCarmine. "His sons, his wife feel the same way. They would be sick. They don't want to see their father die." Angela Basciano had said that she would marry him again if she could, according to DiCarmine.

Summations on the death penalty issue didn't stray much from what the lawyers had said in the penalty phase. Prosecutor Argentieri, taking aim at the argument that the public could be protected from Basciano if he got a life sentence, said he had solicited murders even while in custody. "This is a defendant who will not be stopped and who will not be changed. For all of these reasons, he has earned the sentence of death."

Attacking the government's argument that Basciano would remain a public danger while in prison, Jasper reminded the jurors of the testimony of defense expert and forensic psychologist Thomas Joseph Reidy, who described the draconian conditions of the supermax federal prison where Basciano would go. The layout kept prisoners disoriented and mostly alone. They can't even see the nearby Rocky Mountains from their cells, said Jasper.

While Argentieri drenched her summation in blood by reminding jurors of the killings of Santoro and Pizzolo—as well as Basciano's solicitations to kill others—Jasper played the moral card. The death penalty isn't an accounting game, where jurors tot up points to see whether death wins out or life. It is at its very core a moral decision, which Jasper constantly reminded the jury. One juror, standing fast on a decision to sentence Basciano to life in prison, would spare his life. Just one vote among the panel could stop the death penalty.

"I am asking you to say no to death. I am asking you to say yes to life," said Jasper.

Jasper also hit heavily on facts quite clear from the testimony: Killers like Massino weren't facing the death penalty. Others involved in Pizzolo's murder weren't facing capital punishment either. If the government was asking that Basciano be executed because he "killed and killed again," then what about Massino? He also killed repeatedly.

After the summations, the jury left the courtroom at 3:45 p.m. on June 1, 2011. They held the life of Vincent Basciano in their hands. Then, to the surprise of many, the panel sent out a note at 5:32 p.m.—just about the time that Garaufis was going to send them home for the day. They announced that they had reached a verdict. The deliberations on Basciano's life had taken less than two hours.

On the verdict sheet, jurors had to indicate whether they thought that they had found beyond a reasonable doubt that Basciano had killed Pizzolo and Santoro and had participated in other uncharged murders. The jurors all answered "yes" to those questions. As to the uncharged murders, attempted murders, and murder solicitations—including Andres—the jury said that the government had proved that aggravating factor beyond a reasonable doubt. However, the verdict form had only the option to say yes or no. It didn't indicate which of those separate serious crimes had been proved to the jury's satisfaction. In a twist, the jury voted "no" to the question of whether Basciano would commit acts of violence in the future while in jail, a signal of what was coming next.

By a majority, the jury voted to spare the life of Basciano and send him to another life term in prison. They unanimously agreed that Pizzolo's life of crime had contributed to his death.

Then, on their own, ten jurors noted on page six of the verdict sheet another factor that had swayed them. "There are other members of organized crime that have admitted to an equal or greater number of serious crimes that are not facing the death penalty, much less incarcerated." By that statement, the jurors showed that the conduct of Massino and Vitale in taking part in numerous homicides had weighed in the calculation that death for Basciano was the wrong decision. The defense had clearly blunted the impact of Massino's testimony in the penalty phase by stressing his own body count and the good deal that he had negotiated for the financial well-being of his wife and family.

By notching up bodies and staying away from capital punishment in the process, Joseph Massino had given the jury enough justification to save Basciano's life. It was another significant irony. The government tried to use him as an instrument for the death penalty, but Massino begot Basciano's salvation.

Defense attorneys Jasper, Goltzer, and Stafford and paralegal Lucy Kim rejoiced at the verdict. Basciano shot a smile to his sons in the courtroom. He had confided to friends and acquaintances that he didn't think the jury would vote for the death penalty. On East Tremont Avenue later that day, people went up to Angela Basciano and told her that they had prayed for Vincent. The old neighborhood where Vinny Gorgeous once held sway exuded a collective sigh of relief. The real battle all along had been over whether the defendant would be executed. Basciano had won. He had his life, such as it would be.

Garaufis allowed the jurors to meet with the defense and government attorneys in private to discuss the verdict. The defense agreed. The government didn't at first but tagged along, remembered Goltzer.

"Can I meet with the jurors too, judge?" asked Basciano.

"There's no chance in the world," answered Garaufis.

23

Because of the jury's decision, the sentencing of Vincent Basciano on July 20, 2011, was a foregone conclusion. Garaufis gave him life without parole. Basciano was Colorado-bound. But that didn't make the day a nonevent.

Constance Cordero addressed the court to say how the death of her father had created a void in her life that couldn't be filled. When once she could pick up the telephone and talk to her father about the good and the bad in life, now there was nothing.

As was his right, Basciano stood up to speak on his own behalf. He rambled about minutiae. He never apologized for anything, nor did he even mention the Pizzolo homicide. Instead he complained that solitary conditions had hamstrung his ability to defend himself. Ironically, the government had offered earlier in the case to lift the special administrative measures if Basciano agreed to monitored visits. In what may have been an irrational decision borne of so much time in solitude, Basciano refused the government's request. He also stated that the Massino tapes had done him in.

Garaufis could have pronounced the sentence without fanfare. But instead, as he has often done in the Bonanno crime family cases, he read from prepared remarks shaped by his experience of handling over one hundred prosecutions of borgata members. Three of those trials gave Garaufis a unique perspective on Basciano.

Said Garaufis: "Basciano is intelligent and has many other qualities that would have permitted him to live a productive and law-abiding life.

Yet he did not choose such a life. He chose a life of crime, violence, and greed. He chose to wound, maim, and kill—all to enrich himself and advance in organized crime."

Garaufis also had words for future mobsters, warning them from a career in crime. There was nothing romantic or redeeming about organized crime, and there was nothing to its code of conduct. It was life without love and honor in the blood that it spilled, the judge said.

"However La Cosa Nostra may be portrayed on the popular screen, Basciano stands here today, proof of its reality—a crumbling facade, beneath which lies a bleak, pathetic, and ignorant life. It is time that the mob's members abandon La Cosa Nostra—'this thing of ours'—and find something that is actually worth calling their own."

Garaufis harbored no illusions that the mob would dry up, its members turning to lawful lives. Yet he hit Basciano with the life sentence, imposing no fine since the defendant seemed not to have any money. Earlier in the case, the government had secured an order that forced Basciano to forfeit $5 million, a Pyrrhic victory since Basciano didn't have any more assets. Basciano had to pay a $300 mandatory assessment, although it was unclear how he would cover even that.

There had been a time when Basciano had money coming in hand over fist. He had numerous businesses that made him a good living. The construction work alone was doing extremely well, and he could have become a noteworthy developer in the Bronx if he had the time or inclination. He knew that the legitimate life was the better way to go, even if he did a bit of tax cheating by skimming from a business. At least the prison time for tax evasion wasn't as bad as racketeering.

"We have to have legitimate rackets. Why can't you and I have something so if we get pinched we see daylight?" Basciano once mused to Tartaglione. "You and I open up a topless joint, put it under somebody else's name. We're taking $30,000 a week from the joint, you and I. Big fucking deal. We get pinched, what's we gonna get, two year?"

Between business deals and his rackets in the Bronx, Basciano had a life that could have kept him in the middle level of the crime family and off the radar of law enforcement. But after Massino's arrest in 2003, Basciano's hunger for power pushed him into the administration of the Bonanno family. But that also put him in a position for Tartaglione to tape him. Basciano's bravado about the Santoro homicide gave the FBI enough to arrest him in 2004. Then followed the fateful conversations with Massino. In the end, Massino did Basciano no favors by giving him the power that he craved.

Had Basciano not taken a leadership position in the Bonanno family, he likely would have stayed outside the FBI crosshairs—perhaps for years. But eventually he would have been arrested for something. The domino effect of informants would have implicated him at some point in the Santoro and Pizzolo murders. Basciano rose in the mob at a time when turning cooperating witness offered the best retirement plan around for old gangsters like Massino. Newer members like Cicale, brought into the life by nothing more than the quest for money, had no deep-seated loyalty and also easily became turncoats.

Basciano remains a true believer to this day.

"I feel like I lived my life in vain," said Basciano in a letter to Kalb. "All the things I believed in and held sacred seem to have been a fraud. It seems that I only believed in them and I'm one of the few that followed the rules. But I'd rather die than to compromise my values!"

It would be easy at this point to wrap up the story of Vinny Gorgeous as another morality tale about the Mafia and how it leads its members to lives that end in prison or on a morgue table. But as the case unfolded over nearly seven years, more than that happened. The government had a duty to bring the killers of Randy Pizzolo and Frank Santoro to justice. The resulting indictment and conviction of Basciano demonstrated the FBI's winning approach to building racketeering cases against the mob as well as the strength of the prosecution. Rather than take little bites, the

FBI thought grandly and used old files, photographs, and the testimony of retired agents to make big cases. The approach had worked against the late John Gotti, Joseph Massino, and now Vincent Basciano.

However, the Department of Justice's use of the death penalty seems suspect on a number of levels. First, it looks like the decision to pursue capital punishment against Basciano came from a desire to punish him for his alleged aim of killing prosecutor Greg Andres. Ephraim Savitt's recollection of questions raised to him about the so-called "hit list" during his meeting with the department's death penalty committee strongly suggested that officials had that in the forefront of their minds.

As it emerged during Basciano's case, the hit list represented nothing more than a legal red herring. Still, prosecutors used it for a long time as a rationale for keeping him in solitary. In the end, the government never used the list in the trial, which Basciano believed, in a convoluted way, would have shown to the jury that the government's case rose up on a foundation of falsehoods. Then the allegation that Basciano had solicited Massino for permission to kill Andres became part of the indictment against him, only to be dropped after an appeals court dismissed parts of the charges. We may never know what actually happened in that jailhouse conversation between Massino and Basciano on November 23, 2004. The talk wasn't recorded, and failing two lie detector tests called Massino's recollection into doubt. But it is entirely possible that Massino later played the role of marionette to Basciano as puppet. In the January 3, 2005, jailhouse tape, Massino finesses words and connotations in such a way that suggested that Basciano had broached the subject of "taking out" the prosecutor. Massino had spent a lifetime playing lesser men to his advantage.

We also have to give consideration to the race card. The vast majority of federal defendants who receive death penalty eligibility are either black or Hispanic. The only person ever to get the death penalty in Brooklyn had been the young black man Ronell Wilson. Basciano was the second white defendant certified for the death penalty in the Brooklyn federal district in nearly two decades. The defense bar's conventional wisdom—unsubstantiated in the Basciano case—holds that the Department of Justice was looking for a man of Basciano's demographics to help balance the racial disparity in federal death penalty cases. As of June 2012, according to the Federal Death Penalty Resource Counsel, the attorney general had authorized for the death penalty some 484 defendants. Of those, 247 (51 percent) were black and 127 (26 percent) were white, with the remainder (27 percent) being Hispanic or belonging to other ethnic groups.

But the real lesson in the Basciano case may be that the government may have come to rely too much over the years on cooperating witnesses, failing to see how much trouble they gave jurors trying to balance the moral equation in a capital punishment case. It's not impossible for a jury to sentence a defendant to death in a federal case when the prosecution relies on cooperating witnesses who also commit heinous crimes. Around the same time that the jury spared Basciano's life, a different jury in New Haven, Connecticut, voted for death in the case of the head of a crack distribution ring convicted of two brutal murders. The defendant had hog-tied and beat his victims to death with a baseball bat. A key government witness had pleaded guilty to murder but didn't face the death penalty.

Yet there comes a point when the wrongs of the witness override the crimes of the defendant, as happened in the penalty phase in Basciano's case. No matter how truthful Massino may have been in the guilt phase of the trial—and he did seem to be a good witness—the man had a lot of blood on his hands. While the government argued about the strength of his credibility, it couldn't shift the moral weight toward death for the defendant, even after spending an estimated $5 million to $10 million on the prosecution. It didn't seem to matter how many acts of murder, attempted murder, or solicitations to commit murder the jury may have put on Basciano's shoulders. Crimes of violence remain, regardless of whether the perpetrator suddenly sees the light and cooperates against someone else who committed the same crimes.

In *No Simple Victory: World War Two In Europe 1939–1945*, historian Norman Davies grapples with the notion that the conflict in that part of the world didn't take place just between our enemy Adolph Hitler and our ally Joseph Stalin, both in their own strange alliance once. That struggle also took place between two similarly evil men. As one reviewer noted, the moral equation didn't change. "If one finds two gangsters fighting each other, it is no valid approach at all to round on one and lay off the other. The only valid test is whether they deserve the label of gangsters," writes Davies.

As the jury found in Basciano's case, it really was hard to distinguish him from Massino on one basic level. Both were gangsters—successful, yes—but gangsters nevertheless. But when it came time to weigh the morality of the death penalty, it was impossible to overlook what Massino had done in his life of crime in order to take his loyal and eager supplicant's life. Massino admitted to twelve murders; Basciano was convicted of two and may have committed more, attempted others, and solicited permission to do yet more. We may never know what the jury found on that element of the case, but we do know that the death penalty couldn't win on that kind of score. It was Vincent Basciano's one victory.

Epilogue

VINCENT BASCIANO ARRIVED AT ADX FLORENCE, THE MOST SECURE FEDERAL prison in America, in August 2011. A cell of about seven feet by twelve—roughly eighty-seven square feet of living space—circumscribes his life most of the time. The poured concrete slabs allow no edges or places to hide things. He has a television set, shower stall, sink, and a toilet without a seat. The shower, according to an expert familiar with the facility, comes on for about ten minutes and then turns off automatically to prevent inmates from clogging the drains and flooding the cell. He takes his meals in his cell, and there is a daily pickup for outgoing mail. He can exercise outdoors in a special pen or cage and does that on average about five times a week for two hours at a time. During recreation he is allowed to communicate with other prisoners, something he couldn't do while under solitary in New York. The exercise yard is situated so the inmates can't see the Rocky Mountain range to the west.

I asked Basciano for an interview and for comments about his situation. He courteously declined. According to friends and those who know him, Basciano seems to be adjusting well to life in Florence, even though he remains in his cell for on average twenty-three hours a day. The food is to his liking—exercise keeps his weight down—and he is taking part in various prison televised courses such as astronomy, geography, and history that he hopes will allow him to step down into less-restrictive housing. Basciano can have visitors, although he is not allowed physical contact and must speak over a telephone in a secure and monitored visiting area. He spends his time reading, exercising, and writing to family and friends. He finds writing cumbersome, though, since he can only use pens or pencils about four inches long.

Meanwhile, Joseph Massino has snatched a victory of sorts. Under his deal with the government, Massino's wife was shielded from any risk of prosecution for money laundering. He also kept eight pieces of real estate in the family, some of which no doubt spin off rental income. Massino at some point will ask the court for a reduction in his life sentence, a motion granted with regularity to other cooperating witnesses in organized crime cases.

In January 2012 Basciano filed with the court a lengthy motion attacking his sentence and the verdict in this case. The seventy-five-page handwritten document reveals many of what Basciano believes were inequities in his case. Boiled down to its essentials, Basciano's motion contends that the government consciously withheld from the defense information that would have shown that Cicale had testified falsely or at the very least had been contradicted by other witnesses, notably Gambina. Translated into legalese, the argument alleges that prosecutors committed a so-called *Brady* violation, which appeals courts take seriously. Basciano's arguments are intricate, sometimes convoluted, and not expressed with the skills of an attorney. But he believes that evidence exists, improperly withheld from his lawyers in the 2006 trial, that thereby polluted his later cases.

"Due to the prosecutors continued non-compliance, the court's decision making process was effected and my constitutional due process rights denied," wrote Basciano.

Limited to a cumbersome writing implement and the sparse amount of legal material he can have in his cell, Basciano asked the court to appoint legal counsel to help him. The court system had already appointed him counsel to handle his appeal in the Pizzolo murder case. Still, that didn't stop Basciano from filing another motion seeking to disqualify Garaufis from deciding his January 2012 motion on the grounds that the jurist was biased against him.

It will take years for the various appeals to be adjudicated. In the meantime, if he can't see the nearby Rockies, Vincent Basciano can at least continue to breathe the fresh Colorado mountain air.

Anthony Aiello (Bonanno soldier), after pleading guilty in 2008 to conspiracy in the murder of Randolph Pizzolo, was sentenced to thirty years. He is serving his time at Raybrook Federal Correctional Institution in upstate New York. He is scheduled for release in May 2031.

Greg Andres (prosecutor), after a career as an assistant US attorney in Brooklyn dismantling the Bonanno crime family, did a stint as a deputy attorney general in Washington, D.C., during the tenure of US Attorney General Eric Holder. In 2012 Andres resigned from government service and became counsel in the litigation department of the New York law firm of Davis, Polk, & Wardell, LLP.

Nicole Argentieri (prosecutor) is deputy chief of the organized crime and gang section of the Brooklyn US Attorney's Office.

Angela Basciano (ex-wife) remains a resident of the Bronx and keeps in touch with her former spouse. In Bronx State Supreme Court, she sued her former business partner, Kim Van Zandt, over hundreds of thousands of dollars allegedly owed her. Van Zandt's husband, Robert Jr., was found shot dead in the swimming pool of his Scarsdale, New York, home in September 2011. He was under investigation at the time for running a Ponzi scheme. Investigators consider Van Zandt's death a suicide.

Benjamin Brafman (defense attorney) maintains a high-profile white-collar defense practice in Manhattan. In 2011 Brafman helped defend former World Bank president Dominique Strauss-Kahn against charges involving an alleged sexual assault of a maid in the Sofitel Hotel. The case made international headlines, ending after prosecutors dropped the case against Strauss-Kahn when problems developed with the credibility of the complaining witness.

Michael Breslin (FBI agent) is a supervisory special agent for the FBI in Philadelphia.

Joseph Cammarano Sr. (Bonanno captain) pleaded guilty in February 2005 to a charge of racketeering for conspiracy to commit murder and a charge of illegal gambling. He received a sentence of fifteen years in prison, serving his time in Butner Federal Correctional Institution in North Carolina, the same complex where infamous Ponzi schemer Bernard Madoff is serving his 150-year sentence. His attorney says that Cammarano has a number of health problems.

Dominick Cicale (former Bonanno captain), after testifying against Basciano and at one of the federal trials of John Gotti Jr., was sentenced in January 2012 to ten years in prison by Judge Nicholas Garaufis in Brooklyn federal court. With credit for time already served, Cicale is expected to get out of custody in mid-2013. He is serving his time in a witness security facility.

Patrick DeFilippo (Bonanno captain) was sentenced to forty years in prison for his 2006 federal racketeering conviction. While the jury couldn't agree whether he took part in the murder of Gerlando Scascia, the sentencing judge used evidence from the trial on that charge in fashioning his sentence. DeFilippo's projected release date is June 2038. DeFilippo has filed court papers challenging his case on the grounds of ineffective assistance of counsel, arguing that he wasn't fully counseled on his sentence exposure after rejecting a plea deal that would have given him no more than fifteen years. His attorneys have filed papers noting that he is suffering from congestive heart failure and once "died" in prison before being revived.

Jack Dennehy (prosecutor) is an assistant US attorney in the Brooklyn US Attorney's Office and handles organized crime cases.

James DeStefano (FBI agent) is a supervisory agent in the FBI's New York City office.

Anthony Donato (Bonanno soldier) received a sentence of three hundred months for racketeering. He is serving his time in Sandstone Federal Correctional Institution, a facility for low-risk offenders in Minnesota.

Donato is seeking to vacate his sentence on a number of grounds, including a claim that the government withheld evidence helpful to his defense.

Stephen Frank (prosecutor) works as an assistant US attorney in Boston, Massachusetts.

Giuseppe "Joey" Gambina (former Bonanno associate) is awaiting sentencing for his guilty plea to a violence and racketeering charge, for which he faces a possible twenty-year term. A protected witness, he is believed to have moved from the New York City area.

Nicholas Garaufis (federal judge) is still a federal judge in Brooklyn, where he has been assigned since his appointment in 2000. After presiding over scores of Bonanno crime family cases, Garaufis has been handling an active caseload. Recently his docket included a lawsuit by black firefighters against the New York City Fire Department over bias in its entrance examination.

George Goltzer (defense attorney) maintains an active criminal defense practice in Manhattan. Since the day Basciano was sentenced, he has never spoken a word to his former client.

Anthony Indelicato (Bonanno soldier) is serving a twenty-year sentence after pleading guilty in August 2008 to a count of racketeering for conspiracy to commit murder and a charge of conspiracy to distribute marijuana. He is incarcerated at the Fairton Federal Correctional Institution in New Jersey. He is scheduled to be released in 2023. Indelicato filed court papers in 2009 challenging his plea on the grounds that the government withheld an exculpatory letter from a cooperating witness. His request was denied in May 2012.

Richard Jasper (defense attorney) maintains an active criminal defense practice in Manhattan.

James Kousouros (defense attorney) maintains an active criminal defense practice with offices in Manhattan and Queens.

Thomas Lee (witness), after pleading guilty in 2005, was automatically disbarred in New York State. He and his family have relocated, although old friends say they have seen him visiting the Bronx.

Barry Levin (defense attorney), after defending Basciano in 2006, went on to handle a number of high-profile cases. He successfully defended reputed Genovese crime family captain Barney Bellomo on a federal murder charge. Levin also defended accused "black widow" murderer Barbara Kogan. During her state trial, Kogan pleaded guilty to manslaughter in 2010 for killing her husband. Kogan is set to be released from prison as early as 2020.

Michael Mancuso (Bonanno captain, former acting boss) is serving a fifteen-year sentence for admitting his role in the killing of Randolph Pizzolo. He is incarcerated at the Edgefield Federal Correctional Institution in South Carolina. His scheduled release date is March 2019.

Joseph Massino (former Bonanno boss) is currently in the federal witness security program. He is expected to testify in the federal death penalty racketeering murder trial of reputed acting Colombo crime family boss Joel Cacace in Brooklyn federal court either in 2012 or 2013. In late 2012 he testified for about three hours in the federal extortion trial of reputed Genovese crime family member Anthony Romanello in Brooklyn federal court. Romanello was acquitted in a case many trial observers thought was weak. Massino is expected at some point to make a motion to reduce his life sentence in the hopes of getting out of prison sometime before he dies.

Kimberly McCaffrey (FBI agent) has been assigned as a special agent to the FBI's Baltimore division.

Taryn Merkl (prosecutor) is chief of the organized crime and gang section of the Brooklyn US Attorney's Office.

Murray Richman (defense attorney) maintains an active criminal defense practice in the Bronx, where he is known affectionately as the "mayor of the Bronx." He professes to have represented one-third of the New York State legislature at one time or another. Richman hosts a weekly radio show, *Don't Worry Murray,* on WVOX radio in Westchester County that deals with a wide range of legal and political issues.

Jeffrey Sallett (FBI agent) is assistant special agent in charge of the FBI's Boston division.

Ying Stafford (defense attorney) maintains an active criminal defense practice in Manhattan.

James Tartaglione (former Bonanno captain) remains a cooperating witness for the government.

Anthony Urso (Bonanno captain, underboss) pleaded guilty to one count of federal racketeering conspiracy in February 2005. Now aged seventy-six, Urso is serving a twenty-year sentence at Elkton Federal Correctional Institution in Ohio, a facility for low-risk inmates. He is scheduled for release in December 2021. Before he was sentenced in 2005, he wrote a letter to the court saying that Massino used him as his driver and did so to shield himself from illegal activities.

Salvatore Vitale (former Bonanno underboss), after testifying in many federal trials, was sentenced to time served in 2010 for numerous murders and other crimes. Now a relocated government witness, he is still called up at times to testify.

ACKNOWLEDGMENTS

THIS BOOK COVERS SOME OF THE MOST IMPORTANT DEVELOPMENTS EVER to occur in organized crime in America and took a great deal of work. It covers four major federal criminal trials, not counting selected cases that took place over a period of decades. As a result, the records examined were voluminous. Many people helped me along the way, and I thank them.

As mentioned previously, Vincent Basciano politely declined to sit for an interview, nor would he comment for this book. True to the life he had lived in the mob, Basciano didn't want to tell tales. It wouldn't look good on his résumé, said one mobster. Nevertheless, through thorough reporting, interviews with others, and crucial documents, I was able to learn much about Basciano's thinking and state of mind. Sources of those materials remain confidential.

Angela Basciano granted me an interview in November 2006 that ran in *Newsday*. She didn't take lightly her decision to go public. She is a private woman, who showed a lot of grace and class under very trying times. This time around, Angela decided not to comment for this book.

Those whom I can thank publicly largely work in law enforcement and the legal professions. At the FBI, Betsy Glick, James Margolin, and Gregory Comcowich helped me get the official clearances to talk with a number of special agents. Among the agents I interviewed were Michael Breslin, James DeStefano (no relation), and Jeffrey Sallett. Former agents Charles Rooney, John Stubing, and Jack Garcia also provided valuable historical perspective.

At the Brooklyn US Attorney's Office, official spokesman Robert Nardoza helped steer me to the right resources. Thanks also are due to assistant US attorney Taryn Merkl, head of the organized crime and gang unit, and paralegal Samantha Ward.

Among the lawyers who helped me in my research were Frank Bari, Benjamin Brafman, James DiPietro, George Goltzer, Richard Jasper,

Susan Kellman, James Kousouros, Barry Levin, Richard Ware Levitt, Edward McDonald, Patrick Parrotta, Murray Richman, Roland C. Riopelle, Ephraim Savitt, Maurice H. Sercarz, and Ying Stafford.

Thanks are also due to private investigator Gerard Gardner of Gardner Investigative Services for his help in providing perspective on the Basciano case.

Journalists and writers whose works I consulted include Ralph Blumenthal, Jerry Capeci, Stefanie Cohen, Kati Cornell, Lee A. Daniels, Norman Davies, Iris Derouex, Jim Dwyer, Alan Feuer, Tom Hays, Meryl Gordon, Scott Ladd, Lee Lamothe, Zach Haberman, Adrian Humphreys, Bob Kappstatter, Mitch Maddux, John Marzulli, Larry McShane, Alexandra Mosca, Rocco Parascandola, Selwyn Raab, William Rashbaum, John Riley, Greg Smith, Gay Talese, and Murray Weiss.

Newsday editor Deborah Henley and assistant managing editor Maryann Skinner are to be thanked for getting me approval to write this book. My immediate *Newsday* editor, Monica Quintanilla, put up with my requests for time off. Cathy Mahon, *Newsday*'s permission coordinator, easily found me a key photographic resource.

Lastly, I want to thank my agent, Jill Marsal, for her persistence in pushing this project, and my editor, James Jayo of Lyons Press, for seeing the merits to the unique story of Vinny Gorgeous.

NOTES

Chapter 1: Details of the murder of Randolph Pizzolo, as well as a reconstruction of his final hours, derive principally from his autopsy report and the testimony of Dominick Cicale in *U.S. v. Basciano*, 03-cr-929, (EDNY) and *U.S. v. Basciano*, 05-cr-60 (EDNY). Cicale's testimony also provided information about Pizzolo's uneven career in construction and his troubles with various mob associates. FBI agent James DeStefano discussed Pizzolo's final days in an interview.

Chapter 2: The spine for this chapter is the secret tape made by Joseph Massino on January 3, 2005, when he recorded Vincent Basciano in the recreation cages of the federal Metropolitan Detention Center in Brooklyn. The tape is about 150 minutes long, but only about an hour of it contains the important conversation. Background material on Massino's thoughts about Basciano comes from the testimony of Richard Cantarella in various Bonanno crime family cases. Basciano's private thoughts about Massino derive from material provided to the author by a confidential news source. Interviews with FBI agents Jeffrey Sallett and James DeStefano fleshed out details about how Massino was wired up to tape Basciano.

Chapter 3: Former FBI agent Charles Rooney's interview with the author gave details about the discovery of the photograph of Basciano during the Pizza Connection investigation. Details of the Pizza Connection case can be found in Ralph Blumenthal's *Last Days of the Sicilians*. Details of Basciano's early life occur in various law enforcement documents prepared after he was arrested in 1985 for the attempted murder of David Nunez. Details of Anthony Colangelo's life and death exist in law enforcement files prepared during the murder investigation. Details of the Nunez attempted murder case come from *New York v. Vincent Basciano, et al.*, 5726/1985, Bronx County State Supreme Court.

Chapter 4: Details about Basciano's early business holdings and his family life come from court filings in *U.S. v. Millan, et al.*, 91-cr-685, United States District Court for The Southern District of New York, as well as law enforcement and corrections files prepared in connection with the Nunez attempted murder case. Details of the Bonanno crime family wars of the 1960s come from Gay Talese's *Honor Thy Father*, while more recent machinations come from my own *King of the Godfathers* (2008). Information about Operation Grand Finale comes from an interview with former FBI agent John Stubing as well as *King of the Godfathers*. Details of Massino's crime family dealings and various inductions into the Bonanno family exist in government law enforcement records.

Chapter 5: The French Connection case details are widely available in various books. I covered many of the cases involving Southeast Asian heroin trafficking to New York City in the late 1980s. The history of the mob's involvement in drugs, as well as the Pizza Connection, can be found in *King of the Godfathers*, *Mafia: The Government's Secret File on Organized Crime* (2007), and *Last Days of the Sicilians*. The Blue Thunder case details come from the extensive filings in *U.S. v. Millan* (1991), including court transcripts and judicial rulings. Attorney Benjamin Brafman provided details of his representation of Basciano in an interview in Manhattan. Background on Brafman comes from a *New York* magazine story written by Meryl Gordon, as well as my coverage in 1986 of the Gambino crime family prosecutions. Law partners Maurice Sercarz and Roland Riopelle in a joint interview provided additional details about how Basciano conducted himself in the Blue Thunder case. A *Los Angeles Times* story by Scott Ladd on December 5, 1993, provided details about the arrests and prosecutions of police officer Jeffrey Beck and others in the Blue Thunder case, as did several decisions by Manhattan federal judge Shirley Wohl Kram.

Chapter 6: This chapter involves a variety of events and relies on a multitude of source materials. The investigation by the Manhattan

District Attorney's Office into mob dealings in the *New York Post* comes from *King of the Godfathers* and Raab's *Five Families*. Patrick DeFilippo's prominence in the Bronx is described in various FBI and government records. The murder of Rosemary and Thomas Uva is described in numerous news accounts as well as government and FBI files. The alleged murder by Basciano of an unidentified man in a Queens club and Massino's concern are also described in government and FBI records. The rise to prominence of Albanian mobsters is illuminated in *U.S. v. Rudaj*, et al. (2003) and the thick trial record. Government and FBI files also provide information about the Albanians and their ties to Basciano. Gaetano Preduto cooperated with the government as a witness, and his testimony is reported in a number of court proceedings, including *U.S. v. Rudaj*, as well as in FBI reports. Details of events leading up to the death of Gerlando Sciascia, as well as his killing, come from the record of *U.S. v. Massino* (2003), mainly through the testimony of cooperating witness Salvatore Vitale. FBI records also contain information about Sciascia's death, while Basciano's ties to Sciascia come from private records made available to me. Lamothe and Humphrey's *Sixth Family* also describes the reaction among Canadian gangsters to Sciascia's death.

Chapter 7: Details about the inside of the Casablanca Restaurant come from *Five Families*. Government and FBI records describe events that took place at the club and were related to investigators by Richard Cantarella. Basciano's various business holdings and construction projects come from files prepared by his attorneys in *U.S. v. Millan* and *U.S. v. Basciano* (2003). The gambling investigation of the Queens County District Attorney into Taylor Breton and Basciano is detailed in wiretap affidavits and supporting documents filed with various judges in Queens State Supreme Court. Breton's guilty plea and sentence are reported in newspaper accounts of 2001 and related to the author by the Queens District Attorneys Office. New Jersey Casino Control Commission records reveal that Breton was placed on the agency's exclusion list in

2002. Cicale also testified about Basciano's dealings with Breton in *U.S. v. Basciano* (2003 and 2005).

Chapter 8: The description of the Manhattan Grille comes from an Internet review and the author's personal visit made some years before it closed. Details of Cicale's criminal history and family life, as well as the meeting between Basciano, Cicale, and Indelicato at the Manhattan Grille come from Cicale's testimony in the trials of *U.S. v. Basciano* (for indictments in 2003 and 2005). I covered the murder of Salvatore Montagna in November 2011.

Chapter 9: Details of the murder of Frank Santoro come from the testimony of Cicale in all of Basciano's trials from 2006 through 2011. Santoro's wife, Maria, also testified in 2007. Other information about the shooting comes from NYPD interview reports and autopsy reports. Santoro's criminal record is also contained in court filings and police reports. Cicale described in his testimony the post-murder meeting following the death of Santoro. Additional details also come from witness reports provided to the NYPD and FBI.

Chapter 10: Details about the meetings that Massino had with various Bonanno crime family members about Santoro's murder are contained in FBI reports. I have done wide-ranging reporting about the genesis of the FBI investigation into Massino and the Bonanno family. Much of the information in this chapter comes from *King of the Godfathers* and *Five Families*, as well as interviews with agents Jeffrey Sallett and Kimberly McCaffrey in 2004 at FBI headquarters in New York. I reinterviewed former agent John Stubing in 2012 about the Grand Finale investigation. Salvatore Vitale's 2001 federal criminal case is described in *Five Families*, *King of the Godfathers*, the record in *U.S. v. Vitale*, 01-cr-383 (EDNY, 2001), and contemporaneous news media accounts. Testimony in the trial of *U.S. v. Massino*, which took place in 2004, also related the way Sallett and McCaffrey did the forensic accounting investigation, which in turn developed informants Barry Weinberg and Agostino Scozzari. Additional material on the use of Weinberg and Scozzari comes from *Five Families* and *King of the Godfathers*, as well as the author's interview with a confidential source. Frank Coppa and Cantarella each testified about their decisions to cooperate during the trial of Massino in 2004. Government files, as well as private summaries given to me, provided information about the conversations Massino had with Basciano and others before he was arrested on January 9, 2003. The description of the sequence of events on the morning Massino was arrested comes from *King of the Godfathers*, based on interviews with agents Sallett and McCaffrey. Anthony Urso's remark that Vitale was to become an informant is found on tapes made by James Tartaglione.

Chapter 11: The description of the arraignment of Massino and Vitale comes from *King of the Godfathers*, as do the events surrounding the decision by Vitale to become a cooperating witness. The recorded conversation involving Tartaglione, Basciano, and others on December 21, 2003, can be found in the record of *U.S. v. Basciano*, 03-cr-939.

Chapter 12: Cicale's recollection of Basciano's suspicions about Tartaglione occurs in his testimony at Basciano's trials in 2006 and 2007. The recorded conversation on January 18, 2004, comes from the record of *U.S. v. Basciano*, 03-cr-939. Ruth Nordenbrook's compassion with Tartaglione comes from *King of the Godfathers*.

Chapter 13: A description of the arrest in January 2004 of Urso and other members of the Bonanno family comes from a news release prepared by the Brooklyn US Attorney's Office. Ben Brafman's interaction with Basciano in 2004 comes from an interview with the attorney in 2012. Cicale testified in detail in 2006, 2007, and 2011 about the aftermath of the arrests of Basciano and others. Attorney Thomas Lee's history and dealings with Basciano and Massino come from his debriefings by the FBI and government documents. I covered Massino's trial and wrote about it in *King of the Godfathers*, as did Raab in *Five Families*.

Chapter 14: FBI agent Michael Breslin talked about the formulation of the investigation into Basciano and his colleagues during an interview in 2012. The description of Pizzolo's tortured relationship with Basciano on construction projects, as well as in the mob, comes from Cicale's testimony in all of Basciano's federal trials. Joey Gambina described his own life of crime in the 2011 trial of Basciano.

Chapter 15: Michael Breslin and Jeff Sallett described the arrest of Basciano in interviews. Breslin also testified about the arrest in the 2011 trial of Basciano. Cicale testified in Basciano's 2011 trial about his frantic activity when his boss was arrested. Cicale also testified in detail about the plot to kill Pizzolo. Gambina testified in Basciano's 2011 trial about the plot to kill Pizzolo and of his refusal to take part in the murder. James DeStefano described in an interview the day Cicale was arrested.

Chapter 16: Massino's jailhouse meetings come from his testimony in Basciano's 2011 trial, as well as from a private summary of those events. The decision to fit Massino with a recording device and the actual taping were described by agents DeStefano and Sallett in an interview. Tape transcripts and the recordings all provide details of what was said in the taped meetings.

Chapter 17: I covered the news that Massino had turned cooperating witness for *Newsday*. Thomas Lee's arrest was described in various news accounts, and his case is part of the federal court record. Anthony Aiello's charges and arrest are described in court records. Barry Levin described in an interview how Basciano hired him for his 2006 trial. Events in Basciano's 2006 trial are contained in the record of *U.S. v. Basciano*, contemporaneous news accounts, and my reporting on it for *Newsday*. Levin discussed with me his relationship with Basciano during the trial and the public tiffs he had with his client. The most notable testimony was provided by Cicale in describing the murders of Santoro and Pizzolo.

Chapter 18: Case file in *U.S. v. Basciano* (2003) and contemporaneous news accounts. Trial transcript and author's notes.

Chapter 19: Case file *U.S. v. Basciano* (2005) and contemporaneous news accounts. For the views of some federal judges on the death penalty,

I consulted Block's *Disrobed: An Inside Look at the Life and Work of a Federal Trial Judge* and Morris's *Leadership on the Federal Bench: The Craft and Activism of Jack Weinstein.*

Chapters 20–2 : Case file *U.S. v. Basciano* (2005), trial transcript, and contemporaneous news accounts, as well as my notes.

Chapter 23: Case file *U.S. v. Basciano* (2005), trial transcript, and contemporaneous news accounts, as well as my notes. Statistics on federal death penalty cases since 1988 came from the website of the Federal Death Penalty Resource Counsel, a group that assists federal courts in assigning death penalty attorneys and advises on capital punishment issues.

Epilogue: Expert testimony in penalty phase, *U.S. v. Basciano* (2005). Rule 2255 motion by Vincent Basciano.

BIBLIOGRAPHY

Books

Block, Frederic. *Disrobed: An Inside Look at the Life and Work of a Federal Trial Judge.* New York: Thomson Reuters Westlaw, 2012.

Blumenthal, Ralph. *Last Days of the Sicilians: At War with the Mafia: The FBI Assault on the Pizza Connection.* New York: Times Books, 1988.

Davies, Norman. *No Simple Victory: World War II in Europe, 1939-1945.* New York: Penguin Books, 2008.

DeStefano, Anthony M. *King of the Godfathers: "Big Joey" Massino and the Fall of the Bonanno Crime Family.* New York: Citadel Press, 2008.

Jackson, Kenneth T. *The Encyclopedia of New York City.* New Haven, CT: Yale University Press, 1995.

Lamothe, Lee, and Humphreys, Adrian. *The Sixth Family: The Collapse of the New York Mafia and the Rise of Vito Rizzuto.* Mississauga, ON: John Wiley & Sons Canada Ltd., 2006.

Mass, Peter. *The Valachi Papers.* New York: Bantam Books, 1969.

Morris, Jeremy B. *Leadership on the Federal Bench: The Craft and Activism of Jack Weinstein.* New York: Oxford University Press, 2011.

Pistone, Joseph D., and Woodley, Richard. *Donnie Brasco: My Undercover Life in the Mafia.* New York: New American Library, 1987.

Raab, Selwyn. *Five Families: The Rise, Decline, and Resurgence of America's Most Powerful Mafia Empires.* New York: St. Martins Press, 2005.

Talese, Gay. *Honor Thy Father.* New York: Dell Publishing Co., 1981.

United States Treasury Department, Bureau of Narcotics. *Mafia: United States Treasury Department Bureau of Narcotics, The Government's Secret File on Organized Crime.* New York: HarperCollins Publishers, 2007.

Court Documents and Cases

Angela Basciano v. Kimmarie Van Zandt, et al., 301221/2008, Bronx County State Supreme Court.

Patrick DeFilippo v. U.S.A., 09-cv-41534, United States District Court for The Eastern District of New York.

Anthony Donato v. U.S.A., 09-cv-5617, United States District Court for The Eastern District of New York.

Anthony Indelicato v. U.S.A., 09-cv-5228, United States District Court for The Eastern District of New York.

People of The State of New York v. Vincent Basciano, et al., 3K009469 (1983), Kings County Criminal Court.

People of The State of New York v. Vincent Basciano, et al., 5726/1985, Bronx County State Supreme Court.

Resorts International v. Vincent J. Basciano, 21639/1999, Bronx County State Supreme Court.

Ralph Rivera v. U.S.A., 98-civ-7322, United States District Court for The Southern District of New York.

Trump Taj Mahal Casino v. Vincent Basciano, 22997/1998, Bronx County State Supreme Court.

U.S. v. Anthony Aiello, 05-132M, United States District Court for The Eastern District of New York.

U.S. v. Antonino Aiello, 864 F.2d 257, United States Court of Appeals for The Second Circuit.

U.S. v. Vincent Basciano, et al., 03-cr-929, United States District Court for The Eastern District of New York.

U.S. v. Vincent Basciano, et al., 05-cr-60, United States District Court for The Eastern District of New York.

U.S. v. Frank Caruso, et al., 75-cr-1157, United States District Court for The Southern District of New York.

U.S. v. Joseph Manfredi, et al., 488 F. 2d 588, United States Court of Appeals for The Second Circuit.

U.S. v. Joseph Massino, et al., 02-cr-307, United States District Court for The Eastern District of New York.

U.S. v. Eric Millan, et al., 91-cr-685, United States District Court for The Southern District of New York.

U.S. v. Gaetano Peduto, 94-cr-204, United States District Court for The Eastern District of New York.

U.S. v. Alex Rudaj, et al., 03-cr-1110, United States District Court for The Southern District of New York.

U.S. v. Anthony Urso, et al., 03-cr-1382, United States District Court for The Eastern District of New York.

U.S. v. Salvatore Vitale, et al., 01-cr-382, United States District Court for The Eastern District of New York.

Government Publications

New York State Joint Legislative Committee on Crime, Its Causes, Control and Effect on Society. Report for 1970, September 1970.

Newspapers and News Organizations Consulted

Associated Press
Daily Mail (UK)
Los Angeles Times
Newsday (Long Island)
New York Daily News
New York Magazine
New York Newsday
New York Post
New York Sun
New York Times
Reuters

Websites

www.bop.gov
www.court.state.ny.us
www.dos.state.ny.us
www.fbi.gov
www.findagrave.com
www.ganglandnews.com
www.Lexis.com
www.Nexis.com
www.nj.gov/casinos
www.usdoj.gov/usai/nye (US Attorney's Office, Eastern District of New York)

INDEX